# CAPE VERDE, LET'S GO

INTERPRETATIONS OF CULTURE
IN THE NEW MILLENNIUM

Norman E. Whitten Jr.,
General Editor

*A list of books in the series appears
at the end of the book.*

# CAPE VERDE, LET'S GO

Creole Rappers and Citizenship in Portugal

DEREK PARDUE

UNIVERSITY OF ILLINOIS PRESS
Urbana, Chicago, and Springfield

© 2015 by the Board of Trustees
of the University of Illinois
All rights reserved

1 2 3 4 5 C P 5 4 3 2 1
♾ This book is printed on acid-free paper.

Library of Congress Control Number: 2015951273
ISBN 978-0-252-03967-6 (hardcover)
ISBN 978-0-252-08117-0 (paperback)
ISBN 978-0-252-09776-8 (e-book)

# Contents

List of Illustrations   vii

Note on Orthography   ix

List of Frequently Used Acronyms   xi

Introduction   1

CHAPTER 1. Creole's Historical Presences   27

CHAPTER 2. Kriolu Interruptions of Luso   59

CHAPTER 3. Lisbon Rappers and the Labor of Location   84

CHAPTER 4. Spatial Politics of Kriolu Presence in Lisbon   105

CHAPTER 5. Kriolu and European Interculturality   132

Suggestive Conclusions   153

Notes   157

References   165

Index   185

# Illustrations

FIGURE 1. Cabo da Roca   2
FIGURE 2. Uncle C   3
FIGURE 3. Lusophone space worldwide   5
FIGURE 4. Lisbon street signs   30
FIGURE 5. Praga, Kriolu rapper   85
FIGURE 6. The division between Prior Velho and Quinta da Serra   107
FIGURE 7. Scenes of demolition on the way to Quinta da Lage   110
FIGURE 8. B-boy Zé Macaco   110
FIGURE 9. Alvalade, a former social housing project   118
FIGURE 10. Damaia, another social housing project   119
FIGURE 11. Mural project on residential buildings in BSF   120
FIGURE 12. Casal da Boba, Amadora   122
FIGURE 13. The main entrance into Kova M   126
FIGURE 14. Moinho da Juventude in Kova M   126
FIGURE 15. The main entrance into the Talude community center   134
FIGURE 16. The Talude neighborhood from the community center   135

# Note on Orthography

Because Cape Verdean Creole has never been recognized officially, its orthography varies, including the name of the language itself. The two most common spellings are *Kriolu* and *Crioulo*. I opt for the former because it is most common in Lisbon. In part, this spelling stems from a particular politics related to the island of Santiago, often in distinction or opposition to the island of São Vicente. Linguists and Kriolu activists have developed and sporadically implemented the orthographic system of the Unified Alphabet for the Writing of Cape Verdean (ALUPEK). However, very few of my interlocutors practiced ALUPEK, even those who support it politically. Therefore, many words, in practice, contain options for $c/k, s/z, n/m$, among other variations. This is all to say that Kriolu fosters neologisms, and rappers, the main sociocultural group in focus in this book, exploit this structural opportunity.

I use *Creole* to refer to Creole language, in general, and to the social, cultural, historical, and other related phenomena conventionally indicated by the term. I use *Kriolu* to refer more particularly to aspects of Cape Verdean language and identity. Moreover, I am trying to assert the importance of Kriolu and Creole as significant and complex concepts through the use of capitalization as would be the case with *English* or, more pertinent, *Portuguese*.

# List of Frequently Used Acronyms

| | |
|---|---|
| ACIDI | Alta Comissariado para a Imigração e o Diálogo Intercultural (High Commission of Immigration and Intercultural Dialogue); renamed as ACM, Alto Comissariado para as Migrações (High Commission for Migration), on February 27, 2014 |
| ACIME | Alto Comissariado para a Imigração e as Minorias Étnicas (High Commission of Immigration and Ethnic Minorities) |
| ALUPEK | Alfabeto Unificado para a Escrita do Kauberdianu (Unified Alphabet for the Writing of Cape Verdean) |
| CPLP | Comunidade de Países de Língua Portuguesa (Community of Portuguese Language Countries) |
| EU | European Union |
| PAICV | Partido Africano da Independência de Cabo Verde (African Party for the Independence of Cape Verde) |
| PAIGCV | Partido Africano da Independência de Guinea-Bissau e Cabo Verde (African Independence Party of Guinea Bissau and Cape Verde) |
| PALOP | Países Africanos de Língua Oficial Portuguesa (African Countries with Portuguese as the Official Language) |
| SEF | Serviço de Estrangeiros e Fronteiras (Immigration and Border Service) |
| SGL | Sociedade de Geografia de Lisboa (Geographical Society of Lisbon) |

# Introduction

When one is standing at the cliffs at the Roca Cape (Cabo da Roca, figure 1), it is easy to imagine that one is at the end of the world. The sixteenth-century Portuguese writer Luís Vaz de Camões famously describes that this is "where land ends and the sea begins." The constant gusts sweeping across the ocean dramatize the act of historiography, the recording and archiving of Iberian, European, and African journeys at this southwestern extreme of Europe. One can imagine the excitement of modernity on the threshold of discovery. I witnessed that vast sea, an immensity that elicits reflection on the whole nature of things.

A couple of years later, I recalled those moments of seemingly floating above the ocean, navigating time in individual imagination, as Corsino ("Uncle C") (figure 2), a hip-hop activist and documentary filmmaker, and I stepped out onto the roof of a friend's house in a now demolished, "improvised" neighborhood of Bairro de Santa Filomena in the greater Lisbon metro area.[1] The clotheslines swayed under a stiff breeze as Uncle C checked his cell phone to search for funds to send to his family in Cape Verde and the Azores. Meanwhile, I looked out under a clear, cobalt-blue sky onto the Bairro de Santa Filomena (BSF) dwellings. Night was falling, and I felt I had come to another sort of precipice, increasingly aware of the complexity of migration webs and networks that make up the idea of being Portuguese and being Cape Verdean. I left for Praia, the capital city of the Cape Verde archipelago the next morning.

FIGURE 1. Cabo da Roca, the westernmost point of Europe. Photo by author, 2015.

I had begun to realize that Creole, as a sentiment and history, is both as expansive as the ocean and as intimate as colonialism. In scholarly circles, *Creole* is a by-product of colonialism and a serendipitous identity category of seemingly everyone in the fast-paced globalized world. Watching Uncle C at work on his phone and listening to the Cape Verdean braggarts in the alleyways below, I began to see the story of Kriolu, the Cape Verdean language-identity, as a Creole interruption and, thus, a contingent break from the mimesis of Portugal's "soft" power of inclusion. *Cape Verde, Let's Go: Creole Rappers and Citizenship in Portugal* is about the history of encounters and the politics of difference. It is about an Eastern Atlantic Creole that deserves consideration among scholars of (post)colonial citizenship.

## A Shift in Demographic Tide and the Steadfastness of Paradigm

Portugal was once a giant of European conquest and benefactor of colonial largesse. Thus begins an old Iberian tale that produced decades of nostalgic public policy and state ideology during the waning generation of the late nineteenth-century monarchy, the early republic, and the Antonio Salazar dictatorship of the twentieth century. Whether the key words are *discovery* and *civilization* or *remittances* and *diaspora* (Feldman-Bianca 1993; Baganha 1999), the idea of Portugal has been

FIGURE 2. Uncle C. Reprinted by permission of Corsino Furtado.

until relatively recently a concept of emigration and spreading out. The notion of Lusophone space is far from negligible. According to Jorge Fernandes Alves (1999), with over two hundred million speakers and occupying over four million square miles on four continents, Portugueseness, in some fashion or another, represents 7 percent of the globe's land mass.

Figure 3 is a snapshot of Portuguese space around the world. Contrary to many advocates of *Lusofonia*, or Portugueseness, including the Community of Portuguese Language Countries (CPLP), the differences among the so-called members of the CPLP often outweigh the linguistic similarities. Therefore, I do not intend to espouse any sort of "baseline" of Portuguese "culture" vis-à-vis language. Similar to most languages, Portuguese varies widely between continents, and, of course, the Creoles of Cape Verde, highlighted in this book, along with those of São Tomé e Príncipe (a smaller archipelago off the coast of Gabon), Guinea-Bissau, and Curaçao, disrupt even further any sort of notion of homogeneity. It is in contrast to the ideology that Portugueseness (and by extrapolation, Englishness, Frenchness, and so on) is by nature disseminating and cohesive that I wrote this book. The particularities of Portuguese colonialism and the unique relationship between Cape Verde and Portugal reveal a general lesson: citizenship is a dynamic encounter in which hybridity and distinction are complementary, not oppositional.

At the end of the twentieth century, after generations of Portuguese emigration, official and clandestine, a reversal of migration flows occurred (Malheiros 2002; S. Pereira 2013). Despite a relatively low percentage of non-nationals within the European context (hovering around 5 percent, according to Eurostat 2011), the late twentieth-century demographic shift significantly influenced ideas, experiences, and policies of Portuguese citizenship. In the 1980s and 1990s, Portugal became increasingly multicultural as immigration intensified not only among African Countries with Portuguese as the Official Language (PALOP), including Angola, Cape Verde, Guinea-Bissau, Mozambique, and other Portuguese colonies, Brazil, East Timor, Goa, and Macau, but also among migrants from China, India, Moldova, Romania, and Ukraine, to name but a few. Until the late 1990s, a third of these countries' immigrants were from Cape Verde (Pires 1999).

Certainly, the relatively rapid influx of migrants, both "familiar" and "different," has led to tension with occasionally violent outcomes. However, at the level of law, Portugal has been a leader among European countries to change immigration laws and public policy in adjustment to the new demographic and cultural realities. According to the Migrant Integration Policy Index (MIPEX), a quantitative assessment based on 148 policy variables, Portugal is unique in that it is one of the most greatly affected countries during the present economic recession and yet consistently progressive in its policies toward immigrants. MIPEX tracks this attitude toward immigrants through such indicators as antidiscrimination laws, employment opportunities, and intercultural education. Portugal's performance (since 2009) is surprising given that the economic crisis—with unemployment around 18 percent—has been a "push" force not only for some immigrants to return to "home" countries but also for many young Portuguese to migrate to former Portuguese colonies, particularly Angola (Malheiros 2011).

What is, perhaps, unexpected in the case of Portugal makes sense from another perspective. If the relationships among migration, policy, and identity are considered from a more humanistic view including social history and expressive culture and not simply employment demography, we find another paradigm. This para-

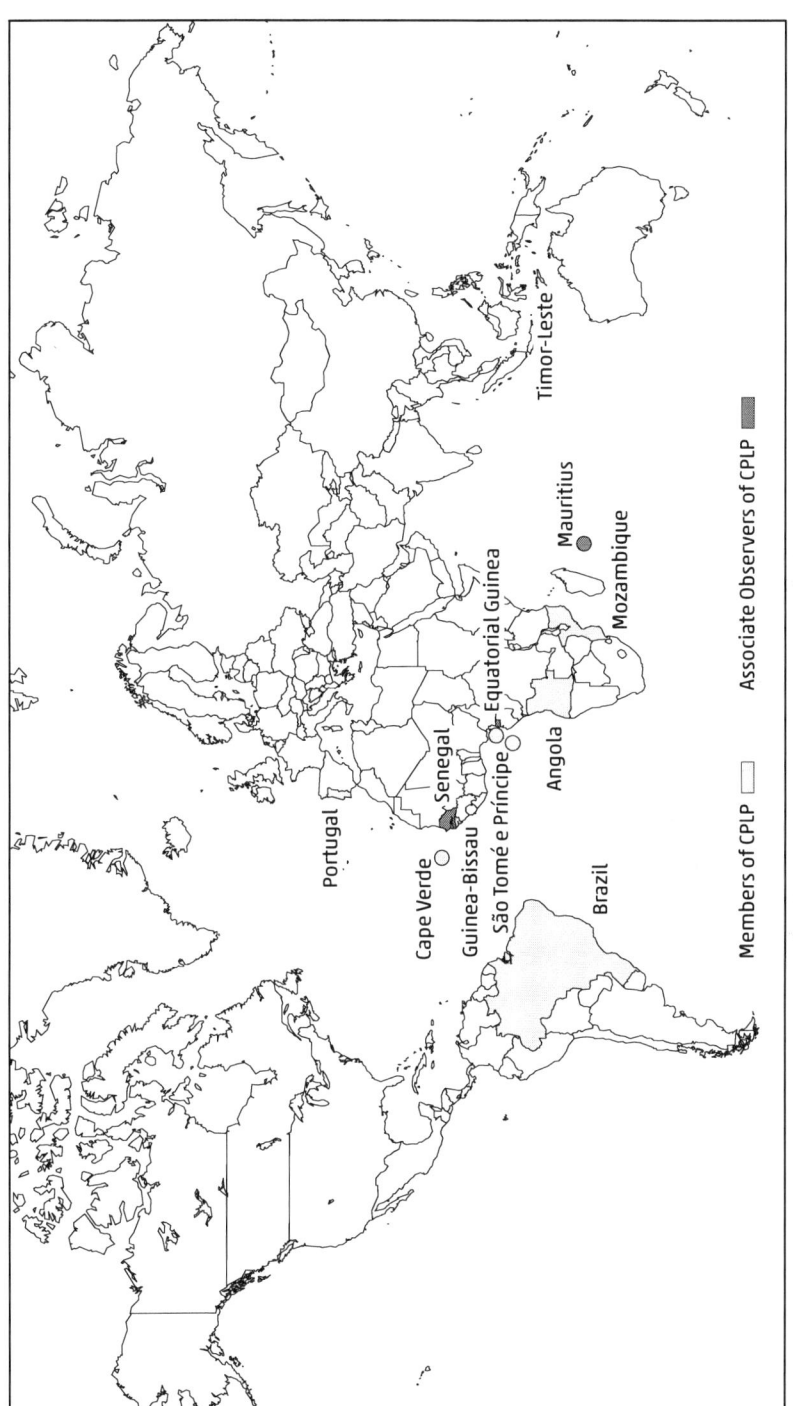

FIGURE 3. Lusophone space worldwide. Re-creation of a CPLP map.

Introduction

digm is based on the *encounter* or what Portuguese scholar Boaventura de Sousa Santos describes as an "inter-identity . . . , a complex identity constellation that combines traces of the colonizer and the colonized" (2002:16). In lived reality, the articulation of language, identity, territory, and rights is not as straightforward as census statistics or identity politics. It is not simple, because each one of these categories is contingent on dynamic social relationships influenced by histories of labor, migration, hierarchy, and expressive culture.

## The Project

Based on field and archival work in Portugal and Cape Verde, *Cape Verde, Let's Go* is an account of Kriolu rappers in Lisbon, Portugal, and their roles in challenging and potentially transforming metropolitan Portuguese identities with implications for what it means to be European in the twenty-first century. The term *Kriolu* refers to the language, culture, and history of a predominantly diasporic community originating from Cape Verde, the Atlantic Ocean archipelago, located 350 miles west of Dakar, Senegal. All Cape Verdeans, either native to the archipelago or located in diasporic communities, speak Kriolu, a hybrid language that emerged in the late fifteenth century through Portuguese colonialism in West Africa and as a result of the Iberian expulsion of Jews and Muslims under the purview of the Spanish Inquisition. The language is influenced by Portuguese vocabulary and the grammar and phonemic systems of West African languages, such as Mandingo, Temne, and Wolof, and other pidgin and Creole languages.

*Cape Verde, Let's Go* is neither a tale of Portuguese nostalgia nor a script of immigrant squalor. Rather, it is a rumination on the epistemology of the encounter, the main lens, I argue, through which one can more fully appreciate the rubric of Creole and understand Portugueseness and its constitutive discontents and marginalia. Beyond the current theories of citizenship in contemporary Europe, such as "postnational" citizenship as social rights (Soysal 1994; Bosniak 2006) and multicultural citizenship (Kymlicka 1995), this book extends Christian Joppke's interpretation of citizenship in direct terms of migration by making the encounter the theoretical focus (2010). I do that by highlighting *Creole*, an originally Euro-African formation on the eastern side of the Atlantic, not the Caribbean,[2] and grounding the theory in the unique experiences and histories of Cape Verdeans. In a twist on a typical phrase of propaganda during twentieth-century Portuguese colonialism, the case of Portugal and Creole citizenship offers a chance to "show the world to the world" (*mostrar o mundo ao mundo*) in a way that the current literature either fails to capture or has yet to imagine.[3]

To "show the world," I discuss the Cape Verdean presence in Portugal, particularly its capital Lisbon, where roughly 30 percent of the national population and the great majority of immigrants reside. There are but sixty-five thousand estimated Lisbon residents of Cape Verdean descent. Yet, the distinct contours of Cape Verdean history and its language of Kriolu reveal the ideals and realities of "Portuguese" formation as well as constitute a model for contemporary citizenship. The aim of this book is to demonstrate that from the relatively minuscule figure of Cape Verde, an obscure archipelago off the coast of Senegal, come large lessons about not simply identification but also the politics of experience and social agency within a poorly understood postcolonial context.

Neither Cape Verdeans nor the Portuguese are heroes of humanity in any sense, nor are they homogenous cultures. Certainly, both groups are heterogeneous, as individual identity is obviously contextual, a combination of "sameness and difference," following Georg Simmel's classic definition ([1908] 1971). For example, several Cape Verdeans in Lisbon explained to me that for them, socioeconomic class was the determining factor in their relationships and that language, race, and diaspora only occasionally made any difference to them at all. Similarly, a Portuguese social worker very much sympathetic to my efforts to understand paths to citizenship and social organizing among local youth, once turned to me and said, "You know, sometimes, like in health situations, it doesn't matter if you're from Cape Verde, Angola, China, or Lithuania. Identity doesn't matter. The system just sees you as an immigrant and that's it." It is a valid point, and the experience she describes is a great arbiter of truth.

However, there are general lessons about migration and identity that make sense only in terms of culture and history. The relationship between "Portuguese" and "Cape Verdean" is unique, but, I argue, one can draw certain generalizations that speak beyond the small, esoteric time-space of contemporary citizenship laws in this southwest corner of Europe. By knowing more about the mutual constitution of each loosely defined group, that is, Portuguese and Cape Verdean, we might better assess the general relationship between the experiences and policies of migration and, thus, better gauge citizenship as a balance of achievement and ascription.

## Citizenship

What sort of citizenship do I mean by Creole citizenship? I approach *citizenship* primarily as a *condition* of rights, status, belonging, and participation, which changes based on contextual factors, such as political and legal histories, as well as the realities of labor chances and cultural expressions. By formulating citizenship in this way, I differ slightly from the major model of citizenship theory, which posits that citizenship *is* a universal right, itself a conscious detour from the late nineteenth- and early twentieth-century model of citizenship as a status provided by the state to members that then affords a set of rights. Citizenship as a condition means that it is not a simply a static list of laws, duties, and benefits, decreed by the state or deserved for all people, but, rather, citizenship emerges from a set of practices and social relationships constitutive of civil society. Citizenship includes belonging and identity, and my goal is to represent the contextual nature of these categories and their relationship with the codified, regulatory, and structural aspects of politics. Based on social agency and cultural practice, my perspective on citizenship intersects with my view of Creole.

Citizenship is not only a set of practices motivated by a range of individual and collective interests; it is also a chronotopic formation, that is, citizenship's meaning and efficacy are situated in particular articulations of time and space (Sassen 2001). The chronotope guides my analysis in chapters 3 and 4. *Creolization*, the term referring to the social process of encounter, transculturation, and resulting power, offers particular insight into such contours of citizenship because it implies identity and spatial formation over time. Creolization also suggests movement toward encounter, a meeting point, in which representations, such as languages and religions of local and other spaces, are exchanged.

While creolization appears to escape the state or a bounded polity, citizenship, as Joppke reminds us in his scholarship on the landscape of migration in Europe, is "hardened" by the state (2010). That is to say, while identity claims and other forms of membership may circumvent the state, it still exerts a pragmatic and ideological force on citizenship as a set of rights, a mark of status, and a medium of identification. For this reason, I focus my analysis on the dynamic parameters of the Portuguese state and, ultimately, interpret diasporic claims or postcolonial hybridity made by Cape Verdean rappers, in terms of localized meanings inside Portugal. In the final analysis, I suggest that there exists a difference between Portuguese citizenship and citizenship in Portugal. It is the latter that Creole favors and could act as a model for contemporary citizenship, more generally.

Citizenship is a political and cultural project of membership that consists of everyday life moments and long-standing historical dynamics. *Cape Verde, Let's Go* is about a "New Europe," one where multiculturalism is polemical and unavoidable due to the heightened visibility of difference and the frequent tensions regarding the ethics and moralities of "modern" ways of life. It is about a part of Europe that is, perhaps, least understood in current anthropology, as Iberia's former colonies are seen as more significant than the old and faded Castilian and Lusitanian territories.

The ideology of Lusotropicalism (and other "Luso" discourses), a set of myths celebrating Portuguese colonialism and postcolonial society as exceptionally "congenial" and "open" to difference among, particularly, black African subjects, represent one such cluster of historical depth and everyday presence. Luso, thus, stands as a central point of debate in the book. I explore this hallmark of "modernity" and its ongoing legacy through terms such as *interculturality* in order to highlight Kriolu as a curiously uncomfortable difference not only in the specific case of Portugal but also in the grand matrix of creolization and postcolonial reconciliation with past eras and former European metropoles. Interculturality is a recent term employed by the European Union and European Commission, intended to capture the zeitgeist of early twenty-first-century social life, a period of intense and visible immigration from Africa, the Middle East, Eastern Europe, and South and East Asia. The *inter* prefix connotes a desire for sociocultural connections among peoples of different ethnicities, as opposed to the mosaic-inspired designs under multiculturalism. Interculturality is a political term circulated in the European public sphere by heads of state, culture ministers, and a range of culture agencies across Europe. Its politics are part of an inherited "liberal" tradition and demonstrate a selective view of immigration and inclusion.

Citizenship as a condition is made material through spatial occupation, a presence that marks places and forces us to reckon the city as a palimpsest. I focus particular attention on the spatial aspects of two historically complementary dimensions of citizenship—language and expressive culture. To frame citizenship in Europe in terms of language is a departure from the majority of scholarship that explains language difference in terms of a "functional capacity of the newcomer" (Joppke 2010:134). For reasons of supposed singularity and cosmological "thickness," Europeanist scholars have focused their theories on states' reactions to *religious* difference as identity and not *language*.[4] The view that language is but a thin smile of identity ignores the copious evidence provided by cultural anthropologists and social linguists.

Cape Verdean-ness in Portugal is essentially entangled in the performance of Kriolu, a language and identity born and developed in the colonial encounter. Of course, here, too, we find a great deal of heterogeneity. Kriolu, or Crioulo, varies significantly from one Cape Verdean island to the next and from diasporic location to another. The two spellings themselves refer to a general break between the Creole spoken in the northern ring of islands called the *barlavento,* or windward islands (Crioulo), and the southern, *sotavento,* or leeward islands (Kriolu). Since I conducted fieldwork in Praia, the birthplace or "home" of the majority of Cape Verdeans in Lisbon, I use the *K* orthography throughout the text. Such variability is not simply island pride; it is rooted in the logistics of diaspora and migration, such as transportation. For example, in an interview collected by a Cape Verdean sociologist, the physician Antonio Saint Aubyn described his journey to get back to São Nicolau (barlavento) from Portugal at a time in the 1990s before there were airports of any size in the major cities of Praia and Mindelo. Aubyn flew to Sal, a small barlavento island developed into a tourist destination in the 1980s, and then used his influence to board a military plane and then a boat to arrive in São Nicolau (in G. Raimundo 2008). The logistics of Aubyn's journey are central to his memory of Cape Verde, his sense of island variability, and his relative class standing. There are many Kriolus/Crioulos among the roughly five hundred thousand Cape Verdean living on the archipelago, and this periodically becomes an obstacle to, for example, the politics of language in public education. Nevertheless, it is the fundamental experience of the encounter and migration mediated by a mode of K/Crioulo that binds the island nation together and provides a measure of cohesion for the diasporic communities abroad.

## Migration

As we begin to sketch out the operative relationships between contemporary citizenship in multicultural nation-states, it is important to remember what is involved in migration. Following Miguel Vale de Almeida, "migrations are not a simple spatial transference of a work force. This transferal constitutes a social movement through which working classes on a global level are restructured within the system of production" (2007:109). Cape Verdeans are not political refugees or part of a forced migration based on religious persecution. They constitute the dominant category of migration in the contemporary world, movement related primarily to labor and culture. From this perspective, migration is a variable response to socioeconomic conditions accompanied by an equally dynamic process of cultural production.

This book is an attempt to bring together two bodies of knowledge that rarely meet in any systematic way, migrant experiences and migration policy. An integration of these two spheres of life is essential in understanding the relationship between identity formation and citizenship practices. In his introduction to the *Cambridge Survey of World Migration*, Robin Cohen reminds the reader that the emergence of a "European World Economy," borrowing from Emmanuel Wallerstein, was not just a development of trade routes and commodity markets but also an intensification of human traffic (1995:2). The complex intersectionality of motivations, geographies, temporalities, types, regulations, and experiences of migration is the basis of citizenship.

Mobility and border crossing both complicate and enrich citizenship by simultaneously peaking xenophobic anxieties and affording opportunities to expand one's skill set. For example, in Portugal the rise in popularity of Paulo Portas and his anti-immigration "people's party" with over 10 percent of the vote for assembly members and over 8 percent for the European Parliament in 2009, coincided with improved educational options for immigrants in Portugal after legislators passed the new National Citizenship Laws in December 2006.

## Introduction

Europe is at the center of discussions around citizenship and belonging because it is here where mobility and the encounter are increasingly the shaping forces of identity categories and ideologies. It is here where many of the conventions of modern identity and the public sphere are both a sense of pride and a target of scrutiny. Despite its peripheral status within Europe, Portugal, through its internal debates on the Lusotropical mythology of cultural mixture and the organizational attempts to recuperate a linguistic-cultural-territorial solidarity of Lusofonia, illuminates distinctively the "identity problem" of not only Europe but also the postcolonial moment, more generally.

As signaled above, the aim of this book is to dismantle the oppositional understanding of identity within a context of encounter and appreciate equally the experiences and policies of migration so that we may formulate a more meaningful set of theories of citizenship. This requires an appreciation of materials, as well. I present the reader a wide range of sources, including fiction, historical documents, ethnographic field notes, song lyrics, and political theory. For example, *Cape Verde, Let's Go* can be read as a scholarly response to what one literary character observes, "But, alas, Portugal doesn't really colonize, it just spreads. . . . [This] means that wherever the Portuguese manage to get (and we have got quite far), not only do they forget their civilizing—that is, colonizing—mission, but they quickly allow themselves to be colonized—that is, decivilized—by the local people" (Agualusa 2002:124).[5] What is this unique characteristic of Portuguese encounters? How does this real and imagined notion of interculturality (glossed in Portugal as Lusofonia) play a role in ideas and policies of "Portugueseness" from migrant and state perspectives? Is there something in the "Portuguese" identity that could be a general model of identity, a relationship that Phillip Rothwell describes as an unconscious contradiction of "synthesis and separation" (2000)?

Through careful consideration of colonial and postcolonial Portuguese history, it is clear that creolization is central to identity formation and cultural production. We know from linguistic evidence and cases, such as Haiti, Cape Verde, and Mauritius, that Creole can function as a principle of identity with empirical political vestiges. Caribbean fiction writers Raphael Confiänt and Ernest Pépin put the driving question of *creolité*, an indigenization of creolization, in this manner: "How can we approach, today, politics in a Creole way? What world should we build while taking into account these facts? Here are, we think, the stakes of Creolité" (Pépin and Confiänt 1998:100). Or, paraphrasing Caribbeanist scholar Aisha Khan, can Creole be both a model of and model for society?

As we tack back and forth between Lisbon-based ethnography, Lusophone histories, and theories of identity formation, the ultimate question remains: does a category of encounter warrant a set of rights, entitlements, and other forms of formal recognition? This question is part of a more general analytical puzzle: does citizenship in the contemporary world, especially in places such as the European Union, the "New Europe," challenge the nation-state (Bellamy 2004; Soysal 1994)? In the case of Portugal, is Lusofonia, the most contemporary term in the Portuguese lexicon to describe a flexible but cohesive linguistic-cultural-territorial community, egalitarian or at least substantively inclusive of the increasingly heterogeneous populations that make up "Portugal"? Or is the idea of Portugal simply an ideology of paternalism, a resilient episteme bridging colonial and postcolonial periods?

## Portugal and Luso-Africa in Fiction

Such questions are particularly salient for Portugal and Portuguese relationships with migrants from former African colonies. At one time the Portuguese empire stretched its sphere of influence from the Southeast Asia point of Macau and Goa to the massive territory of Brazil in South America. Yet, it is Portugal's contact and mediation of Africa that continues to be both a point of intercultural pride and a source of anxiety as the Portugal administration constantly worries about its socio-economic and political footing as a contributing member of the European Union.

Despite its relatively small size, Cape Verde was a central and initial focal point of global and colonial creolization. Based on slave-trade records, we know that during the fifteenth and sixteenth centuries, when Spain and Portugal dominated the sea and expanded trade routes, slave ships stopped in Cape Verde before making their way to the labor camps of the New World. By the seventeenth century, the Dutch and British naval forces increasingly were successful in stealing African slaves from Portuguese vessels and selling them back to interested parties in Italy and Europe, more generally. In the nineteenth and twentieth centuries, the Portuguese depended on Cape Verde the place and various Creoles as communicative codes to manage labor populations and products connected to São Tomé e Príncipe and Angola. Again and again, Cape Verde was the major point of mediation and encounter.

Something seems to just happen "out there" in places like Cape Verde, which has been simultaneously the most proximate to Portugal, signifying a historical place of trade, mixture, and the evolutionary "Creole nation," as well as a mysterious Other with particularly strong tendencies toward identity politics. As several participants in a survey I conducted in 2013 reported, "Cape Verdeans do seem to have their *own culture*. Their presence is diverse in Lisbon but whatever and wherever it is, it seems to be something not-Portuguese." Expressed in a different register, acclaimed Angolan fiction writer José Eduardo Agualusa, in his book *Creole*, selects Cape Verde as the place for the protagonist Fradique Mendes to give homage to an old, faithful servant: "I threw Cornélio's head in the sea. It was a heavy, moonless night off the Cape Verde Islands. Iemanjá, the *quiandas* [water goddess], all the powerful divinities of Africa's hot waters will accompany his spirit back to the land of the Hausa" (2002:98).⁶

In Agualusa's novel, Fradique's transatlantic travels between Luanda, Angola; Recife, Brazil; and Lisbon, Portugal, turn violent due to his controversial stance as an antislavery advocate. Fradique's abolitionism comes through as personal in his letters, which amounts to the substance of the novel, and he directs much of the correspondence to Ana Olímpia, the Creole goddess and former Congolese princess. In the last chapter of *Creole*, the only letter written by Ana Olímpia, she reminds the reader that in most West African languages, the "same word is used for 'the sea' and 'death': *calunga*. So for most slaves the journey was a passage across death. The life they had left behind in Africa was Life; the one they found in America or Brazil, a Rebirth" (2002:151–52).

Acclaimed Angolan writer Pepetela (Artur Carlos Maurício Pestana), in his novel *Mayombe* about the interpersonal relationships among revolutionary guerrilla fighters in the Angolan independence movement of the 1960s, reflects on the double-edged nature of the sea through the minor character Muatianvua.

> The immensity of the sea that nothing can change taught me patience. The sea unites, the sea narrows, the sea joins. We too have an interior sea, which is not the Kuanza, nor Loje, nor Kunene. Our sea, made of diamond-drops, sweat and crushed tears, our sea is the sparkle of a well-oiled weapon that flashes in the midst of the Mayombe greenery, casting diamond scintillations at the Luanda sun. (1996:103)

Just as I had stood on an improvised roof pondering Kriolu, the Atlantic, and migrancy, societies in so-called Luso Africa continue to work through the sociogeographical metaphors of Portuguese colonialism. The sea as a unifying force and historical archive both soothes tensions and incites a politics of difference. One might, then, infer that Cape Verde, as a central archipelago in the transatlantic slave trade not only to the Americas but to Western Europe, is a precarious site between life and death yet one essential to the rebirth of creolization, again, not only in the Americas and the well-documented site of the Caribbean but also the vibrant but sporadically interpreted locale of Portugal and the former metropole of Lisbon.

To push the metaphor a bit further, Lisbon within the context of Europe has also figured consistently as a conduit, a suspect but inviting place for characters in transition. One finds this sentiment, particularly, in crime fiction set during World War II. For example, in the gumshoe novels *The Lisbon Crossing*, *A Night Train to Lisbon*, and *The Two Hotel Francforts* as well as the more sophisticated historical fiction *A Small Death in Lisbon*, the Lusophone capital is an intriguing safe haven, a precarious port within a notoriously porous state under the fascist dictator Salazar.[7] As the public intellectual Neill Lochery describes, Lisbon was often referred to as "Casablanca II," filled with black marketeers, hopeful migrants, undercover spies, and open, contradictory wartime propaganda. A setting of dubious encounters, Lisbon was the Creole city that inspired the young British intelligence officer Ian Fleming, author of the wildly successful James Bond novels.

The politics of the period and, in the case of Lochery, the individual maneuverings of Salazar make for the drama of these works of pop scholarship and historical fiction, but it is the deeper history of Lisbon's cross-cultural or, in contemporary European discourse, "intercultural" landscape that make Lisbon a more believable setting. The period of World War II is timely because this marked the beginning of an important trend of Portuguese domestic rural–urban migration as well as a preview of the immigration of Luso-Africans to the metropole. By the 1950s, such places as Alto da Cova da Moura, or what Cape Verdean youth now refer to as "Kova M," would start to become improvised neighborhoods, a new development and problem of Lisbon urbanization and a new chapter in the history of Portuguese interculturality. Lisbon as well as most European cities is still living this moment and attempting to manage the spatial arrangement of improvisation in addition to the accompanying cultural expressions of such encounters (Banting and Kymlicka 2013). This leads us to an introduction of the ethnographic foci in this book, Cape Verdean Kriolu rap music and daily life in the improvised and social neighborhoods, or project housing, of Lisbon.

## Kriolu inside Portugal

In his 2001 song "Nu bai" (Let's go), Lisbon rapper Chullage, with these apparently innocuous opening words in Kriolu, captures the energy of urban youth and raises awareness about a current problem of identity and belonging.

*Kabu verdi*
*Nu bai*
*Gosi nu sta na Portugei*
*Nu bai*
*Es ta ben y sai.*

[Cape Verde
Let's go
Now, we're in Portugal
Let's go
They (my people) come and go.]

## Introduction

The issue of Chullage's generation, those Cape Verdeans who migrated to Portugal as children during the 1980s, is tied to labor dynamics and urbanization. The immigrant population of this boom period consisted of predominantly manual laborers with an informal education. As INE (National Statistical Institute) reported in 1981, almost 80 percent of Cape Verdeans in Portugal worked in the service industry, construction, or manufacturing, and only 4 percent owned a business or worked in some capacity for themselves (INE 1981). Based on a survey conducted in the 1990s, Ana de Saint-Maurice reports that Cape Verdeans and migrants from São Tomé led the list of lowest-earning migrant groups in Lisbon with a roughly 40 percent rate of poverty and that these rates had worsened over the previous generation (1997:97). While this sort of space-labor dynamic compares with other cases in Europe and the Cape Verdean diaspora, the situation in Portugal is distinct. Its particularities are evident in the social life of language and, consequently, identity politics.

Cape Verdeans are highly diasporic; virtually every family can count on at least one migrant in the immediate family circle. There are significant communities in New England (particularly in the Boston and Providence areas), Paris, Rotterdam, Madrid, Coruña, Brussels, Dakar, Buenos Aires, and Santo André (part of São Paulo, Brazil, metro area). Cape Verdeans in these locales have integrated themselves conventionally into mainstream society through labor, education, language, and religion. As one particularly prideful Cape Verdean man told me, "when I lived in Sweden [during the 1970s] ... you know, there were South Americans, they'd complain about the dictatorships, the Africans would complain about the weather, the French would complain about the food.... Everyone complaining... and looking forward to returning as soon as possible, except the Cape Verdeans, we could stay. We're used to that." In the case of the United States and Boston, in particular, Cape Verdean integration was mediated by race so that Cape Verdean experiences became part of "Black Boston." One can find this in the testimonies of Cape Verdean migrants during the twentieth century (Britto 2002) and cultural management in institutions, such as the Boston Children's Museum, which dedicates a large playroom to Black Boston, including an African American barbershop, a Haitian carnival float, a Dominican market, and a Cape Verdean café.

Returning to Chullage's song, the language of Kriolu is significant given the fact that this hybrid combination of Portuguese and West African languages has no official status in Portugal or in native Cape Verde. Nevertheless, the ubiquitous Kriolu phrase nu bai became a call for greater attention to daily life of residents in the periphery neighborhoods of Lisbon not only among rappers but also in underground cinema and general Cape Verdean cultural events. These two small words of nu bai contain three large questions: who, exactly, are "we" (identity), where are we going (location), and what is the role of movement in identity formation (migration and policy)? Chullage, in particular, but scores of other Kriolu rappers in the first decades of the twenty-first century would go on to make explicit links among migration, living conditions in peripheral Lisbon, and identity. Kriolu rappers, through their language and a rhetorical style that emphasizes both space and mobility, actively perform the question of citizenship. In so doing, they challenge the dominant discourses on identity built around conventional concepts of race, class, ethnicity, and property.

## Rap

Rap music is one of the only forms of popular expressive culture that makes issues of encounter transparent and readily consumable as stylized rhetoric. This genre of transnational popular culture, while significantly variable in style, message, and politics, does cohere around a few characteristics. Rappers emphasize the text and rhetorical style. More specifically, all rappers, at some point in performance or recording, address space when making claims to authority, glossed as "who I am and the place to be." For example, one can find this consistently in the lyrics of Kriolu rapper Kromo, "I'm always representing Kova M. We don't have nostalgia; we have soldiers." Kromo plays with the Portuguese and Kriolu words of *saudade* and *sodadi* (nostalgia) and *soldado* and *soldadu* (soldier) to portray his neighborhood as less about the classic Portuguese sentiment of nostalgia and the past (*sodadi*) but, rather, more about an immediacy of public strength represented in the soldier (*soldadu*). Kriolu rapper Lord G, part of TWA (Third World Answer), put time and place in an even more dramatic frame: "Nigga, death to me could happen at any time. Bitch, you never sensed that we exist. It's here right now that broadcasts" ("Miraflor" 2002, translated from Kriolu; English words *nigga* and *bitch* in original). Kromo and Lord G, like most rappers, propose such claims to listeners as "real" in the sense that the words are factual or emotionally felt as true. Finally, rap is a genre that demands a skill set of rhetorical flow and neologisms. Therefore, rap's defining features of space and reality expressed through an aesthetics of flow and linguistic creativity make rap attractive to youth looking to link their sense of self to collective membership through a shared pleasure and pride in language.

Rappers are adamant about speaking and, more to the point, are forceful in bringing awareness to how they speak. In the case of young, underemployed rappers, marked as immigrants, dangerous, and African, the manner of rhymed speech reflects the challenging realities of postcolonial conditions in Europe. Karlos, a Kriolu rapper emigré living in Belfast, Ireland, pointed out to me on a visit to Lisbon that "*ma, ka, ta, sa*—these are all little stepping-stone Kriolu sounds that I use to get to the main idea of *djuguta* [daily struggle]." It is this sort of phonemic flow coupled with key words of displacement, emplacement (the practices of making place), collectivity, and stigma that Kriolu rappers explore in rhetoric. While they might not offer concrete answers, Kriolu rappers, at the very least, demand a reassessment of the parameters of formal belonging. I suggest that the tension between citizenship ideologies and lived experience can produce theories of identity.

## Fundamental Claims

*Cape Verde, Let's Go* is a response to two basic research questions that surfaced during my exploratory fieldwork in Lisbon in 2007: What effect, if any, do speaking and rapping in the Euro-African language of Cape Verdean Kriolu have on identity politics in Portugal, and what might the evidence from this Creole case contribute to a general understanding of identity formation? Based on methodologies, including interviews, archival research, lyrical analysis, surveys, participation in targeted internet social networks, and textual review of governmental policies, I formulated two arguments.

First, Kriolu rap in Lisbon has affected, albeit indirectly, the terms that shape law, popular discourse, and politics around what it is to be Portuguese. Cape Verdeans are unique in the history of European colonialism because their lingua franca was already a hybrid with Portuguese and a range of established African languages. This presented a special problem and opportunity for the Portuguese as they desperately tried to maintain their colonial ties to Africa in the twentieth century. Cape Verdeans became both irritating as black, semi-acculturated Portuguese and useful as strategic intermediaries between Portugal forces (the *tugas*) and presumably wholly "other" people, such as the various "tribes" of Bantu speakers (Kimbundu, Kikongo) of modern-day Angola, Congo, and Mozambique. With the decolonization wars of the 1960s and 1970s leading up to the regimes changes of 1974, populist leaders in Cape Verde and Guinea-Bissau significantly highlighted Kriolu/Kriol as essential to cultural nationalism.

An analysis of the politics of the Kriolu language as performed by rappers residing in the Lisbon metropolitan area shows that Kriolu has impacted Portuguese national identity. Although Cape Verdeans, along with other Luso-Africans, have been present in urban Portugal, especially Lisbon, since the late fifteenth century, the great majority of contemporary Kriolu speakers and rappers are first- or second-generation Cape Verdean immigrants. Families arrived in Lisbon during the 1960s as a labor force for public works and large-scale construction projects in the 1970s due to the destruction resulting from decolonization wars back "at home" and again in the late 1980s, when Portugal entered the European Union and reappeared as a potential solution to underemployment on the archipelago. Many

## Introduction

Cape Verdeans, regardless of where they were born, do not possess Portuguese citizenship. Their anxieties around belonging and rights have resonated within a national debate about immigration and citizenship in a postcolonial Portugal. This milieu is a shared situation among Western European nation-states as political administrations respond to divergent concerns in their constituencies regarding a perceived "invasion" of former colonial subjects and other, "more foreign" transnational laborers.

Rap is an essential field of inquiry regarding citizenship because this genre of music and spoken poetry highlights the aesthetic and political power of language and is deeply interwoven into youth and popular culture both at the level of commercial circuits and quotidian practices. Rappers create a sense of membership through stylized language and, at times, use such style to demand civic and political rights. Rappers' success in the globalized music industry depends on rhetorical art of flow, that is, being able to combine a variety of rhythmic rhymes with a flair for the turn of phrase and occasional neologism. Within this field of artistic production, some rappers go further and articulate ideologies of place, politics, and/or violence to an aesthetics of flow. As mentioned above, Kriolu contains certain differences in its linguistic structure that local rappers explore within an aesthetic of rhyme flow in order to attract listeners, Kriolu and non-Kriolu speakers, as not only supportive fans but also potential sympathizers for Kriolu legitimacy. Rapper Chullage explained to me, "It's not just that I feel more comfortable rapping in Kriolu, it's about getting everybody [non-Kriolu speakers in Portugal and rap fans around the world] to listen and go search for the meaning. It's what we all did when we first heard Public Enemy. We didn't understand English. We looked it up. People can do that with Kriolu."

Such legitimacy involves claims on the Portuguese state, ranging from official linguistic, historical, and cultural recognition to state-subsidized Kriolu centers to state-sponsored antiracism campaigns intended to combat everyday stigma. For other Kriolu youth, legitimacy and authenticity come in the form of strengthening diasporic ties to not only Cape Verde but to the widespread diaspora. In addition, some Kriolu rappers cast their identity nets wider to include non-Kriolu hip-hop and internationally recognized "black" centers of cultural production, such as Brazil and Jamaica. In sum, rap is a particularly effective and affective vehicle for Creole citizenship across various community objectives from Kriolu as part of Portugal to Cape Verdean diaspora to Kriolu as part of global negritude.

> It becomes more than ever urgent to develop a framework of thinking that makes the migrant central, not ancillary, to historical processes. We need to disarm the genealogical rhetoric of blood, property and frontiers and to substitute for

it a lateral account of social relations, one that stresses the contingency of all definitions of self and the other, and the necessity always to tread lightly. (P. Carter 1992:7–8)

Paul Carter's musings allude to the second claim of this book, a theoretical argument about citizenship and identity, more generally. In his book of essays, he describes a "migrant aesthetic" as a cultural manifestation of the "dialogic space" created in travel. Again, in the spirit of juxtaposing the spaces of imagination and poetics with the materiality of labor and housing, I suggest that migrancy is an episteme, a paradigm of being that is central to identity formation in the contemporary world.

Kriolu in Portugal and in the homeland of Cape Verde suggests that Creole, in a more global sense, is an epistemology of lived and imagined realities and has been essential in not only colonial but also postcolonial identity formation. Creole identities and languages developed historically from sustained relationships of power inequality under the auspices of slavery and colonialism. More specifically, Creole as a type of identity formation emerged from the self-other dynamic and has been entangled in the negotiation of labor from slavery and other colonial trade to modernization and urbanization projects in Lisbon to contemporary service industries to elite forms of art and scholarship. This is what Pépin and Confiänt called an "identity of coexistence" (1998:98).

> That stranger, as the ghost that shadows every discourse, is the disturbing interrogation, the estrangement that potentially exists within us all. It is a presence that persists, that cannot be effaced that draws me out of myself towards another. ... This decentering of the classical "individual" leads also to the weakening and dispersal of the rationalist *episteme*, of the Western *cogito*, that once anchored and warranted the subject as the privileged fulcrum of knowledge, truth and being. (Chambers 1994:6–7, italics in original)

Iain Chambers describes the centrality of the encounter as not only a transgressive experience but also as a theoretical challenge. In a complementary fashion, local housing activist and Cape Verdean émigré Rolando reflects: "It is this mixture of Cape Verde and Portugal that makes me feel more human. I feel like this background has made me more open and sensitive to dialogue. Look, I am critical but this comes after opening myself up to interaction with others" (personal communication, 2011). This sort of intercultural perspective on identity is part of a nationally articulated ideology of Portuguese identity and is rhetorically part of citizenship policies since the early twentieth century. Writing in the late colonial period of the early 1970s, journalist Nuno de Miranda adds a spatial element to the identity component of the encounter. He does this, unsurprisingly, through the trope of the sea (*o mar*).

> The sea is more than a geographical symbol, it is an element of characterization. ... The sea incarnates our historical desires, the kernels of truth and reality of our nationality.... The sea, which is a point of connection, is the fiber with and through which we bind all these idiosyncratic forces of social and economic import, and maintain a unifying equilibrium and harmonic development of the country. (1971:31)

Portuguese and Cape Verdeans share the collective trope of the sea. Kriolu takes these relationships of encounter and transnational or transcontinental migration as a basis. The language and identity not only embody the fundamental relationship of self and other but also concerns the dynamics of power and place.

## Methods

Ideally, those in the business of cultural representation and interpretation, including anthropologists, develop a methodology from primarily inductive reasoning. Experiences on the ground play a significant if not determinative role in how we go about conducting research. In previous research carried out in São Paulo, Brazil, I depended almost exclusively on the classical methods of cultural anthropology, including participant observations, surveys, and informal interviews. Most of my analysis emerged from knowledge gained in situ. This made sense given the topics of daily life and popular youth culture, but certainly there are other perspectives on the subject given only passing acknowledgment in those publications. For example, if we think chronotopically, São Paulo is an ephemeral city of advertising and urban Post-Its. Billboards and graffiti tags are everywhere, and despite its significant history (founded in 1554), one rarely feels such historical depth. São Paulo, then, is what French novelist André Gidé once mused, in reference to Paris, as "a lively city where the past is not a tyrant" (1949:201).

Lisbon couldn't be more different, as residents cannot help but feel history. Monuments are everywhere, and nostalgia is the state's consistent aesthetic palette to remind residents of identity. While this layer of visual history thins out as one moves to the peripheral districts and municipalities where many Cape Verdeans live, the chronotopic sentiment of colonial intimacy still pervades. A significant portion of the African émigré community in Lisbon lived through independence wars and experienced the pain and triumph of decolonization in the 1960s and 1970s. Such experiential and spatial parameters call for a complementary methodology and, more specifically, a healthy incorporation of textual research at state and community archives.

## Introduction

I conducted fieldwork in Lisbon on four separate occasions, 2007, 2009, 2011, and 2013. Each period ranged from ten days to ten weeks. I also conducted fieldwork in Praia, Cape Verde, on two occasions, 2009 and 2011, for a total of eight weeks. Taken together, I held targeted but informal interviews with thirty-four rappers, three graffiti artists, one DJ, and two street dancers. I also interviewed a dozen members of state agencies that work with immigrants in Lisbon and another ten people who work for nongovernmental organizations (NGOs) related to immigration and interculturality. The focus of this book is squarely on rappers and is significantly gendered given the population pool. Twenty-eight of the thirty-four rappers are male. This sort of information provides a baseline for the reader to gauge the kind of fieldwork interactions from which I induce a set of social theories.

In addition, since 2009 I have consulted a range of archives located in state-sponsored institutions, such as national libraries and collections of colonial documents, as well as much-smaller community archives located in neighborhood and "intercultural" organizations. It is worth reflecting briefly on the organization of the archives as a trace of bureaucracy (Crooks and Parsons 2014) and the general frame of knowledge production. For example, I visited several times the archives of the Sociedade de Geografia de Lisboa (Geographical Society of Lisbon) (SGL), created in 1875 and modeled on the Geographical Society archive in London. As Miguel Bandeira Jerónimo outlines in his essay on the role of missionaries in the production of colonial knowledge during the turn of the twentieth century in Luso-Africa, the SGL and subsequent state-sponsored institutions, such as the Colonial and Ethnographic Museum (1892), Colonial School (1906), and Overseas Archives (1931), helped generate a new "economy of information" and "propagate a semantics of colonization" (2006:30–31, see also João 1998; Guimarães 1984).

The forces of institutions and language frame not only history (what Michel-Rolph Trouillot describes as the "archival power" [1995] in relation to what we know about Haiti) but also identity and citizenship. As described in detail in chapters 1 and 2, the SGL is home to several periodicals published by Portuguese state agencies responsible for legitimizing and reinvigorating Portugal's reinvestment in Africa as part of the so-called scramble for Africa in the late nineteenth and early twentieth centuries. Referring to the "crisis" of Africa, the paternalist Prime Minister Salazar confessed about the maintenance of Lusotropical hegemony over Luso-Africa, "This is the mission of our life" (quoted in Duffy 1961a).

Given this context, it is fascinating to see how SGL staff crafted annual bulletins concerning the great promise of Cape Verde in the late nineteenth century as compared to the other African colonies. Such magazines as *Permanence*, published during the final years of Portuguese colonialism in the early 1970s, display a "cultural design" of Lusotropicalism, highlighting, for example, the "natural" camaraderie of white Portuguese and black African youth in school as an attractive cover print for the periodical. This stands in contrast to the testimonies and folkloric documents I discovered in the neighborhood archives both in Lisbon and Praia detailing the infamous droughts of the 1890s and 1940s and the abandonment of Portuguese aid. Such axes of power and experience became central to my fieldwork methodology by shaping the questions I asked and informing the subsequent theories of my interpretation.

The realities of Lisbon have influenced my methodology not only in terms of looking back and becoming attuned to archival protocols but also in terms of social networks and information technology as they relate to cultural production in rap music and community building in the Cape Verdean presence in Lisbon and to Kriolu identification throughout the diaspora. We can substitute *YouTube* and *Facebook* for *Walkman* in the following rumination Chambers wrote in 1994: "Like Walter Benjamin's description of the Parisian arcades that let light into their interiors, the Walkman brings the external world into the interior design of identities." YouTube, blogs, and Facebook have become alternative "sites of dwelling" (1994:50, 52) and have influenced the conceptualization of the "field" in cultural studies. For example, savvy Cape Verdean youth used Facebook and to a lesser extent Twitter in the early months of 2013 to mobilize PALOP residents in Lisbon as a form of political lobby after local police killed a Cape Verdean resident of an improvised neighborhood. In addition, these youth tried to motivate those sympathetic to the situation to convene in a neighborhood cultural organization and daycare to watch documentary films on Marcus Garvey and the Black Panthers. They call this "Marcus Garvey University," an alternative site of popular education. Moreover, I utilized the virtual and material sites to conduct surveys about the image and presence of Cape Verdeans in Lisbon. Information technology, thus, facilitates the refashioning of conventional sites (day-care facilities, neighborhood gathering sites) into new political and ethnographic sites. In addition, the technology itself becomes a site of sociality. In the words of Cape Verdean Kriolu rapper Hezbollah, "Facebook allowed us to make our idea of 'ghetto platform' into something more real and effective" (personal conversation).

As explained above, I define citizenship as a set of conditions emergent through a relationship of policy and practice. Throughout the current volume, I employ such terms as *presence* and *performance* to capture the action-based dynamics of this relationship and, thus, bring an ethnographic perspective to the material. The ethnographic data comes from a set of Kriolu places, ranging from the most transparently performative, that is, commercial and state-sponsored rap concerts, to the most disembodied, that is, Facebook networks and other social-media interaction. However, my primary settings of interaction were in neighborhood public spaces and inside the apartments and home studios of Kriolu rappers. Yet, the street and the studio are fluid spaces of sociality bending to the occasional obligations of family (siblings making requests), the watchful and often respectful eyes of community elders, and the unexpected visits of friends and rivals.[8]

Such a cultural landscape argues for a methodological approach based on the everyday rather than the event. Other researchers in Lisbon have, likewise, noted that due to the long, repressive dictatorship of Salazar-Caetano (1932–1974), combined with a subsequent large-scale wave of immigration in the 1980s and 1990s, conventional sociopolitical mobilization has been slow in coming. Hip-hop, along with other youth and popular expressive cultures, has been effective in creating venues for community building and occasional citizenship mobilization (Durão 2011; Fradique 2003).

## Relevance of Portugal and Cape Verde to Citizenship Debate

Policy analysts and scholars have focused their discussions on citizenship and migration in Europe on England, France, Germany, and, to a lesser extent, Holland, Belgium, and Scandinavian countries (Bowen 2007; Bosniak 2006; Koopman 2010; Parekh 2000; Brochmann and Seland 2010). Heavy on policy interpretation and political theory highlighting such keywords as *multiculturalism*, *pluralism*, and *liberalism*, this literature gives only passing treatment of daily life and expressive culture. For the most part, culture is limited to visible ethnicity and, more specifically, religious practices in the public sphere.

Although Portugal occupies a marginal position within the current political economics of Europe, Portuguese colonialism and its complex relationship with various types of migration warrant scrutiny. Similar to Spain, Portugal passed through periods of relative insularism under fascist regimes. Moreover, in part due to its own dependent relationship with the United Kingdom and France, Portugal was itself a country of significant emigration consequent of labor pressures. Yet, by the late 1980s, both Spain and Portugal became target destinations for an increasingly diverse group of immigrants. Unlike Spain, Portugal's long-standing relationship with its sub-Saharan African colonies provides a generative and dynamic sense of historicity to the current demographic shifts. It is here where Cape Verde becomes salient.

In distinction to Portugal's policies and mindset toward its other African territories, Cape Verde and Cape Verdeans were never completely "othered." Cape Verdean alterity has always been a (potentially) passing category. In short, this is the "Creole" benefit, represented by the privilege of Shakespeare's character Ariel, the mobile intermediary between the grounded Caliban and omnipotent Prospero in *The Tempest*. However, the drama of Cape Verdean-ness moves through many acts indexing cleavages of class, race, and geography (i.e., a hierarchical stratification of the islands). As chapter 3 discusses in detail, Kriolu speech and expressive culture have a tradition of high art and literature, which was embraced as part of what would be termed in the 1950s as Lusotropicalism, an intended emblem of Portuguese "soft" power representing colonial stewardship in Africa and postcolonial partnership in the current times of globalization.

Kriolu is also a Calibanesque brand of rebellious backtalk against contemporary discourses and policies based on racialized stigma that purports that African immigrants tend to be more violent, less educated, more criminal, more promiscuous, and, overall, more marginal to a suddenly desirable and ambiguous Portuguese citizenship. For example, the High Commission of Immigration and Ethnic Minorities (ACIME), renamed in 2007 as the High Commission of Immigration and Intercultural Dialogue (ACIDI), an organization usually positive about Portugal's immigration policies and the relative congeniality of Portuguese people, published a critical report on media representation of immigrants (ACIME 2006). Through an analysis of mostly newspaper articles and television programs and commercials, the ACIME research team discovered that "Portuguese" viewers find it "difficult" to relate to "Africans" because they appear to be "less competent" and have less drive toward accomplishment than Brazilians and Eastern Europeans, respectively.

In summary, the relationship between Portugal and Cape Verde is both intimate and contradictory. Yet, it is definitely not silent. There is pressure on state agencies to define and categorize its citizens. Given the palpable tension around such a project in contemporary Europe, it is significant that since 2006 the Portuguese government through new, more inclusive laws and a rebranding of Lisbon as distinctively "multicultural" has begun to address the contemporary demographics of the country and update its definitions and parameters of citizenship. Kriolu exemplifies both the Portuguese ideal of identity and membership as mixture and the postcolonial rub of identity politics based on the "human rights logic" of contemporary citizenship (Joppke 2010:27). The reasoning here is that everyone deserves official recognition and, thus, a robust sense of citizenship, but such recognition does not translate into assimilation or mixture but acknowledgment of difference. This is what Kymlicka (1995) critically describes as "benign neglect" on the part of states. In short, Kriolu seemingly represents both inclusion and exclusion. How is this possible? What sort of model for citizenship does Kriolu represent?

## Chapter Summaries

Chapter 1, "Creole's Historical Presences," provides historical depth to the claim of a Creole citizenship by delineating the spatial presence of Africanity inside

Introduction

Lisbon and detailing the special relationship Portugal has had with Cape Verde. Creole presence and the very notion of Creole connect directly to the organization of labor and the language of encounter. Moreover, both language and labor were (and continue to be) significant categories in evaluating membership, one of the defining markers of modern citizenship.

As Portuguese colonial regimes attempted to adapt to market demands and European competitors, they changed state approaches to citizenship. The intimacy of Portugal–Cape Verde influenced colonial policies in the definitions of important categories, such as *indigenous* and *assimilated*. I argue that the factors of Lisbon spatiality and colonial management of space, language, and education suggest that Creole has been a significant presence in the formation of "Portuguese" identity. Following historians of the Black Atlantic, such as Linda Heywood and John K. Thornton (2007), I root my discussion in the historical fact that Portugal preceded all other European countries by at least a century in exchange and conflict with West and Central Western Africa. Such encounters and displacements created Creole.

Chapter 2, "Kriolu Interruptions of Luso," contributes to the discussion of Creole citizenship by addressing the new challenges of identity politics after 1974 with the official end of Portuguese colonialism and the implosion of the Salazar-Caetano fascist regime. The 1980s witnessed a gradual disintegration of the Marxist-inspired government alliances throughout the newly independent African nation-states with a marked intensification of civil wars in Angola and Mozambique. The demographic effects of this turmoil, that is, emigration to predominantly Lisbon, reignited discourses around Kriolu as both black otherness and part of Portugal's unique multiculturalism. To this end, I analyze the power of Lusotropicalism as an organizing ideology that has survived political shifts and continues to inform Portuguese notions of national identity. Chapter 2 introduces more systematically Kriolu rappers and their challenges to Lusotropicalism and other Luso discourses, such as Lusofonia.

Chapters 3 and 4, "Lisbon Rappers and the Labor of Location" and "Spatial Politics of Kriolu Presence in Lisbon," respectively, continue the ethnographic focus on Kriolu rappers and concentrate on the dimension of space in Cape Verdean identity formation. These chapters contribute to the overall analysis of citizenship and identity formation by arguing that belonging, rights, and outside recognition depend on spatial occupation in the form of cultural centers, neighborhood streets, and studios. Once established that Kriolu is a historical force, albeit ambiguous, in shaping Portuguese sense of national identity in various global and regional contexts, the questions remain: What is the local presence of Kriolu in contemporary Lisbon? How do Kriolu rappers delineate space and difference through rap rhetoric? In other words, is there a Kriolu rap "scene," and, if so, how might one describe its parameters?

Chapter 3 focuses on the links between the microstructures of Kriolu phonemes and morphemes and Kriolu rap's narrative themes of discontented diaspora and unfulfilled membership. Chapter 4 marks a transition from linguistics and discourse to the more overt politics of space evident in the current demolition and relocation campaigns that city urbanization agencies engineered. Kriolu also plays a significant role in understanding the differences between autoconstructed neighborhoods and social or state-sponsored project housing.

Chapter 5, "Kriolu and European Interculturality," builds from previous analyses of Lusotropicalism and other Luso discourses of Portuguese inclusion by interrogating the ideas and policies of interculturality. This term is a key word the European Union and other agencies proposed to address the everyday tensions around multiculturalism and difference. With a solid understanding of the history and national ramifications of Kriolu, we can begin to apply a theory of identity vis-à-vis encounter, migration, and interruption to assess the potential lessons of Kriolu and, more broadly, Creole citizenship in a postcolonial Europe. To this end, I juxtapose a set of life stories from Cape Verdean rappers and their families against policy documents from the European Commission (EC) and the Portuguese state agency ACIDI.

In the final section, "Suggestive Conclusions," I provide a culminating set of theoretical conclusions and policy deliverables that bring together anthropological concepts and life experiences of Kriolu.

## CHAPTER 1

# Creole's Historical Presences

> *O sangue e as almas, as vozes e as histórias, a música e as saudades, o amor e os versos,—são Portugal e África fundidos, afeiçoados pelo mesmo destêrro nostálgico, consolado e dorido,—resignado, sem revolta, nas ilhas que são cárceres, conventos e mirantes perdidas ao meio da vastidão do mar.*
>
> The blood and soul, the voices and histories, the music and longing, the love and verses—[all of this] roots Portugal and Africa, blessed by the same nostalgic exile, consoled and pained,—resigned, without revolt, on the islands that are prisons, convents and lookouts lost in the middle of the vast sea.
>
> —Augusto Casimiro

This passage from the Portuguese chronicler Augusto Casimiro exemplifies the typical story of blood and soul constitutive of the ideal Portuguese collective self. Moreover, Casimiro depicts what Eric Morier-Genoud and Michel Cahen call the "social space of migration [within the] imagined entity of the empire. And this is particularly true in the Portuguese case, with a historically deep integration of Africa into the national imagining" (2012:19).

Portuguese collective memory, particularly as it relates to Luso-Africa, often begins with the Moorish occupation of Iberia, which lasted for several centuries until the late thirteenth century when King Alonso recaptured Lisbon and the southern region called Algarve, a nominal Arabic holdover. The idea of Portugal as a geopolitical entity was born. The Moorish period was a time of what in the Brazilian context would later be termed *mestiçagem*, or racial mixing.

For its part, Cape Verde emerged as a place name and social construct in the late fifteenth century. It was a place created from Luso-Afro trade and encounter and then left to creolize for a time with other populations, especially after Portugal's formal abolition of the slave trade and Brazil's independence in 1822. Along with Belgium, England, France, and Italy, Portugal redirected its efforts toward Africa in the late nineteenth and early twentieth centuries. For Casimiro, a popular writer of his time, Portugal's identity is essentially lodged in African encounters mediated by the ur-metaphor of the island, a nod to the pain of voyage and the beacon of discovery. Cape Verde is the archetype of the encounter, the primary figure of Portugal's national construction.

The notion that Portugal is a product of long, sustained intercultural encounters with Africa is not simply something that happened supposedly out there in the mysterious world of colonialism and early capitalism. The blood and soul of a Luso-Creole were not relegated to territories outside of Europe, whose inhabitants would only return to the metropole in a post–World War II milieu of migration as a result of reorganized capital, labor, and political regimes. Indeed, Africanity has been an intermittent but formative part of, particularly, Lisbon's history for over a millennium, whether it be the "negros" in the era of regional governor Al-Judami,[1] the so-called black moors (*mouros pretos*) during early slavery periods of the late fifteenth century, the roving bards and fishermen of the seventeenth and eighteenth centuries depicted in museum exhibits, the elite Luso-African college students, and future revolutionary leaders of the 1950s or the poor, working-class *badiu* (vagabond; from the Cape Verdean island of Santiago) Kriolu rappers of today.

This chapter provides historical depth to the claim of a Creole citizenship by delineating the spatial presence of Africanity inside Lisbon and detailing the special relationship Portugal had with Cape Verde. As implied above in Casimiro's text, the Luso-African experience is an intimate "exile," one that produces nostalgia via contact linked directly to the organization of labor and the language of encounter. For late nineteenth-century political leaders, such as Antonio Ennes, labor was one of the defining characteristics of the civilizing mission of the Portuguese in Africa. For example, in his 1891 "Mozambique—Report Presented to the Government," Ennes utilizes scientific racism to justify policies of taxation and forced labor campaigns by the Portuguese colonial administration. In Ennes's view, nostalgia and pain are the unavoidable human elements of colonialism and part of the price to forge a strong, modern Portugal ([1893] 1971). However, some of the "voices and histories" of Casimiro's Portugal are in Kriolu, and they interpret the toils of labor, island hardships, and Atlantic travel as ultimately an idiom of emplacement, a discourse that links encounters abroad with social relations inside Portugal. More of Kriolu linguistics as it relates to Lisbon place making, rap rhetoric, and flow is discussed in chapter 3.

## Historical Presences

Historical presences are manifested in symbolic and material forms. For example, figure 4 shows a poster from the exhibit *Os Africanos em Portugal* (Africans in Portugal) held in 2011 at the Torre de Belém (Belém Tower). Belém, a neighborhood on the Tagus River bank, is between major landmarks, such as the Commerce Plaza and Rossio, and the picturesque city of Cascais, the setting for so many World War II historical fiction novels. The poster displays several examples of residential street signs in the Lisbon area, the racialized or African names thereby representing the incorporation of Portuguese colonialism (and, occasionally, African liberation) into everyday Lisbon geography. For example, the poster presents the well-known street *Rua do Poço dos Negros*, which joins *Travessa do Judeu*, literally the intersection of Well of Blacks Street and Jew Crossing. The names represent a time of return in the early eighteenth century, a return of Moors, Africans, and Jews attempting to reestablish residency and legitimacy in Europe after the Inquisition and massive expulsion during the fifteenth and sixteenth centuries. Following the massive earthquake of 1755, a combination of progressive politics and modern urbanization under Sebastião José de Carvalho e Melo, the first Marquess of Pombal (Marquês de Pombal), resulted in an "enlightened" disengagement from the slave trade, thereby diminishing the visible presence of Africans in the metropole and in the process scattering current African residents into fragmented communities (Henriques 2009, 2012). An encore of such race-space politics more than two centuries later with the urbanization campaigns to "integrate" immigrant communities relocated them away from improvised or autoconstructed residences and into social neighborhoods, as chapter 4 describes. Currently, Kriolu rappers and other Cape Verdean youth are attempting to reinsert themselves in the city, giving new meanings to Lisbon race and space through language, music, and grassroots politics. Such action constitutes a type of social agency that helps define the concept of emplacement, a response to the legacy of displacement referenced above.

The history of Africanity in Lisbon is a dynamic process of historiography, culture, and law. The ebbs and flows of Portuguese (and by extension European) interest in Africans inside the metropole coupled with ambiguous terms of classification during colonialism due to shifting state policies of citizenship and formal inclusion have produced many contradictions and complicate the notion of a straightforward account of African presences inside Portugal (Henriques 2009, 2012). Portugal is a fascinating example of racialization and migration because its contradictions are a formative part of national development. Fascism and Lusotropicalism seem to go hand in hand. Scientific racism shares ideological space with Lusotropicalism. Popular press during the first half of the twentieth century

FIGURE 4. Lisbon street signs. Poster from the exhibit Os Africanos em Portugal. Photo by author, 2011.

depicts Africans as happy children, foolish dandies, and terrorizing cannibals. In more recent periods, Portuguese xenophobia and robust multiculturalist policies have operated in a parallel fashion.

The dialectics of African desire and disgust were certainly just as influential in Portugal as in more well-documented areas, such as Latin America (see Skidmore 1992; Graham 1990). Isabel Castro Henriques describes the contradiction involving race and citizenship in this manner: "If Portuguese laws recognized Africans as free and theoretically Portuguese, the secular consolidation of the African image as being naturally a slave made it difficult to consider a change in the African's status" (2012:79). Further back in history are the remarkable antislavery laws Marquês de Pombal issued. On September 19, 1761, the so-called *Leis Pombalinas* (Pombaline reforms) outlawed officially the importation of slaves into Portugal. Pombal's reasoning appears futuristic as it reminds one of the urban sociologists of the 1920s in their explanations of the "problems" of the "negro" and other immigrants in the city as a result of conditions and the environment. Pombal remarks,

> This extraordinary number of black slaves, who are sorely missed abroad in my overseas territories as part of an earthly, rural culture. They come here and oc-

cupy the role of the servant boy struggling for housing. They fall into idleness and tend towards vice, to which they have natural proclivities. (1761)

The logic that construes social problems as activated by environment is a rationale based on space. For Pombal, Walter Reckless ([1933] 1969) or, for that matter, contemporary urban planners in Lisbon, the ills of the city made manifest are a problem of human geography. LBC, an activist Kriolu rapper from the Cape Verdean autoconstructed neighborhood Cova da Moura, provides a contemporary example: "The police last Saturday night [summer of 2013] came up to one black guy at the bottom of the hill near Damaia [an adjacent neighborhood] and said, 'You can't be here. Just you being here, I can hit you.' And he did. This kid obviously didn't know what every youngster here in Cova da Moura grows up knowing—the places where the police can just beat on you and the places where you're supposed to be" (LBC, personal communication, 2013).

The question latent in the accounts of LBC, Henriques, Pombal, and Ennes can be summarized as: what are the social, cultural, and political forces that afford space to some and not to others? What I refer to as "Kriolu presence" addresses this issue of social geography and the processes of dis/emplacement. In figure 4, *poço* (well) refers to what was a large cemetery that once contained the corpses of a substantive African population dating back to the early days of Portuguese expansion and colonialism. Is this street sign a preview of what would become "the growth of a particular black metropolitan aesthetic that gives distinct shape and direction to questions of post-colonial culture and identity" (Chambers 1994:68), what Homi Bhabha theorizes as a "third space" resulting from hybridity and the encounter (1990)? Or is it what Mary Louise Pratt describes, "while the imperial metropolis tends to understand itself as determining the periphery ... it habitually blinds itself to the ways in which the periphery determines the metropolis—beginning, perhaps, with the latter's obsessive need to present and re-present its peripheries and its other continually to itself" (1992:6)? Do common place names and Creole chatter produce civil society, or are these signs just a simple case of patriarchal control, a hegemony located in landmarks and ephemeral talk?

The questions asked in this chapter likewise complement those of Morier-Genoud and Cahen when they reflect historically on the relationship between migration and "autonomous social spaces" in the Portuguese empire (2012:1–30). Do the African occupations in Lisbon of residence and profession, education and expressive culture, take on a life of their own? Do their legacies, evident in Kriolu-speaking youth and robust immigrant neighborhoods, constitute recognized publics with influence on collective notions of the city of Lisbon and ideas of Portuguese citizenship?

CHAPTER 1

## State Representations of Africanity and Space

State-sponsored cultural production in Lisbon has generally portrayed Africanity in Portugal as an exceptional offer by an understanding colonial regime. For example, in 2011 the Torre de Belém, a four-story tower monument that actually sits in the Tagus River, was the site of an attractive retrospective exhibit on Luso-African history inside Lisbon. Since 2006 the Portuguese state and the public postal service (CTT) have commissioned a group of scholars and publicists to produce coffee-table books. *A Herança Africana em Portugal—séculos XV–XX* (The African inheritance in Portugal) presents a heavy tome of thick, glossy paper and is dedicated to the role of the Luso encounter abroad in the making of "Portuguese" culture back "home" in the metropole. The poster session in the tower was essentially a series of cropped and enlarged text highlights and prominent images from the book, which is specifically about the African presence in Lisbon (Henriques 2009).

To see the exhibit, I descended into what resembles a dungeon. Beyond the expected depiction of African religious, culinary, aesthetic, and other ethnic practices that became visible in Portugal and, specifically, Lisbon, the exhibit underscored the importance of place. The visual narrative began with Lagos, in the southern region of the Algarve and the first European port of the slave trade, dating back to 1444. The long centuries of trade structured by a racist market logic of value came through in the documents of African bodies, institutions, and place names.

The exhibit designers transformed what might have appeared as an inauspicious start to any sort of national Africanity narrative into a story of pioneering urban policies regarding residential patterns and linguistic geography. Beginning in 1593 with a royal license, Africans built the Mocambo, a series of what would now be considered neighborhoods, located on a stretch of land adjacent to the city center to the west along the Tagus (Henriques 2009). The better translation of *mocambo*, following the conventional connotation of the Umbundo term, perhaps is *village*. Brazilianists will recognize the Kimbundo cognate of *quilombo*, a word that reveals many layers of race, space, self-liberation, and contemporary identity politics in Brazil (see, for example, Silberling 2003; French 2009; Kenny 2013). The authors of the exhibit concluded by reassuring the public that by the seventeenth century, the population of the Mocambo had become significantly mixed with slaves, freemen, Portuguese, and women participants of religious orders.

The Mocambo is, thus, upheld as a Creole space with folks dedicated to the commerce of the sea, a market organized around the encounter. The implication is that a sense of "black" space existed inside the metropole early in modern immigration history and that interethnic and interracial Creole mixture has always been the Portuguese way. Africanity in Lisbon was not limited to street names, as suggested by figure 4.

Such historical material of race and space echoes in contemporary Portugal, as residents continue to reflect on identity. One can interpret the following 2007 headline from the Lisbon newspaper *Ípsilon* as an attempt to incorporate "outside" influences as self-identification. "Lisbon wants to be black again?" sets the tone for the 2007 review of the third annual Africa Festival, a multiday event featuring world beat musical artists. For this year, journalists invited a number of academics and cultural promoters to discuss race and multiculturalism. What is "black culture"? Is it the same as Africanity? Antonio Contador, a Portuguese sociologist, who has published widely on urban youth culture and rap music in Lisbon, asserts that "Africanity has faded" from a set of cultural expressions that constitute contemporary negritude and added, "Lisbon has been cosmopolitan and black for a long time. It is legitimacy that is slow in coming" (Contador quoted in *Ípsilon* 2007:15). Contador's scholarship contributes to a larger corpus of work that argues that contemporary forms of so-called black culture are more than simply "African" expressions. They are more not because the cultural forms consist of other discrete "elements" from other cultural groups but because "blackness" has been cosmopolitan and part of globalized flows for centuries and has become part of "essential" cultural expressions that represent Europe, the Americas, and so on. One implication of Contador's statements in the *Ípsilon* interview is that the Portuguese have been comfortable with Africanity as a relative ad hoc distinction to national culture but are reticent in accepting the idea that blackness has been formative in what is considered Portuguese and what the Portuguese and foreigners might recognize as Portugal.

## The World of Cape Verde

Africanity-as-Creole begins with Cape Verde. Although most of the action of this book takes place in Portugal, Creole citizenship hinges on the particularities of Cape Verde and Cape Verdeans. Hardly "lost" forever out in the sea, Creole encounters with Cape Verdeans were important to not only enterprising merchants, such as whalers, but also literary figures and public intellectuals, such as Herman Melville. Famous for his novel *Moby-Dick*, Melville was keen to insert social comments related to the milieu of whaling in harbor towns, such as New Bedford, Massachusetts. What Melville leaves implicit in descriptions of Dagoo and the narrator Ishmael's reflections on his other "swarthy" companions before and during the epic sea adventure is made explicit in "The 'Gees," an article published in 1856, five years after *Moby-Dick*.

In this ironic essay, Melville exposes the scientific racism of ethnology through a wry description of this curious people labeled the 'Gees, "an abbreviation, by seamen, of *Portugee*, the corrupt form of *Portuguese*. As the name is a curtailment, so the race is a residuum." Melville, assuming the airs of his contemporary scientists, goes on to explain that "in his best estate the 'Gee is rather small (he admits it) but, with some exceptions, hardy; capable of enduring extreme hard work, hard fare, or hard usage, as the case may be. In fact, upon a scientific view, there would seem a natural adaptability in the 'Gee to hard times generally."[2] Melville seems to enjoy himself as he focuses on the scientific discourse of the day: "His complexion is hybrid; his hair ditto; his mouth disproportionally large, as compared with his stomach; his neck short; but his head round, compact, and betokening a solid understanding. Like the negro, the 'Gee has a peculiar savor, but a different one—a sort of wild, marine, gamey savor, as in the sea-bird called haglet. Like venison, his flesh is firm but lean" ([1856] 2013). Ultimately, the 'Gee, or the Cape Verdean migrant whaler, Melville argues in his facetious jab, has potential for civilization. The 'Gee is the ideal Creole citizen, an insightful laborer, malleable in culture and place. The 'Gee is both remarkable and unnoticed, the perfect diasporic subject.

> Two qualities of the 'Gee which, with his docility, may be justly regarded as furnishing a hopeful basis for his intellectual training, is his excellent memory, and still more excellent credulity. The above account may, perhaps, among the ethnologists, raise some curiosity to see a 'Gee. But to see a 'Gee there is no need to go all the way to Fogo [Cape Verdean island with strongest diasporic connection to the New England region], no more than to see a Chinaman to go all the way to China. 'Gees are occasionally to be encountered in our seaports, but more particularly in Nantucket and New Bedford. But these 'Gees are not the 'Gees of Fogo. That is, they are no longer green 'Gees. They are sophisticated 'Gees, and hence liable to be taken for naturalized citizens badly sunburnt. ([1856] 2013)

Melville's cynical imitation of Darwinian ethnology reveals the racism of the time, but it also, in the case of Cape Verde, demonstrates the documented fascination outsiders have had with this archipelago.

Melville's turn of phrase describing the 'Gees as "naturalized citizens badly sunburnt" captures the Creole dynamic of Cape Verdeans. In the words of one Portuguese colonial officer, the "Cape Verdean showed his African origin only on the skin, when the pigmentation accidentally denounced him" (M. Oliveira 1955:24). Creole citizenship is a racialized process of political belonging shaped by the conditions of labor. To become "naturalized" involves material conditions of labor and histories of migration.

Naturalization also, as Melville implies in his faux ethnological account, emerges through performance, that is, the language and expressive culture in encounters with the other. For the Portuguese, such articulation and recognition come through in mythologies of "discovery." The acclaimed British historian Basil Davidson in his poetic and reflective book on Cape Verdean independence opens the text with a quote from Nobel Prize Portuguese author José Saramago: "As for the Old Discoverers, I think my name should be added to theirs, and with better reason if modesty allows. For they discovered a handful of deserted islands. But in those islands I have discovered a world" (quoted in Davidson 1989:epigraph). What is this "world" of Cape Verde? What could there possibly be in this small scattering of islands located approximately 350 miles off the coast of Dakar, Senegal?

Cape Verde's value and essence can only be understood in terms of the encounter. It has existed as a meeting place, a weigh station for a variety of regional trades, Euro-Afro encounters, and transatlantic campaigns. The role of Cape Verdeans went beyond trade and included a significant number of early Euro-African historians (Mark 2002). Jose da Silva Horta argues similarly that what passed often as "Portuguese" accounts of the Guinean coast were in fact "Luso-African" (2000).

While there are hypotheses that precolonial culture and society existed on the islands,[3] most scholars and Cape Verdeans purport that Cape Verde and Kriolu resulted from early Portuguese colonialism and creolization, a systematic process of mixture and displacement (Rodrigues 2011; Challinor 2008). Interpreting documents from the Catholic Church and trade reports, Brazilian scholar José Ramos Tinhorão explains that the early slave trade by the Portuguese went back as far as the fourteenth century with trading spaces on Rua Nova in Lisbon. With regard to Cape Verde, Ramos discusses the historical documentation around what many Portuguese children learn in school, the year 1444 and the first four officially documented slaves to be brought from sub-Saharan Africa, namely, Senegal and Cape Verde, to Portugal under the direction of Dinis Dias (Tinhorão 1988:47). This Creole formation afforded Cape Verde a distinct place in the *imago mundi* of the Portuguese.

## Language, Education, and History

Language and colonial education reinforce this cultural imagination. Portuguese officials and scholars were quite conscious of the link between language and culture within the colonial paradigm. Angolan writer and critic Mário António Fernandes de Oliveira chronicles the Portuguese efforts in the "diffusion of the Portuguese language as an instrument of cultural and political integration as well as a bridge between the various parcels of the national territory." He claims that even the languages that were not nominally Portuguese spoken in the overseas territories were "politically Portuguese languages" (1970:20, 21).

Cape Verdeans established a relatively privileged position in local and translocal hierarchies. Manuel Brito-Semedo argues that a small cadre of local elite on Cape Verde benefited from the institutions of education on the archipelago during the early period of "Ladinization," defined as Christian and Luso conversion. By 1650 Pedro Semedo Cardoso, a local Creole, was appointed governor. Brito-Semedo cites letters from Padre Sebastião Gomes, who reported that five of the nineteen people of political power were native "crioulos" (1995:107).

The privileged position of Cape Verde in the colonial geographies of education created a precedent of metropolitan concern, at least in some official circles. While, on the whole, it is true that Lisbon frequently abandoned its obligations to take care of its African colonies, and this was acutely felt in Cape Verde during the fierce droughts of the late nineteenth and early twentieth centuries, a cadre of state-sponsored scholars insisted on the maintenance of investment in education on the archipelago.

In a 1938 entry to the activities report of the Lisbon Geographical Society, an anonymous author laments over the Cape Verde governor's decision to close the preparatory high school Liceu São Vicente in Mindelo on São Vicente island. The author rehearses a common theory of culture and intelligence the Portuguese used in their reckoning of Cape Verdeans. First, "the Cape Verdean people, in their tenacious struggle with nature, have assimilated civilization to a point that approximates that of the Metropole." Secondly, the "geographic position of the archipelago places its people in permanent and accessible contact with all the civilization of the new and old worlds. . . . Despite all of this, they never forget patriotically their homeland, however distant and welcoming the host territory may be" ("Actividade" 1938:143). The first claim is reminiscent of nineteenth-century theories of environmental determinism and aligns Cape Verde culturally with Europe in contrast to the prevalent conclusions that explain Latin American and African difference as indicative of laziness due to their relatively easy conditions for survival. The second claim espouses the idea that intercultural contact is a natural value of the Cape Verdean islands and functions as a predictor of intelligence (see also Ezequiel 1944). Contact pulls up culture.

The archival power of lettered Cape Verdean men supports the argument that the "world of Cape Verde" was significant in the Portuguese imagination of not only otherness "out there" but also the imagination of themselves. Born in 1555 of a woman described as *"parda"* (mixed race of black and white) on the Cape Verdean island of Santiago, André Álvares d'Almada represented an intermediary group of Luso-Africans, referred to locally as "Portuguese." Almada consistently refers to "we" when discussing the "Portuguese" and to the Jalofos, a group occasionally proposed as the most direct precursors to the identity label of "Cape Verdeans," as "nearest to us" ([1594] 1984:4). His text is a narrative filled with lengthy descriptions of the various peoples occupying the region of the Guinea rivers in West Africa, ranging from Senegal and Cape Verde to Saint Ann. He aptly describes the rise and fall of local rulers, local laws, physical characteristics of people, and geographical locations of territories.

Periodically, Almada mentions the travels of rulers who visited Lisbon: "The Jalofo king called Bomaim Gelim, who came to Portugal in the time of King Manuel of Glorious Memory, must have been a relative of this king. Bomaim Gelim came to offer his obedience to King Manuel and to beg him to order that a fortress to be built in a kingdom and a trading post established, so that he might have the help of our men against those who had usurped the kingdom of his ancestors." Almada also remarks on the fluidity of languages, "These Jalofos speak their own language and they also understand that of the Fulas, since there is a caste of Black Fulas living among the Jalofos, called Tacurores.... Some of the Jalofos understand the language of the Moors, because the Moors regularly bring horses to sell to the Jalofos, and many of them are always to be found at the court of the king of the land" ([1594] 1984:5, 10).

As historian P. E. H. Hair affirms in his annotations to Almada's book, Almada's treatise on the area of the Guinean rivers became a constant reference in publications on the region well into the nineteenth century and was recognized by the Spanish crown in Madrid, despite the Estatuto de Ordem (protocol statutes) against persons "of color [*de cor*]" (Almada [1594] 1984:5). That these statutes were not implemented in Cape Verde lends credence to the notion that Creole Cape Verdeans like Almada were seen simply as not "colored" (P. Cardoso 1913).

## *Pretuguês*, or Black Portuguese

The intersections of race, education, language, and culture took on other manifestations as Portugal utilized Cape Verde and the Guinean coast as ideological trophies in Portugal's version of civilization. As expected, myths of Portuguese civilization depend on selective historiography, and Jacques Raimundo, a Portuguese scholar of education writing in the early years of the Salazar regime, identifies language instruction as an "adept instrument" (*hábil instrumento*) of Portugal's "soft conquest" (*conquista suave*). In his short dissection of what he calls "pretuguês," a neologism mixing *preto* (black) with *Português* (Portuguese), Raimundo makes a case of Portugal's "vocabulary patrimony" and with it a cultural accompaniment to the civilizing process involved in African colonialism (1933; see also Duffy 1961b). In this respect, "black manners" of speaking Portuguese were thoughtful imitations of culture.

## CHAPTER 1

Raimundo is one of several Portuguese intellectuals who recalled the theatrical plays of Gil Vicente, the canonical sixteenth-century dramaturge. Vicente scripted pretuguês, also called *lingual de guiné* (language of Guinea; see Clements 2009:45–46), as well as occasionally *bozal/boçal* (literally, "of a slave from West Africa"; frequently evoked in contemporary Portuguese vernacular to mean menial, stupid, or a simpleton as both an adjective and noun) language (Lipski 1994), through minor characters in his plays. He was later celebrated as providing remarkable insight into the linguistic and cultural imitations of the colonial subject residing in the metropole (J. Raimundo 1933:14–19). By contrast, the famous poet Bocage, active in the late eighteenth century, publicly denounced Portuguese Creoles and *mestiços* (mixed-race people) as on the side of "Blacks" and, thus, inferior in speech and being (Henriques 2012). In a few select sonnets from his prolific literary production, Bocage was explicit in describing visiting "Brazilian" (code for mulatto, or mestizo) dignitaries as "revolting," "*pardo de feições*" (a cursed half-breed).

In his poem "Os cães domésticos e o cão montanhês" (domestic dogs and the mountain dog), Bocage uses the medium of a fable to convey his notions of race and social stratification. Toward the end of the poem, the domestic dogs are accused of a crime and are queried as to their justification; they respond, "*O nosso jus é a força; O teu delito é a cor*" (Our justification is force; your crime is your color). Bocage then concludes by explicitly drawing attention to his own racial discrimination: "*De homens pretos, e homens brancos / Cuido que fala este autor*" (With respect to black and white men, I take care in what I say) (Bocage [1799] 2007:23–24).

Examples of pretuguês in the dramatic texts of Gil Vicente and Bocage are part of what Iain Chambers terms the "accents of Empire" (1994:68) or what linguist J. Clancy Clements terms the "naturalistic acquisition" of immigrant populations (2009:124). More specifically, the colonial encounter inside Lisbon made its presence as a series of complex imitations, thereby creating an imagination of the Other. Periodically, pretuguês and other imperial accents represented racist theories aligned with Bocage and subaltern twists of meaning for political change, thus moving the idea of "black manners of speech" far away from any sort of supposed Portuguese cordiality.

Such difference frequently surfaced in labor relations resulting from urban migration. For example, in the 1940s and 1950s, *pretuguês* as a term of ridicule was documented among temporary contract workers in the streets of Maputo, Mozambique, and Luanda, Angola (Hamilton 1991), and an increasingly visible group of uneducated, poor Luso-African migrant men in Lisbon. In a Calibanesque moment, the founder of Cape Verdean and Guinea-Bissau nationalism, Amílcar Cabral, famously stated that "language is the best inheritance that we received from the Portuguese" (1974:30). The milieu of independence and decolonization helps contextualize this declaration as an attempt to break down ethnic-linguistic barriers among Luso-Africans in order to achieve a proposed common goal, just as Shakespeare's Caliban recruited Stephano and Trinculo with the hopes of creating a coherent opposition to the master Prospero.

More recently, Cape Verdean linguists and pedagogues have emboldened Cabral's phrase to take control of what Portuguese means in contemporary Cape Verde. In a collection of interviews with Cape Verdeans living in Lisbon about their views and sentiments regarding their "home," an advocate for Kriolu reflects, "We [must] revisit the fact of coexistence between Portuguese and Crioulo in Cape Verde. . . . Considering this evidence that the Cape Verdean language has supplanted that which was dominant until Independence, to banish Portuguese from the archipelago would correspond to a cultural mutilation. That was the most precious inheritance of Portugal" (Viriato de Barros quoted in G. Raimundo 2008:630; see also B. Ramos 1985). Cape Verdean linguist Manuel Veiga is more direct as he recognizes the ambivalent nature of Portuguese as an opportunity actually to claim coauthorship: "The best instrument with which we can share the world of Cape Verde with the Portuguese is precisely the language of Camões, the 'pátria' [fatherland] of Fernando Pessoa, of which, today, we can claim the title of co-ownership" (1982:31).

Current Kriolu rappers, such as Chullage, have taken the idea of controlling linguistic "inheritance" by mimicking what the marginalized character Caliban in *The Tempest* refers to as "cursing." The oft-cited line in Shakespeare's play has Caliban retort to Prospero, "You taught me language; and my profit on't / Is, I know how to curse" (act 1, scene 2, lines 517–18). Kriolu rappers' profit is explicitly the medium with which they can talk back to experienced racial prejudice in Portugal. Implicitly, perhaps, they join the spirit of Veiga and other linguists cited above in asserting that the language Kriolu with all of its social history and cultural performance is a coproducer in the discourse attributed to "Portuguese." In "Pretugal," Chullage raps,

*Koraçon lá e korpo ká em pretugal*
*Mentalmente enkkkarcerados ká em pretugal*
*Sem pão, mas kom veneno e armas p'ra morrermos em pretugal*
*Segregados p'ra n sermos ninguém em pretugal.*

[Heart there and body here in Pretugal
Mentally incarcerated here in Pretugal
No food but with poison and arms for us to die in Pretugal
Segregated so that we are nobodies in Pretugal.]
—(*Rapensar* 2004)

In both cases, Caliban and Chullage, the "profit" is construed from the perspective of the matrix of master/slave, colonizer/colonized, or citizen/migrant relationships. In all cases, the relationship involves race, labor, language, culture, and social action. While this song posits the Kriolu immigrant and Portugal in radical terms of opposition, other raps from Chullage suggest coauthorship in the construction of Creole Lisbon. Chullage, in particular, among Kriolu rappers, tends to rap in a mixture of Portuguese and Kriolu, which in and of itself suggests coproduction in Veiga's sense. Through a creative use of *k*, indexing both the badiu variant of Cape Verdean Kriolu from the island of Santiago and the U.S. style of *k* diacritics, Chullage combines the microstructure of language to the macrostructure of narrative made explicit in the lyrics outlining racism, spatial segregation, and Cape Verdean/general migrant dis/emplacement. Chapter 3 revisits the issue of Kriolu language politics in more detail.

Drawing from my fieldwork among Kriolu rappers in Lisbon and the Cape Verdean capital, Praia, I feel an anxiety to let the voices of Chullage, LBC, and others fill the page. Their use of Kriolu as productive critique is an end point, a constructive expression of Creole citizenship. Their Kriolu diacritics emerge from a postcolonial position, and we cannot fully understand the significance of their words, their actions, and their motivation of migration and emplacement without spending a bit more time thinking about the colonial, particularly, nineteenth and twentieth centuries, relationship between Cape Verde and Portugal.

Individual figures, such as Almada, and institutions, such as *lycées* (high schools), were positive symbols of Cape Verde in the Portuguese worldview. Even during the tensest periods of decolonization in the late 1960s and early 1970s, many Portuguese continued to see Cape Verde as welcoming. In his self-published travel log, the Portuguese journalist Vasco Callixto, a specialist in automobiles and aeronautics, reflects on the importance of Cape Verde as a friendly landing pad during the first transatlantic flights departing from Portugal and Spain in the early 1920s. In between references and advertising logos of Pirelli tires and Land Rover jeeps, Callixto repeatedly alludes to the "Lusitânia," the name of the 1922 hydroplane that traveled from Lisbon to Rio de Janeiro, and "the Portuguese soil of Cape Verde that hosted the heroes of the air so warmly" during that first crossing of the South Atlantic (1974:53). One can hear Callixto's celebratory voice as he sets foot in Nova Sintra, the main town on the island Brava and exclaims, "A breath of fresh air, the biggest avenue in Cape Verde and [full of] American products!" (1974:105). Since the glory days of the whaling industry in the late eighteenth and nineteenth centuries, the islands of Fogo and Brava have been oriented to the United States and, particularly, the New England coastal cities of Boston, New Bedford, Brockton, and Providence.

I digress briefly to tell a bit more of the Callixto story because it demonstrates some of the ubiquitous ironies of Portuguese–Cape Verdean history and the intersecting histories of urban space and self-other representations. Besides being a conduit for the advertising of Pirelli tires and other travel-based merchandising, Callixto fancied himself an accomplished photographer, and upon his return from Cape Verde back to Portugal, he organized an exhibit of his work in Sintra in 1973. The location is significant in that Sintra was the playground of the Portuguese nobility and the magnificent site of their countryside palaces away from the "crowded" confines of Lisbon. Moreover, by the time of Callixto's exhibition, the region between Lisbon and Sintra, approximately twenty-seven kilometers, or about seventeen miles, had started to become the peripheral bedroom communities of immigrants, including substantial pockets of Cape Verdeans (explored in more ethnographic detail in chapter 4). Finally, Callixto was born in Amadora, a place that during his youth was associated with past nobility and remarkable architecture linking Lisbon to the regal hillside community of Sintra. Since the 1980s Amadora has become the municipality with the largest Cape Verdean community in Portugal.

## Cape Verde and Kriolu Identification

Following historians of the Black Atlantic, we know that Portugal preceded all other European countries by at least a century in exchange and conflict with West and Central Western Africa (Sweet 2003). Due to its strategic geographic position for both Iberian and West African traders, militias, refugees, and other migrants, Cape Verde was a central point of creolization and a key intermediary point in the formation of what is now referred to as the "Black Atlantic" (Heywood and Thornton 2007). Based on slave-trade records, we know, for example, that during the fifteenth and sixteenth centuries, when Portugal sought to expand trade routes, most slave ships stopped in Cape Verde before making their way to the New World.[4] Historian Matthias Perl has demonstrated that, more generally, Portuguese Creole was early on a language used by non-Portuguese, such as the Dutch and English (1982:7). It became a recognized trade language to do business in West Africa, and Portuguese Creole was disseminated to various parts of Africa, Asia, and the Americas. Kriolu contracted after the seventeenth century, but it was once a transcontinental primary language of trade and power. In the words of Perl, "the Creole Portuguese languages, or variants of a uniform Creole language still in existence today, are remainders of a communicative medium that functioned on a global scale during the 16th and 17th centuries" (1982:12).[5]

Kriolu as a language and identity originated with displacement in the fifteenth century of *lançados* (literally, "thrown out") in Guinea-Bissau and the parallel process in Cape Verde of *ladinização*, the process of being baptized and other European, Christian rituals that increased the African slave's value. The intensification of contact resulted in a pragmatic linguistics of labor segregation and economic exchange (Holm et al. 2006). The term *lançado* refers to one of the results of the Inquisition in Iberia, that is, a cleansing or "throwing out" (from the Portuguese verb *lançar*) of Jews and Muslims (Forrest 2003; Lobban 1995). In addition, expulsion also took place voluntarily in subsequent generations, as mixed-race men, the offspring of white Portuguese tradesmen and black slave women, left Cape Verde and relocated in Guinea (Bull 1989). Subsequently, they became an integral part of the petty bourgeoisie in coastal economies. While occasionally at odds with the Portuguese, these lançados actually linked the Portuguese via Cape Verde, their archipelago colony, with a sizable territory of West Africa (Batalha 2004a:22–23). Ladinização marked the process by which slaves in Cape Verde were inculcated into Catholicism, the Portuguese language, and basic, manual-labor skills (Carreira 1972; Brito-Semedo 1995).

In a discursive shift from labor to phenotype, *Creole/crioulo/kriolu* in the early seventeenth century quickly became a term of racialization.[6] As Márcia Rego remarks, becoming ladinizado and separating from Kriolu translated into a pragmatic rise in value for the slave (2008:147). Yet, a number of slaves, in fact, used their knowledge of variants of Cape Verdean and (African) continental Creoles along with Portuguese as symbolic capital in exchange for their own manumission. For example, Philip J. Havik discusses the foundational role of local *tangomãos* (renegades) and *grumetes* (hired African seamen) as remunerated rowers, sailors, and interpreters in the articulation and capitalization of Creole (2007:46–52). In sum, Kriolu carried connotations of local breeding, labor management, and emergent racial discourses of colonial populations. Kriolu was also a tool for passing and mobility.

By the end of the nineteenth century, Portuguese colonial officials and scholars as well as Cape Verdean local elite became more confident that Kriolu's value as a language and a kind of person was best thought of as a transitional phase on the way to speaking and being Portuguese. In the words of Casimiro, the poet and chronicler from this chapter's introduction, Kriolu was an "intermediary language" of assimilation within what he described as the "colonial character" of the Lusophone world. On the one hand, the "Creole dialect" represented the "disfiguration and laziness" inherent in the "encounter between those of the Kingdom and the African.... [On the other hand], some words gain a profound meaning and others better preserve, in either sweet or rude ways, the taste of the word" (1940:25).

Casimiro based his ideas on the work of nineteenth-century philologists, such as F. Adolfo Coelho. He remarks that Kriolu lamentably indicated blackness but not necessarily an impenetrable alterity: "They [the Cape Verdeans] substituted a moorish mixture of African terms and antiquated Portuguese pronounced with a reckless abandon with guttural stops. This was called *lingua creola*, without grammar or fixed rules. It spread from island to island." Coelho observes that the locals perform all facets of daily life in this idiom: "The locals don't speak another language: [they] pray in crioulo; the parochial pedagogues teach the Christian doctrine in crioulo.... Those who have traveled abroad understand Portuguese, but do not speak it." He went on: "The whites reinforce this, as they learn crioulo, use it in domestic relationships, and rear their children in crioulo almost to the exclusion of pure Portuguese" (1882:451–52).

This latter perspective from the Portuguese settler position is echoed in novels, such as José Eduardo Agualusa's historical fiction *Creole*. Set in the 1870s, the book is essentially a collection of letters from Fradique Mendes to a number of important people in his life, including his godmother and confidant, his Congolese/Angolan love interest, and a leading Portuguese literary and political figure. It is to the last, Eça de Queirós, that Mendes directs a fascinating rebuke. Queirós had called upon Mendes to send a report on "the current situation of Portugal in Africa," to which Mendes replied: "I cannot.... I'm afraid, my friend, that it's not in Portugal's interest that the world should know the situation in our colonies at this moment.... They [the Portuguese] delve into the bush lands ('God is great,' they say, 'but the bush is greater'), and just as they change their trousers and shirts for animal hides, they abandon the Portuguese language, or use it in tatters mixed up with the resonant languages of Africa" (Agualusa 2002:121,122).

The conflicted intimacy between Cape Verde and Portugal mediated by Kriolu was also apparent in institutions and policies of colonial education. As mentioned above, the Portuguese administration consistently ignored the famines and general chaos caused by droughts on the archipelago. However, official periodicals, such as the bulletin of the Sociedade de Geografia de Lisboa (Geographical Society of Lisbon) (SGL), frequently gave education an undivided attention. For example, on the dawn of the First Republic in Portugal in 1910, SGL writers called for reinvestment specifically in Cape Verde, the archipelago "in crisis," so that "colonial education" could "develop more effectively and in a more civilized fashion" ("Subsidio" 1910:312; see also Keese 2012). Such concern in the metropole about Cape Verdean education had precedent. More than a century prior to the SGL publications, in April 8, 1794, under the auspices of the Fazenda Nacional (federal bank), the Portuguese monarch invited young male Cape Verdeans to study in Lisbon, especially in endeavors of science, art, and other vocational (*ofícios*) studies (Brito-Semedo 1995:109).

Writing on the relationship between colonial education and cultural identity on the archipelago, Manuel Ferreira describes the role of *liceus* (school, from the French *lycées*) during the early twentieth century in Mindelo as a site that influenced the cultural ambiguity of future Cape Verdean literati. Mindelo, a town that by the early twentieth century had become a cultural center of Cape Verde and a harbor of elite islanders, was the center of the literary nationalist movement of the *Claridosos* (a group of literary elite from Cape Verde, who produced an influential periodical during the 1930s and 1940s called *Claridade*). Cape Verdean historian Victor Barros argues that "the publication of *crioulo* [in Claridoso literature] does not constitute a preemptory identification mark of contestation and a necessary rupture from the metropole but rather a demonstration of the adaptation within the encounter" (2009:169). The liceu pedagogy was oriented toward Europe and, unsurprisingly, affected the prose and political discourse of its prized students.

Cape Verdean negritude was slow in coming due to the history of cultural education on the archipelago. Ferreira cites the Angolan nationalist and longtime editor of the famous negritude publication *Présence Africaine*, Mário Coelho Pinto de Andrade: "From Cape Verde, whose literature has distinguished itself for some time, it might be necessary and useful to revisit the process of its social formation and situate blacks and by extension Black African culture as a Creole becoming" (Andrade 1951 quoted in Ferreira 1967:299). Andrade had bracketed Cape Verde from his anthologies of African literatures in the early 1950s, following a Lusotropicalist perspective on Cape Verde. By the end of the decade, he had reconsidered his position. For Ferreira, Andrade's change in classification was due, in part, to the politicization of Cape Verde by Cabral, a colleague of Andrade in the famous Casa dos Estudantes do Império, a student house for elite Luso-Africans in Lisbon, and the founding of the PAIGCV (African Party for the Independence of Guinea-Bissau and Cape Verde) in 1956. This signaled a (re)africanization of Cape Verde, Guinea-Bissau, and, in conjunction with similar movement in southern Africa, Lusophone Africa. In Portugal, the Lusotropicalist view of Cape Verde remained steadfast. For example, the critic and São Tomean poet Francisco José Tenreiro, writing in the 1960s, describes Cape Verdean writers as those who had "drunk from the drama of their surroundings . . . directly from the spectacle of a land where the very trees are thirsty, lacking a poetry with well-articulated regional characteristics, the result of African acculturation on the archipelago" (1963).

The Portuguese claimed Cape Verdean Creole as a generally positive result of their special brand of colonialism and developed the paradigm of "Kriolu as a social fact" in various ways throughout the twentieth century. For the most part, this approach benefitted Cape Verdeans and their life chances in the empire (Keese 2012). For example, Mesquitela Lima, born in Cape Verde on the island of São Vicente, spent a good deal of his professional life in Angola as an administrator and columnist. In one particular essay, he discusses the "admirable" capacity of Cape Verdeans to approximate what the Portuguese do as a "culture," namely, the

Cape Verdeans are a "phenomenon of social coexistence.... These special anthropological characteristics [constitute] the Creole man of Cape Verde" (1959:3, 4).

As political economist Ronald Chilcote summarizes, "according to the official view, [Cape Verdeans were] a culture different from and superior to the rest of Africa. As a result, Cape Verdeans were considered 'civilized' and Portuguese citizens. Speaking a Creole Portuguese and proud of an indigenous literature, they had access to education. Mulatto Cape Verdeans served as administrators in the lower echelons of the African colonial service" (1968:373). Moreover, Portuguese essayist Osorio de Oliveira famously declared: "The Cape Verdean is without a doubt the greatest and most unique treasure of Cape Verde" (1936:4). The editors of SGL's official bulletin, likewise, praised Cape Verdeans for their natural proclivity toward education and patriotism ("Actividade" 1938). Ethnologist Silva Neves added "anthropological" heft to claims of distinct Cape Verdean intelligence, sociability, and culture: "The men, in general, present irregular attributes but without the ugliness [*fealdade*] of the inhabitants of another archipelago, Andaman. They remind one more of the indians in the state of California" (quoted in Leite 1937:203).

## From Kriolu as Colonial Intimacy to Kriolu as "Nigga"

When one spends any considerable time in the peripheral residential plots of contemporary Lisbon, the smooth uplifting story of Cape Verdean Creole falls apart.

> Step into the world of a nigger, figure
> to stay a little while so pack your bag up bigger
> First of all just let me introduce you seduce you
> into a frame of mind that's easy to get used to
> Nigger hasn't always meant a man with melanin
> It used to be a piece of wood that sat on the cotton gin.
> —The Coup, 1993

> Now, as Portuguese Africa enters the most critical decade of its history, Lisbon's goal is to reconcile the two opposing characteristics of Portuguese practice in Africa—the simultaneous acceptance and exploitation of the Africans. The reconciliation is to be accomplished by the assimilation of the Africans into a Portuguese world. What in essence the Government proposes to do is to convince the Africans that it is better to be Portuguese than to be independent.
> —(Duffy 1961a)

As implied by the lyrics to "I Ain't the Nigga" of the Oakland-based U.S. rapper-activist Boots, writer of the song and member of U.S. rap group The Coup, and the Africanist historian James Duffy, we should pay more attention to the intersectionality of race and class in the understanding of terms that seem singular, such as "nigga" as solely "black" or colonial exploitation as purely about labor.

Following a tip from a Facebook group called Plataforma Gueto (Ghetto Platform), I decided to attend an event called Marcus Garvey University (MGU), a virtual institution of education named after the charismatic Jamaican leader for empowerment and an early spokesperson for black nationalism. MGU was created by a group of young activists living in various peripheral neighborhoods of Lisbon. I set out hoping to reconnect with a few friends/consultants in a place I know relatively well, Kova M. Undoubtedly, the most well-known if not often infamous autoconstructed, immigrant neighborhood in Lisbon, Alto da Cova da Moura, or "Kova M," is home to thousands of residents of Cape Verdean descent. Chapter 4 details this Kriolu space in more historical and spatial detail, but suffice it to say here, it was a perfect spot for the virtual Marcus Garvey University to take place.

On the way up the steep hillside on one of the entry roads in Kova M, I overheard several Cape Verdean young men complaining about their own unemployment. They remarked on the ridiculous tone of voice from government officials, coming from the television that was secured to an upper corner of a local bar room. The news program announced as one of its main stories of the day that unemployment during June 2013 had not increased and had kept steady at 17.8 percent. "Where is that?" one man provocatively asked. Answering his own question in Kriolu, he bellowed, "Here it must be close to half." This brief diatribe against the mainstream news media would serve well as an introduction to this particular evening's public discussion.

I entered the stuffy meeting room belonging to the Moinho de Juventude cultural association, a neighborhood organization of Kova M and a central meeting place for various kinds of local events. People were seated in a circle, watching the documentary film *The Story of Marcus Garvey*. Rui, a dogmatic and charismatic speaker, periodically paused the YouTube video to summarize and interpret the documentary film. He occasionally linked the migration story of Garvey and his early challenges to the situation of black immigrants in contemporary Portugal.

> The issue is race and labor. In Garvey's time there were lynchings, his parents were slaves, and there was supreme black poverty in Jamaica. It was about your appearance and where you were at. If you stop and think about it, not that much has changed over here in Portugal in 2013. We are black, poor, and our value in this capitalist system is directly related to the jobs we don't have and the decaying neighborhoods. While there are no lynchings, there is a system of police brutality that seems to justify violence against us just because we are standing

around in a certain neighborhood. What is it about race, labor, and space? This is the system; this is the law. This is not the case of a few corrupt policemen.

Bracketing the fact that, of course, Marcus Garvey was very much invested in capitalism, following his idol Booker T. Washington, and, thus, had no interest in overthrowing capital markets, including the constant instability of employment and speculative whims of property, the prospective links among race, labor, and space are worth pursuing. Given the history offered thus far, why would Luso-Africans, and especially Cape Verdeans, doubt that their brands of Creole had not assuaged the Manichean system in which Garvey circulated? Was not Creole-as-mixture an answer already established in the Luso world?

Cape Verdean rapper Chullage addresses the links among migration, race, and labor poetically a cappella in a song released on his 2012 album *Rapressão*. Posited in what on first glance appears to be the conditional future tense, "what if" (*será que*), the song's title is best translated as a sharp criticism of present realities, more in the line of "is it really [like this]?" Chullage himself would make a strong appearance later in the Marcus Garvey University series of meetings in Kova M when the topic turned to the relationship among race, prisons, and capitalism. For now, a lyrical (translated) passage.

> Skinheads [are] in all cadres, is it really the case that
> This country only accepts an immigrant if he's a soccer star.
> . . . . . . . . . . . .
> Is it really that brothers don't see that
> We have to stop bickering and go out in the streets in protest
> Because it is there that we will end racism, capitalism
> And all other forms of exploitation.
> . . . . . . . . . . . .
> Really? ... What if.[7]

The linguistic formulation of *será que* (Is it really like that?) implies a history. "It" has been a certain way. The "it" of Chullage's lyrics refers to a reality of marginalization. Although he provides examples of violent and prejudicial outcomes, the underlying fabric of this reality has to do with a demographic change that combines class, race, and gender. According to Jorge Macaísta Malheiros (1998), the early 1990s witnessed a rejuvenated construction industry with high numbers of African men recruits and a spike in domestic service with a significant tendency toward the hiring of African and Afro-Brazilian women. Both trends were based increasingly on temporary, informal work contracts accompanied by a complex network of interethnic social relations (Malheiros 1998:179–82). With a growing presence of uneducated Luso-Africans (especially Cape Verdeans) in service or manual-labor positions instead of the university-trained engineers, economists, and lawyers (men), the connotation of Kriolu began to change from the "quasi-Portuguese" to a black "nigga."

Kriolu as articulated by local rappers frequently involves a level of strategic essentialism. For example, not unlike the key word of "nigga" in U.S. rappers' versions of locality as it relates to the "hood" (Perry 2005; Forman 2002), "badiu," a polemical term of black laziness recuperated by contemporary Cape Verdean residents in Lisbon, indexes an assumed masculinity. Men are "niggas" and "badiu." During my fieldwork, I spoke with thirty-four rappers, only six of whom were women. Of course, an anthropological understanding of gender goes beyond demography and includes practice. For example, LBC explained to me why occasionally he uses the English word *bitch* in his rhymes.

> First of all, I got this idea from Tupac [Shakur], who turned people's heads with his NIGGA acronym [Never ignorant about getting goals accomplished]. So, I put in BITCH [translation from Kriolu: your insensitivity made you corrupt and incorrigible (*bu insenbilidadi torna corruptu y horrivel*)].... The other thing is that "bitch" is meant for other men, not women. I'm criticizing them, not young women. (personal communication)

LBC's comments demonstrate the homosocial dimensions of Kriolu rap; it is a discourse overwhelmingly produced by and directed toward men as a series of judgments on masculinity. Moreover, LBC and other Kriolu rappers deploy "bitch" and "nigga" challenges as rhetorical qualifiers of "street" and "thug." In other words, they imagine and propose public space as implicitly masculine and draw on empowering vocabulary etymologically rooted in English but pragmatically part of a Kriolu project to make cultural claims on territory.

In the literature on Cape Verdean identity in the diaspora, authors have contributed rich ethnographic insight into gendered geographies, especially related to labor. For example, Kesha Fikes (2009) deconstructs various scenes from her fieldwork in the Docapesca, a fish market that catered to restaurant buyers as well as a significant number of Kriolu or Kriol-speaking women who subsequently acted as street vendors outside of major transportation hubs across Lisbon. Fikes shows how these women in their negotiations with mostly white, Portuguese men strategically employed signs of Africanity in jokes and gestures in order to establish relations of intimacy and, thus, facilitate trade. Implicit in these scenes is that the market as a socioeconomic space was inflected by a variable Cape Verdean femininity—a Kriolu space, albeit only temporarily, given that the state closed down the Docapesca in 2003.

Another example related to the social geographies involved in Kriolu rap is the practice of *djunta mon* (joining hands). Originally associated with rural feminine labor in Cape Verde, the public works of djunta mon in Lisbon translate into both collective efforts to improve neighborhood infrastructure or even cultivate crops as well as a rhetorical call to arms for Cape Verdean women to overcome any sort of barrier (Évora 2011; Weeks 2012).

Returning to the documentary film about Garvey's life, we never reached minute twenty. What Rui and others in the room wanted to talk about was the state of pan-Africanism in the current reality of global capitalism. One young man reflected, "I understand pan-Africanism to be the process of making a black person into an African. It doesn't matter where you are, in Jamaica, in the U.S., in Portugal. Pan-Africanism is not a 'go back to Africa' slogan but a message of unity among black people wherever you are." We had reached some sort of consensus as every one of the roughly twenty-five young men and women nodded their heads. One woman added, "Like Rui said, where you are is a big deal. It presents different challenges to becoming African. But, yeah, pan-Africanism is about unity, cross-cultural unity of black people."

Over the next weeks, Ghetto Platform members and a few interested bystanders would discuss party politics, police brutality, and other related topics to race and labor. They invited resident scholars, such as geographer Ruth Gilmore, to sit in and give her perspective on current prison construction in Portugal. On another occasion, Rui Skyped two Cuban activists as part of a group discussion on racism in Cuba with the objective of identifying potential points of comparison and contrast with the situation in Lisbon. A common theme in all of these meetings was the idea that blackness, whether Cape Verdean Kriolu, American, Portuguese, Jamaican, or Cuban, began and continues to be shaped by the chronotope of the ghetto, a catch-all term for postcolonial spaces of precarious residence and labor exploitation. The Ghetto Platform's underlying belief is that to move forward, one needs to recognize this sociohistorical fact. Pan-Africanism, however defined, is perhaps a goal, as suggested by the group discussion, but it begins with the localized time-space phenomenon of the ghetto.

## Racialization and Labor Practices: The Foundation of Citizenship

Kriolu was a unique formation in Portuguese colonialism, and its intricacies and intimacies of social relationships contributed to the overarching ideology of Portuguese "civilization" during early colonial periods of the sixteenth and seventeenth centuries as well as the period of colonial reinvigoration and reinvestment in the African continent during the latter stages of the nineteenth and early twentieth centuries.

The question remains: how do presences and intercultural impressions inform national policies of membership, belonging, and rights? In short, the answer in the case of Portugal and Kriolu is that there is more at stake in citizenship than discursive inclusion of Luso-Africans. As demonstrated in Chullage's rap lyrics about race and immigration as well as the heated discussion outside the neighborhood bar about current unemployment, and race and labor related to the Garvey documentary film, there are many obstacles to any sort of implementation of creolization as a set of policies.

A textual review of the historical connections among race, labor, and citizenship shows that the Portuguese state's discourse of hybridity and fruitful Luso-African encounters have been often at odds with the racist and xenophobic policies of membership and rights. In the words of Elizabeth Pilar Challinor, the labor history of Portuguese colonialism and postcolonial capitalism has been "a process in which citizen and migrant emerged as distinctive, disconnected, black and white figures" (2008:91). Chapters 2, 3, and 4 describe that Portuguese administrators, mestizo apologists, such as Brazilian sociologist Gilberto Freyre, and conciliatory Cape Verdean elite, including the Claridoso artists and scholars, employed Lusotropicalism in the 1950s and, subsequently, other Luso discourses to explain away such exploitative labor history. By the same token, as implied above in the description of contemporary activism among Luso-African migrants, this history established a paradigm of belonging, to which Kriolu rappers position themselves as they emphasize their language as a mark of difference. Kriolu was once a social fact of effective colonialism and promised assimilation into Portuguese identity and citizenship. For some contemporary migrants, Kriolu is now a medium of critique and territorial claims.

The policies of Portuguese citizenship were contradictory. The confusion centered around the identity categories of indigenous (*indigenato*) and assimilated (*assimilado*). On the surface, the words appear to indicate the ascribed status of birth and processes of acculturation. Under this logic, one would expect the rise of Cape Verdeans over the "rooted" Luso-Africans of the continent. In practice, these terms became marks of legal status in what Michel Cahen describes as the "colonial capitalism" of early and mid-twentieth century Portugal. The indigenous were black Africans who were not able or were unwilling to participate in the capitalist economy. Citing the 1926 law, *indígenas* were "those born of native parents and who by education and habits were not distinct from the common of their race" (in Rosas and Brito 1996:320, Article 3, Estatuto Político, Civil e Criminal dos Indígenas de Angola e Moçambique).

Cahen points out that the reality of late nineteenth-century labor demography contradicts the notion that "indigenous" Portuguese were solely locals. For example, many of the indígenas working in São Tomé e Príncipe, another Creole archipelago and former Portuguese colony located off the coast of Gabon, were contract laborers from Angola and Mozambique as well as Cape Verde (Cahen 2012:150). Although in previous eras, the Portuguese forged political-economic alliances with various African states and participated in the slave market, the classification of indígena meant that all black Africans were "natives" unless they could pass out of this supposed stable category. Passing the assimilation tests of the late 1920s and early 1930s included a demonstration of "abandoning indigenous habits and customs" and, consequently, proof of "the ability to speak Portuguese," later to be qualified under the 1954 Native Statute as "accurately" (Rosas and Brito 1996:381–82).

However, as certain popular cartoons of the 1930s demonstrate, "assimilated" Africans in the metropole were expected still to possess savage ways. For example, a particularly striking comic charge, "The Cannibal's Lunch," depicts an African dandy as a potential customer in an upstanding restaurant who mistakes an irate gentleman customer as the waiter and orders a selection of typical Portuguese dishes (e.g., sardines) with a busboy in a stew accompanied by potatoes (*Almoço do Antropófago* 1934 in Henriques 2011:68).

As Cahen and others, Douglas L. Wheeler and Walter C. Opello Jr. (2010), James Duffy (1961a), and Marilyn Newitt (2004), explain, the definitions of operative terms, such as "practicing a profession" as part of being "assimilated," were important sites where the Portuguese segregated purported racial populations. This addendum of "profession" proved to be a way to maximize profit from a skilled but "indigenous" black labor force and avert racial tensions between the blacks and petty white workers due to economic competition for wages. Exploitation could continue, and relatively unskilled white workers could enjoy a mixed but hierarchical relationship with local Africans. By 1961 the indigenato became moot as decolonization wars heated up and Salazar's state issued a blanket law incorporating or "recognizing" local habits and customs from the overseas provinces. *Indigenous* and *assimilated* were out as labels, and, in their place, *rural* emerged as a key word in the 1962 Labor Code. Again, misleading in its meaning, *rural* coded black and periphery.

The clunky Labor Codes of the 1960s did not represent the reality on the ground. A growing informal economy based in emergent (sub)urban communities demonstrated that Lusotropicalism and assimilation were farces (Castelo 1998). No matter the local African's linguistic proficiency in Portuguese, cultural competency in Eurocentric practices, such as Catholicism, or, indeed, one's profession, they were "niggas."

The development of a Creole elite, albeit small at .008 percent in Mozambique and .75 percent in Angola (Cahen 2012:162), distinguished Portuguese Africa from the rest of European-controlled Africa. However, these Creole intermediaries did not serve to "transition" the local economies from one of slavery to one of forced labor; rather, they enabled a kind of "social racism" where categories of place, such as "indigenous," blocked working Africans from any sort of meaningful inclusion.

The association between labor and identity is deeper historically than it may appear. Art historian Peter Mark argues that the labels of *Portuguese* and *Luso-African* (or *noirs lusitanisés*, as uttered by the astonished French in the eighteenth and nineteenth centuries, see Mark 2002:140) were initially linked to the profession of trader. The Creole communities of Cape Verde and various locales within the Senegambia region mixed architectural styles, languages, dress, social etiquette, and religions through encounter and trade. In so doing, they designed identities as cumulative and fluid projects of form and function.

While Mark underscores the social agency of labor and encounter, Shubi L. Ishemo points to the limiting force of Portuguese incursions into Africa. He argues that the lack of infrastructure within Portuguese colonialism may have fostered a fluidity of styles, languages, and so on, but it also produced long-lasting legacies of identity vis-à-vis migrant labor. Ishemo asserts that "the origins of [forced labor] lay in the specific characteristics of the Portuguese capitalist formation and the mode of its penetration and accumulation in the colonies. The consequent social formation that this engendered in each colony explains why, in some post-colonial states [such as Cape Verde], labor migration persists as a structural feature of the economy" (1995:162). It continues to be the case that Cape Verdeans, especially males but females as well, incorporate migration as a rite of passage. Migration is part of becoming an adult.[8]

In the summer of 2007, I finally became adept at managing cellular-phone texts, a helpful side effect of Lisbon fieldwork. Before the Facebook boom and accompanying social-media apps, there were few virtual venues outside of Myspace to do public networking. Rappers (and everyone else) depended on texts to set up live conversations. During those weeks in June, it had been hard to pin down rapper Gilson, but he finally agreed to a chat between his work at the Casa das Sandes sandwich shop in the tourist-filled Rossio plaza and at an electronics booth in an informal mall in a corridor attached to the relatively new subway station of *Parque das Nações* (Park of nations), a planned commercial and residential neighborhood catering to the Lisbon nouveau riche. With a bright sun filling up the late afternoon sky, we talked on the steps leading up to the massive apartment building where Gilson resided in the social neighborhood called Chelas. He opened up about his life.

Yeah, there are lots of Cape Verdeans here in Chelas, and we often run into each other going to and from work down in the tourist centers of Lisbon. Many of them work out near the airport, too, which is near Parque das Nações. You know, the big Vasco da Gama mall. I see kids from Chelas there wandering around. I came to Lisbon with my big sister when I was five years old. She took care of me, and then my mom came. I got a brother in Rotterdam, a cousin in Boston, and a sister in Paris. My dad goes back and forth between Lisbon and Santiago. I was born in Órgãos on the island of Santiago.

Sometimes I think about going to Rotterdam or Paris for a better wage, but there's something about Lisbon. I mean, we're used to Portugal and the Portuguese on some level, and they're used to us. The Kriolu we speak here is more to my taste. It's more me. We take the tuga [white Portuguese, colloquialism], and we don't reject it. We take what we want, add Kriolu, spin it around, and make it rough. On the everyday level, life is easier here in the tuga, and our Kriolu seems more sinister, more prideful. I rap about what all these Chelas kids know. What I am telling you. Making a little [bit of] money, sending some back to family.... It's about the Lisbon relax and the cool rip of Kriolu.

Gilson's story, like many others in the outskirts of Lisbon, is the complementary narrative component to the immigration reports of the *Serviço de Estrangeiros e Fronteiras* (Immigration and Border Service) (SEF).[9] Gilson hardly claims any sort of exceptional status. On the contrary, he sees himself as following a common path among Kriolu youth residing in Lisbon. In accordance with the histories of Portugal–Cape Verde or tuga-Kriolu intimacy, Gilson finds both a comfort and an irritation in Lisbon life. His Kriolu rap reflects the cultural inclusion that gives the Portuguese pride as well as the barbed rhetoric that represents an incompleteness of belonging and clamors for a new model of inclusion.

## A Spatial Reading of Kriolu and "Portugal"

The case of Portugal demonstrates a sociopolitical difference between two concepts that are often conflated—nationality and citizenship. Cahen quips about the time of Portuguese colonialism of Africa, "'race' was used almost exclusively to designate black people, while the Portuguese people were a *nation*" (2012:170, italics in original; see also Carvalhais 2007). Such factors as demography, religion, colonialism, and ideology played significant roles in shaping not only the laws of inclusion/exclusion but also the sentiment of "Portuguese." Until the 1980s, Portuguese history was predominantly one of emigration: pioneering merchants during the fifteenth to seventeenth centuries, tardy capitalists in the nineteenth and twentieth centuries, and migrant labor forces in post–World War II Europe.

CHAPTER 1

Unlike most traditions of "modern citizenship" in Europe, Portugal bracketed conventional social categories of race, religion, and ethnicity as national metrics and, instead, employed a principle of territory, or jus solis, to incorporate its various overseas dominions. This was particularly clear during the decolonization wars throughout Africa during the 1950s and 1960s and into the 1970s. The Salazar-Caetano regime used mouthpieces, such as *Permanência* (permanence), a magazine of current news in the overseas territories. The key word certainly is "permanence." The editorial staff of the magazine asks, "What does Portugal signify?" The columnist answers.

> What does Portugal signify? A country of Europe, no doubt, but one that goes beyond Europe, and completes itself and personalizes itself through encounters with peoples from other continents. A convergence of ethnicities, expressed in multi-secular human relations that overcome distance and racial oppositions. Therefore, it is true that the Overseas territories are an integral part of the Nation. This has nothing to do with colonialism, in which passionate observers try to include such trivial differences due to their lack of a general philosophy of culture. Why not simply admit that the seas are just as if not more unifying as land continuities? (Carneiro 1970)[10]

The principle of territory, even if one considers the seas as conduits of membership as the *Permanence* editors suggest, is not as solidly grounded in terra firma as it may seem.[11] The difference between "Portuguese" (i.e., national identity or membership) and being able to exercise *rights* (i.e., a more robust sense of Portuguese citizenship) is in large part defined by connotations of space and place.

Portugal did follow a similar path as the majority of emerging nation-states in establishing citizenship hierarchy based on property and education. The "liberal" idea was that contributing persons should be afforded civic rights, where "contributing" means propertied, literate gentlemen (R. Ramos 2004). Consequently, a minuscule elite group of "white" (relatively speaking) men was formed. However, even in its early iterations, Portuguese citizenship construed territory slightly more broadly than most. For example, residents who were not of the nobility or clergy could mobilize the term *vizinhança* (neighborhood) to gain status and exercise certain "community" rights (Moura-Ramos 1984).[12] Under the fascist "New State" regime of Antonio Salazar, the language of "natural citizen" was replaced with so-called natural groups and moral and economic associations, thereby introducing aspects of jus sanguinis into the citizenship equation (Salazar 1939).

The peculiarity of Portugal comes in the state's use of *territory* as an orientation. When Portugal turned its attention more directly to its African colonies in the early twentieth century, one's status became increasingly significant if one was "assimilated," that is, a conceptual move to the metropole, or if one was "indigenous," a hopeless native and static African other. Although members of both categories were "Portuguese" nationals, the assimilated were given, at least, rhetorical liberties of access to education and increased salaries. Both types of Luso-Africans were expected to "contribute" through labor to the Portuguese state, and in this way, even though the indigenous were considered separate, wholly other Africans, the Portuguese state could justify forced labor in a postslavery era. The obligation to contribute is codified in the vagrancy laws of the late 1870s and again in 1899 (Jerónimo 2012).

More specific to Cape Verde, Deirdre Meintel (1984) points out that the Portuguese were quick to capitalize on even the tragic famines and droughts that ravaged the archipelago during the 1770s, 1830s, and 1860s. By the late nineteenth century, the Portuguese deployed the key word *vagrancy* to force into submission legally those who were not actively part of labor projects on the islands or on the plantations of São Tomé e Príncipe or Angola. Ishemo estimates that between 1903 and 1970, roughly eighty thousand Cape Verdeans were "forcibly transported to São Tomé" under the vagrancy laws. In sum, Portugal's efforts to modernize and improve its position within global capitalism were more pervasive demographically and spatially in the daily lives of African workers than during the slavery period.

In the 1970s, with the implosion of the fascist regime inside Portugal and the decolonization wars among the overseas territories in Africa, the concept and accompanying laws of citizenship began to change. The 1981 Law of Nationality codifies a shift from jus solis to jus sanguinis as the Portuguese attempted to reconcile a broadening of the "civic community" along lines of gender and class inside Portugal, given a new influx of African migrants. Over the 1980s, immigrants to Portugal became more diverse with an increase from 102 to 129 different countries of origin of residents. Portugal shared such aspects with Spain, Italy, and Greece, which helped foster the idea of a "Southern Europe" (Pedaliu 2013; Malheiros 2010).

Portugal, thus, became, in part, an ethnic imagination. The 1981 law facilitated citizenship for someone born of Portuguese parents abroad, but for someone born of foreign parents residing in Portugal, citizenship remained allusive. The law directly aided children of *retornados*, the thousands of white "returnees" who had been living for generations in Africa.[13] However, it is the second scenario in which many Cape Verdeans found themselves, between logics and between categories.

Who showed you this long path?
Who showed you this long path?
This way to São Tomé!

# CHAPTER 1

> Longing, longing, longing (*sodadi*)
> for our land of San Nikolau
>
> If you write me, I'll write you
> If you forget me, I'll forget you
> Until one day upon your return
> Longing, longing, longing (*sodadi*)
> for our land of San Nikolau.
> —(Soares 1950s)

Any Cape Verdean and many Portuguese would recognize these lyrics. One of the most famous *mornas* (a musical genre), "sodadi" (nostalgic blues) conveys the sentiment of separation from family and friends resulting from labor migration. In this case, as explained by the song's author, Armando Soares, the song refers to the recruitment of Cape Verdean laborers in the 1950s by the Portuguese government to work in the mines of São Tomé e Principe.

Beyond the obvious significance of the song's lyrics, the context in which I first heard the song is noteworthy. While in Boston during June 2009, in preparation for fieldwork in Lisbon and Praia, I attended a luncheon organized by local Cape Verdean associations in honor of a visit by Aristides Lima, the Cape Verdean Parliament leader. The husband of one of the main-event organizers and I chatted over lunch as a house band played through several mornas and *coladeras* (another musical genre from Cape Verde), a few originally by the famous diva Cesária Évora. Brito, my lunch companion, suddenly stopped when the band transitioned into "Sodadi," what turned out to be the final song before Lima's presentation. Brito was touched and felt it an obligation to explain what this song of migration meant to him.

Hardly a representative of impoverished manual labor, Brito had done well for himself in New England. He described the long, arduous travels of his parents and the wide dispersal of his relatives across Europe and the Americas and commented, "This song captures Cape Verde. You have to understand this if you want to understand Cape Verde and the expression of Kriolu." Lima also reflected on the song's continued resonance in an allusion to "Sodadi" in his opening remarks: "A wonderful morna, a moving song. Thank you for inviting me to speak today ... and while Cape Verde continues to be diasporic, we in the Parliament and I as leader are committed to providing the education and local infrastructure so that the partnership between the Cape Verdean government and the upstanding Cape Verdean organizations in historically strongholds such as here in Boston can grow in strength and make for a more effective nation and identity. I am honored to be here to tell you about the current debates in the Parliament."

Statistics from Portuguese government agencies, such as the National Statistical Institute (INE) and the SEF, make it clear that while the relative level of formal education and skill of immigrant laborers in Portugal rose during the 1980s and early 1990s, Cape Verdean and African Countries with Portuguese as the Official Language (PALOP) residents overall continue to make up the bulk of lower-paid, manual laborers in the "new" Portugal (Malheiros 1998). In addition, a significant growth industry during the 1980s was domestic services, which attracted a new wave of Luso-African women, many of whom are Cape Verdean.

Beyond the statistics, the "vagrant," a typical Portuguese euphemism for "nigga," remained current during the 1980s and 1990s in the face of these demographic changes. The terms *vagrant* and *vagabond* (badiu) became culturally meaningful, particularly on the Cape Verdean island of Santiago, as linguistic dialect and identity markers. The term *vagabond* is but one example of the convergence of migration experience and public policy that shape notions of identity, belonging, and a formalized citizenship.

## A Reconsideration of Kriolu Identity

If we take a moment to reflect on this policy history, we begin to appreciate the complexity of Creole as a category of status and creolization as a processual condition of citizenship. What was generally regarded as part of Portugal's colonial mindset and emerging national sense of self came to symbolize the "dangerous" inclusion of African others. The basis of Creole and Kriolu is labor often mediated by trade and migration. As the story about "Sodadi" at the luncheon for middle-class Cape Verdeans and the invited Cape Verdean politician demonstrates, Creole and migrant labor continue to have a hold on identity.

As Portuguese colonialism became more aggressive (and arguably desperate during the twentieth century), Kriolu increasingly came to represent an exploited, African other, someone who is still not yet a contributing member of Portugal worthy of citizenship rights but certainly able to call him- or herself "Portuguese." This identity represented a claim to the future, a goal to be achieved someday in terms of culture, language, and morality. At a fundamental level, this contradiction in Portuguese policy and attitude contextualizes the sentiment behind the emotional charges of the youth in twenty-first-century Kova M. To paraphrase one spirited rapper during the Marcus Garvey University gathering, "Blackness *is* part of Portugal. We come from Creole. Where is the result of all this for me, for us here in this neighborhood? Am I just a nigga?" The consciousness activated by Cape Verdean and Luso-African activists suggests that Kriolu offers something else.

## CHAPTER 1

The next three chapters delineate the emergence and development of a robust, critical Kriolu identity at a time when Portugal, at the macro level of national policy and law, has become one of the most progressive countries in immigration and citizenship. With Portugal's entry into the European Union in 1986, its adoption of the Schengen Treaty in 1991, and its reinvigorated participation in European debates on immigration (instead of its traditional role as emigrant labor force for other, more economically powerful European nations), Portugal relaxed its citizenship laws, which had focused on jus sanguinis and being able to speak "good Portuguese." For example, the current National Citizenship Law, Decreto Lei no. 308-A/75, passed in December 2006, states that an individual who was born in Portugal but of foreign-born parents need only reside inside Portuguese territory for five years and declare a willingness (*vontade*) to be a Portuguese citizen in order to be a viable candidate for citizenship. This reduction of five years was coupled with more-lenient language requirements in terms of proficiency.[14] In addition, the Portuguese state followed other Western European nation-states by including a clause implying that citizenship is a universal right so that Portuguese citizenship would be an option in cases of individuals without any citizenship (*apatriados*) (chapter 5 discusses more on state policies of citizenship and accompanying discourses of interculturality). The contradictions in the intimate relations between Portugal and Cape Verde are historical in their dynamics but ultimately are made manifest in place (from territory to neighborhood) and language (from "black Portuguese" to Kriolu).

*Ami e kriolu.* A simple statement, "I am Kriolu," opens up a complex set of questions and life narratives. How is it that Kriolu, a prototypical Creole classification and, thus, a mark of crossover, could be such a strong identity category? Especially, among early-generation immigrants, what is at stake in Kriolu? This chapter provides historical depth to the idea and practice of citizenship as a condition of rights and identity claims. Portuguese officials racialized citizenship and linked rights to labor and education as they simultaneously propagated Portugal as a unique mixture born out of Euro-African encounters. The next chapter concentrates on the contingencies among an overarching national ideology, Lusotropicalism, and an emerging politics of identity, Kriolu. Once familiar with this relationship, we will hear contemporary Cape Verdean youth and Kriolu rappers more clearly.

CHAPTER 2

# Kriolu Interruptions of Luso

> As a young man, in the 1920s, [Jorge Luís] Borges prowled the obscure barrios of Buenos Aires, seeking the company of *cuchilleros*, knife fighters, who represented to him a form of authentic *criollo* nativism that he wished to know and absorb.... He saw it as a way to reflect the city's essence, as Joyce had done with Dublin, a way to establish a lasting cultural identity that Argentina did not yet possess in the world. His aim, in part, was to enshrine the urban descendent of the *criollo*, with his ubiquitous dagger and supposedly honorable outlaw ways.
>
> —Michael Greenberg

The knife appears repeatedly in Cape Verdean folklore and in news reports about crime and violence in European peripheral urban areas where immigrant populations reside and in the literary texts of modernist masters (Filho 1995). The knife-wielding Creole is, as Michael Greenberg interprets Borges's intentions in the epigraph, a creative oxymoron, full of "honorable outlaw ways." In Lisbon, Cape Verdean presence is like a knife with two blades. Kriolu is both a medium of inclusive citizenship accentuated by a playful folklore and an idiom of violent discomfort. Kriolu seems to cut both ways.

Examples of knives in folklore include that a *guarda* (protective talisman) might be worn around the neck to preclude a knife thrust: "The knife would be turned back" (Parsons 1921:91). In a folk tale from the Cape Verdean island of San Nicolão (Niklau), "Mesiana pours boiling oil into barrels in which male robbers are hiding. They kick and kick. 'You may kick as much as you like,' says Mesiana. She puts a knife in her belt and dances before the chief. As he is pulling out money for her, she dances up close to him and stabs him.... Ali Baba marries Mesiana to his son" (Parsons 1923:5).

A Cape Verdean man was accused years later of being "the author of Maddie McCann's abduction," according to a more recent news report featuring the accusation by the parents of the English girl who was abducted in 2007 in the southern region of the Algarve in Portugal. And the internet gets in on the discussion of violence through an online post in a heated debate about the causes of a 2009 skirmish in a periphery neighborhood to Stockholm, Sweden, police: "I bet you're dying for someone to confirm your suspicions: apparently said man is of African, Cape-Verdean descent. Turns out he emigrated from Cape Verde to Portugal, got his Portuguese nationality/EU citizenship on the grounds of having been born in the late Portuguese Empire and thus in the Portuguese Commonwealth, emigrated to Sweden and married a Finnish woman.... The police went to their house and the [Afro–Cape Verdean] man, thinking it was the gang that threatened them [he and his wife], opened the door holding a hunting knife in his hand. The police shot him" (Gaspar 2013).

Kriolu, like other Creole formations, emerges from intense relations of encounter. However, the intensity of such cross-cultural contact is dynamic, and there are periods of consolidation and differentiation. Once the encounter has been incorporated and routinized as a matrix of language, culture, and identity, Creole can develop in a "dialectical movement" (Vergès 2007:144), involving creative tensions around dis/emplacement.[1] For example, discussing Indian-Oceanic creolization on Réunion Island, François Vergès argues that Creole becomes a vocabulary of suffering and agency, involving loss, exile, memory, traces, adaptation, and inequality. Similarly, Cape Verdean Kriolu's conflicted essence both reinforces and interrupts the national paradigm of Portuguese belonging and inclusion represented in a host of Luso categories and discourses. I turn again to local rappers for inspiration, this one LBC: "I think it [Kriolu rap] is a [response to] Lusotropicalism. They try to limit Kriolu by inclusion, but, for me, Kriolu is not only Cape Verde and our diaspora, but much more... from Brazil to Jamaica" (personal communication).

Lisbon-based and Cape Verdean émigré rapper LBC defines Kriolu rap as a form of spatial politics that, essentially, is a response to Lusotropicalism. This chapter focuses on Kriolu as an expression of historicity in the transition from coloniality to postcoloniality in terms of an interruption of the national marker of Creole, that is, Lusotropicalism. Kriolu interruptions in the form of Cape Verdean high art and working-class screams from immigrant rappers, while certainly responses to national mythologies, are relations and share critical references with an expansive Creole geography, including the Indian and Atlantic regions.

## Ideologies and Interruptions as (Un)satisfying Relations

Even in the most radical expressions of Kriolu-as-difference, there is an awareness of the interdependency between Kriolu and Portuguese, Cape Verde and Portugal. Through themes of blackness, immigrants, and the poor working class, the rap rhetoric of LBC, Hezbollah, Ghoya, Nigga Poison, and Chullage pivots on Luso, *tuga* (a colloquialism for white Portuguese), and Portugal (also sometimes referred to as *tuga*). In my use of the term *relation*, I invoke the prolific Martinican essayist and theorist Edouard Glissant, who posits that "Creole," as well as his more geographically grounded identity label of *antillanité* (Antillean-ness), is more encompassing and representative of identity than "culture." For Glissant,

> "culture" is the precaution of those who claim to think thought but who steer clear of its chaotic journey. Evolving cultures infer Relation, the overstepping that grounds their unity-diversity.... We are not prompted solely by the defining of our identities but by their relation to everything possible as well as the mutual mutations generated by this interplay of relations. Creolizations bring into Relation but not to universalize; the principles of Creoleness regress toward negritudes, ideas of Frenchness, of Latinness, all generalizing concepts more or less innocently. (1997:1, 89)

Glissant focuses on the process by which sociocultural groups mediate the movement of "thought" or in more anthropological terms, social interaction and expressive practices, into bounded entities of "culture" or categories of difference, for example, "negritudes" and so on. The essential hybridity of identity formation, which figures so prominently in Caribbean and Latin American cultural production, more generally, rubs against the geopolitics of reality. Identity as "chaotic journey" of relation conflicts with the regulatory categories and prescriptive procedures of citizenship. The case of Kriolu in Portugal highlights the transatlantic problem Glissant describes.

The moniker LBC is an acronym for "learning black connection," and it is this assertion of difference that interrupts conventional Portuguese identity formation. At first glance, LBC's comments may appear contradictory, "to limit through inclusion," but it is the categorization of Luso and its implied affiliations that rubs LBC the wrong way. Luso is a "precaution," while Kriolu is a dynamic condition. Be that as it may, Kriolu interruption is not an intervention from an unwelcome stranger but a peculiar diversion from a historically close partner. Given the long-term intimacy between Portugal and its former African colonies and the substantial embrace of multiculturalism in postcolonial Portugal by state agencies, such identity politics of Kriolu as "black" difference are not as straightforward as they may initially appear.

Scholars, politicians, and everyday folk have generally narrated the cultural story of Portuguese identity and territorial claim as a manifestation of *Lusotropicalism*, a termed coined in the 1950s by Brazilian sociologist Gilberto Freyre (1953b).[2] *Lusotropicalism* refers to the cordial control of Portuguese (post)colonialism based on "soft" power that translates into racial mixture, lenient laws around civil rights relative to the rest of Western Europe, and a natural predisposition toward intercultural understanding and appreciation. However, as Portuguese historian Isabel Castro Henriques discusses, the Salazar regime adopted the ideology of Lusotropicalism to rationalize the implementation of the 1953 Organic Law on Portuguese Overseas Land as part of a strategy to maintain colonial hegemony in a moment of massive decolonization across the African continent (2012:83).

For his part, LBC interprets Lusotropicalism as control through assimilation when he says, "They try to limit kriolu by inclusion." Although the term *Lusotropicalism* itself has lost favor due to its colonial connotations, newer ones, such as *Lusofonia*, literally the collective identity of Portuguese–speaking countries, have followed suit.[3] The operating logic is that to be Portuguese involves a unique sociohistorical mindset where Creole mixture of European "modernity," Moorish folklore, and African expressive culture constitutes a natural baseline of interaction oriented by the Portuguese language (see Jerónimo 2006). Political scientist Ronald Chilcote synthesizes the theory of Lusotropicalism as the "biological processes of miscegenation and the sociological processes of interpenetration of cultures" (1966:9). He went on to declare that given these parameters, "the Cape Verdean is the most perfect Portuguese human being" (1966:9).

As LBC implies, Kriolu is not simply a language but also an identity. Furthermore, LBC suggests that Kriolu and, particularly, Kriolu rap interrupt Lusotropicalism by drawing attention to a different kind of collective imagination—one that moves away from "Portuguese" parameters of former African colonial encounters and moves toward blackness, that is, Brazil and Jamaica. From an ethnomusicological perspective, Martin Stokes, in his scholarship on world music and cosmopolitan "translations" or recastings of "traditional culture," has argued that "the movement of translations is structured by colonial or neo-colonial fields of power, moving from peripheries to centers and from there to other peripheries" (2007). LBC uses the medium of rap music to "translate" reality and, thus, subscribes to what Miguel Vale de Almeida calls "the projective character of creolization as a form of surpassing nationalism, ethnic exclusivism and racism" (2007:129). For LBC and others, rap exists as a forum through which they can expose the "social rupture" that exists between Kriolu and Luso discourses, a space where belonging is tested and boundaries are negotiated (Siu 2005:28).[4]

Kriolu rappers' voices of discontent with Portuguese "inclusion" are important because they join a range of immigrant experiences across Europe that are forcefully obliging politicians and civic leaders to reassess the parameters and pragmatic function of citizenship. Unlike Angolans in Portugal or Libyans in Italy, Kriolu subjects have historically been considered as quasi-assimilated. Beyond the consideration of national citizenship and identity, the case of current Kriolu rappers also invites a theoretical reconsideration of Creole and the ambiguities of hybridity.

## An Argument for the Significance of Creole

One of the main arguments of this book is that given the current global milieu of intensified migration of people and ideas, we would benefit from a greater understanding of Creole. Like *culture, development,* and *evolution, Creole* is a term that is both descriptive, referring to a historically structured category of people, and evaluative, meaning a judgment of human worth, political legitimacy, and social hierarchy. I hope to persuade the reader of the importance of Creole by employing a strategy used throughout this book: a braiding of history, theory, and ethnography.

In a collection of essays, periodically inspiring and drifting, Iain Chambers summarizes a current paradigm of thought: "Indeed, a significant tendency in present-day critical thought, confronted with the shrinkage of the European rationale that once claimed to speak for all and everything, is to adopt metaphors of movement, migration, maps travel and sometimes a seemingly facile tourism" (1994:2–3). The idiom of movement and migration, including the key word *Creole,* has become a discursive wellspring to make sense of the relationship between demographic and epistemological shifts. In a strong sense, this represents the "post" in postcolonialism. Moreover, historians, such as Jorge Cañizares-Esguerra (2007) and Joyce E. Chaplin (2007), remind us that by the early seventeenth century, Creole had become its own "discourse" of distinction and danger among elites in the Hispanic and British New World, respectively.

Located between modern power and local knowledge, Creole has always demonstrated the potential flexibility evident in identity formation (Cohen 2010). As Guyanese essayist Wilson Harris reflects on his own experiences, the utterance of Creole both reinforces a "reactionary purist logic" of privilege and suggests a way out via interdependency (1999:239). For Harris, fiction serves as a medium to cultivate a "creolization of the chasm" (1999:241), the paradox of identity framed in likenesses and differences.

*Nu ta kanta na kriolu pamodi é revoluson y revolusom.*
*Es som é di imigrantes sima mi, sima nha gentis.*
*Kanta na kriolu ka é pasadu, é di oji, li, gosi.*

## CHAPTER 2

We sing in Kriolu because it is a revolution and revolu-sound.
This sound comes from immigrants like me, like my people.
To rap in Kriolu is not something of the past; it is right now, right here.
—(Karlon, live performance 2009)

Rapper Karlon opened his two-song set with these words. He and his partner, Def, were part of a large youth musical event sponsored by FNAC, the international entertainment retail store. Since the demise of almost all underground music stores and many night clubs in Lisbon toward the end of the 2000s, the FNAC event has become one venue for amateur artists to have a brief moment on stage. Certainly aware of Kriolu's long history in Cape Verde and in the diaspora, Karlon's point here is to convey to the audience of mostly friends, family, social workers, and the occasional drifting Lisbon hipster as well as the downtown bourgeoisie shopper that Kriolu is a vibrant language *here* in Lisbon. Def plays up this idea in one of the song refrains by emphasizing the phrases, *li na tuga, nu é di tuga* (Here in Portugal, we came from Portugal). The first utterance of "Portugal" signifies the country, and the second refers to the encounter. The audience is left with a provocative question, a Creole implication of identity and place.

The proliferation of connotations within Creole is a result of the variety of ways social groups have associated Creole with place, race, class, politics, and ideologies of mixture. Does it become a label of self-ascription to ride the crest of two heroic pasts, in the case of Spanish *criollos*, the Hispanic and Aztec empires, a national treasure lost over the course of modernity in Borges's quote of the epigraph to this chapter, or does it become a forceful point of oppositional relation to which relocated "British bodies" can show their cultural and environmental "seasoning" and "solidify a white hegemony over the land" (Chaplin 2007:51, 55, 62)? Robin Cohen and Olivia Sheringham (2008b) call this process a variable "elective affinity" that combines social actions of identification with creolization, diaspora, and "islandness."

*Creole* and, more forceful, *creolization* surfaced as key words in the 1980s and 1990s among scholars throughout the social sciences and the humanities in their attempts to historically ground and ethnographically describe postcolonial, multicultural populations.[5] What was and continues to be refreshing about the paradigm of creolization is that it provoked a realization that the inner sanctums of "the West" and the bastions of "civilization" had, indeed, become "creolized." Namely, essential aspects of "Western" societies from language to religion to music to sports had been "outed" as longtime, hybrid Calibans, that oft-cited Shakespearean character symbolic of miscegenous nativism, which had, theretofore, been assumed as squarely "French" or "British" or "American."[6]

However, in the process of semiotic consolidation, a simplification has occurred so that *Creole* has come to mean any sort of mixture (Clifford 1988; Hannerz 1987, 1996). What has been lost and what Kriolu rappers and other Cape Verdean migrants reinsert into the discussion of Creole are the elements of history, alterity, and power (W. T. Filho 2009). This is similar to what Aisha Khan calls the "force of abrasion" that is part of the "energy of creolization" (2007:246).

Sidney Mintz reminded us in 1971 that the term *Creole* is a European invention that conflates geographical distinction with essentialist assumptions in the colonial context of hierarchy and social stratification, particularly, in the Caribbean and Latin America, both, of course, equally invented terms of place identity. Similarly, as Stephan Palmié (2006) has discussed, *Creole* refers to "local identity" or indigenization, not hybridity (see also Jackson 2012). Michael Dash (1996) refers to state "ideological appropriations," and Khan discusses Creole as a "master symbol" (2001), which have tended to smooth out the rough edges of Creole as "contention" in favor of a unifying Creole concept emphasizing harmony (see also Khan 2004, 2007; Bolland 1992).

## Kriolu Contentions

On a stifling hot afternoon in August 2009, Kriolu rapper Karlos, hip-hop archivist Uncle C, and I gathered on the steps of the monument dedicated to Luis de Camões. Ironically, we were in the protective shadows of the legendary Portuguese writer, whose sixteenth-century epic poems *Os Lusíadas* (The Lusiads) established the Portuguese paradigm of civilization and grand artistic reflection based on the themes of travel, nostalgia, and the sea. Kriolu and the experience of Cape Verde(ans), in particular, have been the misrecognized partners of such glory and emotion, a story of forced migration and diaspora also linked to the sea and nostalgia. While the pigeons swirled about, Karlos was adamant that I grasp the lack of representation of Cape Verde and African Countries with Portuguese as the Official Language (PALOP), in general, in Lisbon schools and society.

> In school we just learn about Brazil and Goa [a Portuguese territory until 1961, in contemporary southwest India]. It's like Cape Verde and the PALOP are simply part of Portugal. Treated that way. On the way to being Portuguese or something. I don't know what *interculturalidade* [interculturality] is supposed to be. Kriolu is my medium of expression, me and thousands of others. A democracy has the freedom of expression. So, there you have it. The medium though has no support or recognition here. You go through school and through the city with nothing about Cape Verde. The music industry is the same way. When I

read a book by Amílcar Cabral, I knew I had to get out of Portugal. I wanted to spread Kriolu out. I represent the badiu, and, in fact, my experience all over Europe is that they [non-Portuguese Europeans] love Kriolu. Here in Portugal and in Lisbon, there's no interest.

Karlos's comments highlight a number of themes shared by young Cape Verdeans in Portugal. In particular, his references to school education, linguistic stigma, and the vagrant speak to spatial and ideological differences of contemporary Kriolu. Similar to LBC, Karlos expressed his suspicion of assimilationist discourses, such as interculturality and Lusotropicalism. Both rappers cite Cabral, the revolutionary leader of forces in Guinea-Bissau, and, by extension, Cape Verde, as a direct influence.

Although he was born in Portuguese Guinea, Cabral grew up in Cape Verde. His parents were Cape Verdean migrants of educated but modest class backgrounds. This background is significant because in his speeches and writings of the late 1960s and early 1970s, Cabral was particularly sensitive to class divisions in colonial practices of rule and the challenges of bridging such gaps in revolutionary struggles. Cabral focused on *assimilado*, the bureaucratic term for the "good African" often attributed to the Cape Verdean within Portuguese colonialism and used as a tool of alienation. For Cabral, assimilation created a "social gap between the indigenous elites and the popular masses ... [and a mindset with which] the urban or peasant *petite bourgeoisie* considers itself cultural superior to its own people and ignores or looks down upon their cultural values" (1978:45).

Herein lay the revolutionary potential of culture, in general, and Kriol/Kriolu (Kriol is the Guinea-Bissau Creole), more specifically. It is a source of common ground and a medium to "re-Africanise our minds" (Cabral 1974) or what Charles Peterson describes as an "inward turning" (2007:122). Cabral's interruption of assimilation involved a rethinking and reorganization of class and ethnicity for sociopolitical change. For LBC, Karlos, and other Kriolu rappers in Lisbon, the project of interruption also includes an interrogation of space, not simply in terms of "re-Africanization" or a diasporic nostalgia for the maternal archipelago but also a "spreading out," in the words of Karlos, of Kriolu in Europe and a redefinition of various residential areas in the former metropole of Lisbon.

As implied above, the economic and racialized dimensions of Creole and African diasporas are reflected in spatial arrangements. This fact helps explain the variants of Kriolu, both the early linguistic break between Cape Verdean Kriolu and Guinean Kriol, as well as the multiple dialects within Cape Verdean Kriolu. While an extended discussion of the axes of race and class as they relate to the migration trajectories of Cape Verdeans is outside the scope of this chapter, an outline will help to contextualize the Portuguese case.[7]

The archipelago of Cape Verde is divided into two major island groupings, the *sotavento* and *barlavento*, or leeward islands and windward islands, respectively. Travel between the islands remains arduous by boat and expensive and limited by plane. This has contributed to the heterogeneity among Cape Verdeans in their speech and their diasporic connections. In the case of Lisbon, the main émigré population comes from the most populous island, Santiago, located in the windward group. The capital city of Praia, which holds roughly one-third of the national population, is on Santiago.

Both Karlos and Uncle C call themselves badiu, a term referring to both the linguistic variant of Kriolu and the general identity of a person from the island of Santiago, considered by the Portuguese and Cape Verdeans alike as the most "African" island of the archipelago. Karlos was born of Cape Verdean parents from Praia and raised in the improvised neighborhood of Alto de Santa Catarina on the outskirts of Lisbon; Uncle C was born in Praia and came of age in the Azores near a U.S. military base. Uncle C joined Karlos in making the racialized claim that rap is more strongly aligned with badiu than other Cape Verdean islanders and linguistic variants. Cape Verdean literature provides a basis to such sociogeographic claims. For example, in 1898, Cônego A. da Costa Teixeira, the editor of *Almanach Luso-Africano* (Luso-African almanac) from 1895 to 1899, published a version in a Santo Anton variant of Kriolu of Camões's *Lusiadas*. In it Teixeira makes references to Santiago as a nom de guerre, a warrior-like presence that is part of the island identity (Teixeira 1898).

This assertion plays on the persistent stigma against *badiu*, a term that is linguistically akin to the Portuguese word *vadio* (vagabond). As in many cultures, the conflation of laziness and blackness was historically normalized in Portuguese colonial thought and formalized in Creole language, such as the Kriolu term *badiu*. This background helps frame both Gilberto Freyre's tone of disappointment when he describes Santiago as "too negroid" an island (1953) as well as Karlos's affirmation of Santiago as the "real" Cape Verde.

## Creole and Lusotropicalism

Certainly, Creole has carried many different and sometimes opposing meanings. However, at least in the Atlantic regions, a general historical dynamic contextualizes the Portuguese case. As chapter 1 shows, the discursive turn from essential native to productive hybrid hinged upon the idea that Creole signified phenotypic and cultural mixture, which, in theory, was emboldened during certain colonial projects, namely, that of Portugal.

CHAPTER 2

And along came Gilberto Freyre. Freyre is widely known in U.S. anthropological scholarship as that former student of Franz Boas, who returned home to Brazil during the rise of populist dictator Getúlio Vargas during the early 1930s and helped shape what continues to be the dominant nationalist ideology in Brazil, "racial democracy," the emergent ideology during Brazil's experiment with fascism under Getúlio Vargas during the 1930s and 1940s. Less known in the Americas is Freyre's experience in the early 1950s as an invited guest of the Portuguese Ministry of Culture. His assignment was to visit and assess the Portuguese colonies in Africa and Asia. Freyre went on to formulate a related theory of Lusotropicalism, which argues that the Portuguese were historically exceptional, due to their Moorish and generally "mixed" stock, in cultivating the colonial encounter into a creative, Dionysian dance of order and progress.[8]

The timing of the heralded Brazilian sociologist was impeccable. As poet and journalist Rebelo de Bettencourt stated in 1952 during one of Freyre's visits on his worldwide tour of Luso-colonialism, "it's good for us to hear, from time to time, voices like this one [Freyre] that lead us to believe again with optimism in the highest ideals of Portugal" (quoted in Freyre 1953a:425). For Freyre, the Portuguese had a "special transeuropean vocation," an "extra-european" dimension, one that "from the beginning," he stated in his dozens of public speeches to Lusophiles, was a vocation of empathetic love under the sign of "a blackened Venus" (1953b:13, 125–32, 26). This final term refers to what Chilcote describes as the idea that Portuguese were "transforming the tropics, not by introducing European values but by themselves changing into Lusotropicals in body and soul" (1966:9).

Cape Verdeans' identification with Creole afforded a certain degree of privilege toward the latter stages of Portuguese colonialism. Such associations would continue among elite groups of Portuguese and Cape Verdeans as Lusotropicalism emerged as a key word for Portuguese distinction. However, such embrace of the Luso would have divisive effects not only between Cape Verdeans and Portuguese populations but also among Cape Verdeans. Such "internal" divisions reflect class interests and spatial differences based on island affinities.

For example, Manuel Ferreira, a Portuguese scholar and Cape Verde advocate, describes Kriolu as a poetic dialect for natural emotions of local folklore as well as a medium for learning Portuguese and the "modern" pillars of European reason and logic. Ferreira had lived for years in Cape Verde and had witnessed the tragic deaths of hundreds due to droughts and famines during the 1940s, when he was stationed on the islands as part of military service. In his scholarly work and fiction novellas, Ferreira saw Cape Verdean Kriolu as the perfect, modern African language, a window into the ideal type of transition, an ideal postcolonial subject.

He himself mixed Portuguese and Kriolu in his texts as symbolic of the natural mixture of the local and global as well as sentiment and science.

In 1962, Ferreira published *Hora di Bai* (Time to go), an award-winning novel that relates the sentiments of desperation, hunger, poverty, and displacement, as Cape Verdeans move between the islands and emigrate to the labor camps in São Tomé e Príncipe. *Hora di Bai* remains a classic text within the literary canon of African Lusophone literature, representative of the World War II period of "Portuguese" life. Through his protagonists, Ferreira shifts between declarations of sociohistorical facts about one of the great famines in Cape Verdean history and equally accurate narratives of imagination and delirium, sung in the form of mornas, a lyrical song with a lilting melody featuring voice and nylon-string guitar, from the island of São Vicente.

The name of the novel is instructive about the concept of place and belonging. Ferreira's *Hora di Bai* is an homage, in Kriolu, to the Cape Verdean poet Eugênio Tavares (1867–1930), author of dozens of mornas, including one "Hora di Bai." As Cape Verdean scholars have noted, the harsh realities of a long history of diasporic displacement, made poetic by artists such as Tavares, have resulted in an expansion in the connotation of the phrase *hora di bai*. It is not only a time to go; the phrase also indexes a social commitment of saying good-bye, or *a despedida*, and an inevitable time to return. The social fabric of Cape Verdean diaspora is embedded in this ubiquitous Kriolu phrase.

Ferreira employs a number of Kriolu terms and phrases throughout the novel. Yet, curiously, Ferreira frames *Hora di Bai* as an internal story of Cape Verde. The interdependency of Portuguese/Kriolu and colonizer/colonized is absent.[9] In fact, there are no Portuguese characters in the story, and, thus, displacement and despair are local tragedies. Written during the height of the fascist regime of Salazar, *Hora di Bai* demonstrates a familiar tone of Portuguese empathy. Put bluntly, Kriolu and Cape Verdean-ness are unfortunate, but (thankfully) they are located over *there*.

Ferreira's *A Aventura Crioula*, written five years after *Hora di Bai*, demonstrates more critical thinking in his discussion of the effect of Lusotropicalism on Cape Verdean writers. He describes Pedro Cardoso, one of the leaders of the Claridade movement.

> He is, like so many of his generation, a typical intellectual of his land, of the Cape Verdean culture, identified with the drama of his people, an emotional layering of insularity and abandon with a clear notion to live in a specific, delineated, cherished universe, which values and holds sacred his own patria but at the same time ... he is not able to escape the nationalist feeling of the other

patria, parallel and encompassing, which would be the Portuguese patria. . . . No Cape Verdean before the Claridade movement and even among leaders such as Cardoso were ever to resolve this ambiguity. (1967:237)

Moreover,

> Pedro Cardoso, despite all of his limitations concerning history..., will always represent those, and there are so many, who are fatally contradictory but who try to break through the [colonial] fence and give a cultural and sentimental voice to the Cape Verdean universe. (1967:242)[10]

Ferreira was, of course, not Cape Verdean or, by extension, an African nationalist. He represented and was frequently subsidized by the Salazar regime. Yet, his writings were inspired by a group of Cape Verdean intellectuals, predominantly from the island of São Vicente and the city of Mindelo. From the Boston banquet described in the previous chapter, we may recall the role of Mindelo in the nostalgia of Cesária Évora's morna as part of a romantic drama of Cape Verdean identity. This elite group called themselves the Claridosos (the illuminated or enlightened) and published a landmark journal called *Claridade*.

## Cape Verdean Kriolu's Equivocal Rejoinder

Poets, linguists, musicians, and scholars, such as Tavares (whose picture and poem are on a Cape Verdean bank note), Manuel Lopes, Jorge Barbosa, and Baltasar Lopes, are significant in the history of Kriolu because they articulated language and geography as identity. Baltasar Lopes, also a writer, philologist, and a founder of the "enlightenment" movement (Claridosos), describes, "These islands; Creole, by the people's color, white, by the social conditions, and by the language, a Roman experience in the tropics" (1956:15). The "enlightened" Kriolu was one of cultural nationalism in an effort to rework the experiences of colonialism into an expression of high modern art and cultural distinction. From their perspective, being Cape Verdean could be achieved without interrupting Portuguese conventions of racial and linguistic hierarchies.

Baltasar Lopes, who worked for many years as the school principal of one of the most prestigious schools, the Liceu Gil Eanes in São Vicente, was sensitive to Kriolu's role in the classroom. He often remarked that the Creole sentiment was a positive factor in learning because it showed adaptation to the self-other or historically colonial encounter (Barros 2009). For example, in contrast to the 1932 decree that Kriolu should not be spoken in any school setting, Lopes countered by affirming that as professor of Portuguese, he had witnessed on several occasions the "immense possibilities that crioulo offered students.... They discussed Mathematics and even Philosophy coursework" (B. Lopes 1956:12). Be that as it may, the enlightened were not interested in political independence. They simply wanted greater recognition and to secure a place in the cultural patrimony of Portugal (Barros 2008).

A cadre of Portuguese literary critics, such as Amândio César, also found no contradiction in recognizing Kriolu artists while considering their work part of Portuguese cultural production. César's essay on Tavares in celebration of what would be Tavares's hundredth birthday is striking in its hyperbolic language. César, a writer familiar with Angola and hardly an expert on Cape Verde, was curiously impressed by Tavares's rendition of one of Luis de Camões's poems. Amazingly, César remarks that Tavares's reconfiguration of Camões is "sonorously more beautiful than the original." César goes on to make an institutional plea: "Eugénio Tavares is worthy ... of a serious homage, through which the writer would be studied deeply, in his value as a journalist, as a poet of the Portuguese language, as a Kriolu poet, as a creator of popular music and as a man" (1970:26).

Far from an isolated case, Portuguese dignitaries would cite Tavares repeatedly as a symbol of the Lusophone world. In his concluding remarks to the Semana das Colónias (Colonies week) in 1945, professor Mendes Correia ruminated on the real value of wealth and life as part of the moral responsibilities in the Portuguese management of its overseas territories. He asked the audience, including President Antonio Salazar, to consider the British critic John Rushkin's aphorism that "there is no wealth but life" and then cited one of Tavares's sweet mornas: "Life without your love is pain" (in Kriolu: *A vida sem bô amor é dor*). The Cape Verdean poet had described the trump card of love, a reference to Lusotropicalism and its social worth. For Correia, in a nod to Freyre and in support of Salazar, the Portuguese exceptionalism, even or especially when mediated by the Cape Verdean Creole, is the "guarantee of Portugal's eternity" (1945:291).

Lusophone officials and artists of various stripes consistently recognized the special value of Kriolu and utilized their relative influence to advance a different agenda. For example, members of the Luso-African lettered elite occasionally found space in the periodicals of late colonialism to express a poetic national identity. In 1971 Albano Neves de Sousa, an Angolan artist, published a curious obituary essay in tribute to Jorge Barbosa, a famous Cape Verdean poet of the enlightened movement. Sousa inserted a voice of pan-African cultural nationalism in one of the popular Portuguese magazines of propaganda of the time, *Permanência*.

The following two excerpts are particularly striking: "I think I was born with this crazy anxiety to see the person who condemned me to feel well only where I am not present." And, "the painful, melodic *crioulo* of a sweet idiom that is not an African language nor is it simply Portuguese, *morna* that is not *fado* [national music of Portugal] nor *batuque* [percussion-based music of Cape Verde, associated with Africanity].... It is the taste of distance, in the crossroads of the world, a delayed farewell, a hesitant teardrop that has yet to fall" (Sousa 1971:32). Sousa opens his essay with a ponderous claim to the diasporic experience, that is, to feel comfort or familiarity only in another place. He, thus, introduces the fallen poet Barbosa in general terms. How to express the vexing notion of place? The Angolan artist identifies the Kriolu of Barbosa's Cape Verde as the idiom that succeeds in articulating the "taste of distance" not in terms of separation but the trajectory consequent of the *encruzilhada* (crossroads). Kriolu, then, is not simply the drama ensuing a bitter farewell but the drama of a copresence. Cape Verde is both an intersection, a long-standing meeting point of interculturality, and one point in a history of migration. Kriolu is the idiom of wellness "where I am not present."

## Portuguese Misrecognition

While Portuguese officials increasingly praised Cape Verdeans in the array of colonial bulletins as hard workers, poetic artists, and capable managers, the cause of a distinct Kriolu identity on the ground in everyday life seemed to go in the opposite direction. Even members of the privileged classes of Cape Verde, who emigrated to Lisbon for university education, supported Portuguese colonialism, and were invested in procuring middle-class employment for themselves in the metropole, remarked on almost Fanonian moments of misrecognition. The enlightened were not being heard as they intended.

Part of this identity drama was the result of the writings and speeches of the Brazilian scholar Gilberto Freyre. His comments on Cape Verde, published in *Aventura e Rotina* (Adventure and routine), surprised the enlightened, as they fancied themselves the intellectual vanguard of a people who epitomized Lusotropicalism and could potentially share the grandeur with Brazil as a success story of Portuguese colonialism. Freyre disagreed.

> During my first encounter with Cape Verde, I thought initially about the racial mixture, which was rehearsed here in an intense fashion by the Portuguese with Jews and notably black Africans, only to be developed in tropical America, of course mediated by the Amerindian. The first cauldron was here on the island of Santiago, today so negroid: a sign that, unlike what has successfully been happening in Brazil, this place has maintained the African elements of origin.... They had told me that I would find a place reminiscent of the Brazilian northeast here in Cape Verde.... However, this kinship appears to me to be vague and not accentuated. (1953a:290)

The enlightened published editorials of dismay, pondering Cape Verde's place in the Luso worldview (B. Lopes 1956). Were they a relative failure in Lusotropicalism due to underdeveloped practices of mixture, empirically present in Cape Verde's essential blackness? Mário António Fernandes de Oliveira, a mestizo Angolan writer, who, like the Cape Verdean enlightened, struggled with his fascination of Lusotropicalism and his desire to replace European models of literature with nationalist African ones (see Chabal et al. 1996), brought the dilemma back to language. The distinction of Portuguese colonialism, according to Oliveira, was that unlike other powers, Portugal had always been interested in the mixture of "civilization" and "culture" so that there was always a "metropolitan Portuguese" to provide unity to a range of non–Indo-European languages in a political sense: "[Civilization has] a dynamic connotation, related to the process of inserting technology and social organization that are indispensable to development.... [Culture refers to] the differentiation of personality by which men feel a dignity related to their cultural inheritance" (1970:21). For Freyre, the Kriolu language was African gibberish. He quickly left for Guinea-Bissau.

Freyre's impressions notwithstanding, the supposed intimacy of Cape Verdean identity with that of Portuguese became an established hallmark of Lusotropicalism. Remarkably, such Cape Verdean exceptionalism continues to have resonance in some circles of contemporary Portuguese society. During archival research, I came across the work of Rafael Bordalo Pinheiro, a cartoonist and popular artist, who published in Lisbon's leading newspapers during the 1890s and early 1900s. His work at the Museum of the City caught my eye, as the exhibit was starkly critical of the Portuguese monarchy and its policies in Africa and, by extension, toward Africans living in the metropole.[11] After chatting with a researcher at this state institution, I realized that there was an entire museum, the very small Museu Bordalo Pinheiro, dedicated to this Doonesbury-like character. At the gift shop, I struck up a conversation with the store manager and explained my interest in Kriolu, Cape Verde, and their significance in Lisbon. I was taken aback by Pedro's comments.

> You know, I remember in the late '60s, as a boy, I remember our maid. She was Cape Verdean. I could hardly understand what she said. She was not formally educated. Heavens no! But she was incredibly hard-working, and it was obvious that she had an intellect. Cape Verdeans were always ahead of the game. I mean, in relation to other Africans here in Lisbon. And, in general. It came easier to them.

What is striking about the institutional knowledge produced about Cape Verde and Kriolu by Portuguese and Cape Verdean authors is the presence of Creole as natural, ubiquitous, and, ultimately, Portuguese. Most Portuguese, including Pedro, have imagined "it," a reference to assimilation, to be easier for Cape Verdeans. Unlike in the cases of Kimbundo, Umbundo, other languages in the Bantu family, and Fula and Mandjak of Guinea-Bissau under Portuguese dominion, Cape Verdean Kriolu registered with the Portuguese as a social fact of the colonial encounter. Portuguese officials prohibited Kriolu in public institutions, such as schools, but they never entered homes or regulated street banter. The operating logic was that Creole is a remedial language of transition, from Cape Verdean to Portuguese.

After the fall of the Portuguese fascist state in 1974 and the success of decolonization wars in the former African colonies, writers began to reflect more systematically on the contradictions embedded in Lusotropicalism. Some of these came from Brazilians, who had become defensive of their international legacy attached to racial democracy. Freyre had lauded racial democracy publicly as the answer to race relations and cultural nationalism, and such "scientific" praise had captivated Portuguese and elite Cape Verdean Lusotropicalists. For the Brazilian anthropologist Igor José de Renó Machado, Lusotropicalism reveals an effective strategy so that "the Brazilian myth [could be] used as an ideological justification for African oppression" (2004:126). In a similar vein, Portuguese anthropologist Almeida ponders the contradictory uses and interpretations of Lusotropicalism in the form of a question directed particularly at Cape Verdean elite, who considered their country a microcosm of Brazil: "How could a theory of emancipation function at the same time as a theory of colonization?" (2007:127).

In a caustic pivot on Freyre's own fascination with Portuguese "creativity" through interracial sex, contemporary Portuguese novelist Antonio Lobo Antunes utilizes one of his protagonists to provide critique: "I have always supported an installation of a statue or monument in some adequate plaza in this country, a monument in homage to snot, a snot-bust, slime-Marshall, spit-poet, expectorant-man of the State . . . , something that would contribute . . . to the perfect definition of the perfect Portuguese: [someone who] bragged about sex and coughed up phlegm" (2008:24). Antunes, a former military medical doctor stationed in Angola during the decolonization wars, provokes the reader to consider the Portuguese colonial paradigm of desire/disgust of the Other through the coupling of sexual intercourse and hacking mucous.

## Kriolu Agency

Creole agency may be overtly political and/or intimately personal, as the examples below demonstrate. Regardless, any interpretation of Creole must place the actors in the foreground. Anthropologist Richard Price has asked scholars to interrogate the specificities of creolization with regard to not only the demographic heterogeneity within social groups in a particular locale but also the variable processes through which, for example, "Africans became *African Americans*" (2010:57). Historian James H. Sweet phrases the effort in terms of "an emphasis on placing Africans and their descendants at the center of their own histories" (2003:1).

In the wake of newly independent African states, the rearticulation of Kriolu as identity politics paralleled the rising criticism against Lusotropicalism. One of the cultural platforms of the Partido Africano da Independência de Cabo Verde (African Independence Party of Cape Verde) (PAICV) during the early 1980s and after the coup d'état in Guinea and the dissolution of Cape Verde–Guinea into two states, was to affirm independence in language. The idea follows the logic of symbolic capital; that is, a truly independent nation-state must differentiate itself not only in geopolitics but also in language and expressive culture. In so doing, Cape Verde created (or reminded citizens of) its own system of values, a currency of local speech, literature, and, by extension, culture. In more concrete terms, the PAICV subsidized the recuperation and institutionalization of *kriolu fundo* (deep Creole), or, in proper linguistic terms, the basilect register of Cape Verdean Creole. In essence, this meant that the "negroid" island of Santiago with its Kriolu based on empirically more African vocabulary and linguistic structure would take center stage in the national-identity formation. It is into this milieu, what some scholars have called "the Cape Verdean period," that most of the Kriolu rappers I met in Lisbon were born.

As George Lang argues, Creole writers, whether in Cape Verde or the Antilles, often feel the burden of not only narrators but also pedagogues. One of the most forceful examples of this conjuncture in Cape Verde is Manuel Veiga, who acted as minister of culture and published the first modern, Kriolu novel, *Oju d'Agu* (Eye of water) in 1987. Veiga also published a didactic text on the structural linguistics of Kriolu in Kriolu, in which he argues that the badiu dialect from the interior of Santiago island represents the baseline, or "matrix," of all contemporary forms of Cape Verdean Creole (1982).[12]

Creole is a variable chronotope that inevitably conjures time-space sentiments, such as colonialism, migration, and "nigga." Born in the encounter, Creole speakers and writers are acutely aware of the precarious nature of their idiom and the pressure to assimilate into a fully recognized language (Lang 2005). Through the material of folklore, poets, such as Oswaldo Osário (1980), and badiu scholars led by Tomé Varela da Silva (1988) sought to not only produce local cultural material and inspire a new wave of identification but also to do it in a way that linguistically would be as far removed from Luso as realistically possible.

## CHAPTER 2

Demographic studies show that migration from classes of relatively highly educated Cape Verdeans, such as Osário and Silva, to Lisbon slightly declined over the 1980s and early 1990s (Carling and Åkesson 2009:143–44). This stands in contrast to the increased number of working-class Cape Verdeans, especially from the island of Santiago, who saw Lisbon as a promising employment opportunity, even more so after Portugal's entry in the European Union in 1986. The literature from a handful of memoires and oral histories I collected in the field suggests that while badius became the majority of Cape Verdean migrants in Lisbon, this did not mean that they were ashamed of Santiago or sought to assimilate wholeheartedly.

Rather, they brought the sounds of musical groups, such as Ferro Gaita and Bulimundo, with them to the improvised neighborhoods of a growing Lisbon periphery, thus adding to the already established Kriolu musical geography established by Bana and B. Leza (the artistic name of Francisco Xavier da Cruz) of a generation prior. These latter artists and promoters were fundamental in setting up circuits of morna and *coladera* (similar to morna but usually employs a faster tempo), the musical genres strongly associated with the island of São Vicente and the cultural city center of Mindelo. Akin to the poetic contours and political affiliations of the Claridosos, morna singers wielded a kind of soft Kriolu power, a force of sentiment under the emotional label of *sodadi* (longing), both romantic and diasporic. While many readers may be familiar with the individual talents of Cesária Évora during her successful run of world beat recordings and concerts during the late 1990s and early 2000s, it was Bana, B. Leza, Tito Paris, and other smaller players from the centrally located neighborhood of São Bento who had a longer-lasting influence on Kriolu cultural expression in Lisbon.

In contrast, Ferro Gaita and Bulimundo represented the sounds of Santiago island. While there are many other artists one could cite, I selected these to demonstrate two related points. First, Ferro Gaita and Bulimundo are *funaná,* a Cape Verdean musical genre associated traditionally with the island of Santiago musical groups, and their popularity helped catapult badiu from a pejorative term of backward blackness to a symbol of Cape Verdean pride. Funaná has a distinctive sound traditionally built around the iron scraper (*ferro*), accordion (*gaita*), and an upbeat, syncopated dance rhythm. Predominantly a music for dancing, funaná was outlawed during periods of colonialism but now is the most popular music in Cape Verde and in the diaspora. It is the timbre of the ferro and gaita along with the badiu accent in the festive calls to the dance floor that key audiences in to Santiago. In my visits to not only Praia but also the countryside towns of Órgãos, Assomada, and Tarrafal on the island of Santiago, the presence of Ferro Gaita is remarkable. More than just a band, they are an institution of musical education and general Cape Verdean pride.

The second point that these Santiago-based bands illuminate is the issue of the politics of language and territory. Lyrically, Ferro Gaita is more about fun and celebration. For its part, Bulimundo, while also officially a funaná group, was less traditional musically as it incorporated relatively quickly electric guitar, bass, and drum set. In most interviews dating back to the 1980s and 1990s, members describe an "opening" in the musical scene after independence in 1975 and that it was the moment to bring the "deep" Kriolu of Pedra Bedejo, a small village whose historical landmark is a building named Bulimundo, to the city of Praia. The group Bulimundo's first recorded album in 1978 contains these elements. It is less the members' sound per se than their attitude of being *badiu di fora* (marginalized badiu) that is important for the purpose of this section. Their songs immortalize folk music heroes, such as master ferro player Sema Lopi, and underscore Cape Verdean views of struggle in songs about the "long path" (*kaminhu longi*) of funaná and suffering under the label of *deskuidadu* (unkempt delinquent) Portuguese colonialism and Cape Verdean elite imposed.

Critical views of Lusotropicalism, of course, have not been relegated to emboldened scholars, activist artists, and bitter military men. Contemporary rapper Núcleo relates, "It's [speaking crioulo's] something natural. My parents only spoke in crioulo with me. So, it's obvious that I would sing some lyrics in crioulo. It means that I invest all of myself in the product" (2008). In his matter-of-fact reflection, he helps establish a discussion of Kriolu agency as a "natural" interruption resulting from socialization. Despite all the history of Kriolu as assimilation and transition into "Portuguese," Cape Verdeans continue to speak Kriolu proudly and identify themselves as *Kauberdianu*, or Kriolu, even if they are officially Portuguese citizens (Carter and Aulette 2009; Märzhaüser 2009).

Creole interruptions from Cape Verdean migrants in Lisbon demonstrate the general theory that Creole is a mark of change. For Martinican intellectual Edouard Glissant (1989), change is not enough to capture creolization (*creolité*); rather, one must understand Creole as a transformative encounter with necessarily resistant political and cultural ramifications. It is in this spirit that Stuart Hall advocates for a more urgent interpretation of Creole. He famously observes "that these [Creole languages] have become as it were the languages in which important things can be said, in which aspirations and hopes can be formulated, in which an important grasp of the histories that have made these places can be written down, in which artists are willing for the first time, the first generation, to practice and so on, that is what I call a cultural revolution" (1995:13).

Although many Kriolu rappers are not as overtly critical as LBC, recalling the interview excerpt from this chapter's introduction, many recognize that Lusotropicalism contains a negative rub. The presence of Kriolu in Lisbon is reminiscent of Glissant's and Hall's depictions of Creole emergent cultures as expressions that interrupt shallow discourses of national inclusion and ubiquitous chants of democratic globalization.

## Lusofonia

Lusotropicalism was never coherent abroad in the overseas colonies. Moreover, it was not ultimately successful "at home" in Portugal among African immigrant groups or between Luso-Africans and white Portuguese. The ideologically charged morpheme of *Luso* has gained new vigor since the late twentieth century via the discursive recuperation and institutional investment in Lusofonia. Literally translated as *Lusophone*, the term applies to not only language but also political, economic, and cultural spaces of supposed Portuguese influence. Lusofonia is a polemical term of territory.

According to Bart Paul Vanspauwen (2012) and Rui Cidra (2010), the first major step in the concretization of Lusofonia was the creation of the Community of Portuguese Language Countries (CPLP). The Expo event of 1998 in Lisbon provided not only global exposure and an ideological shot in the arm to the Lusofonia cause but also featured Lisbon as its center. The rise of internet technology and social media helped spread the idea of Lisbon as the center of a globalized community. In his research on Lusofonia and musical production, Vanspauwen details the state-sponsored, volunteer, and corporate entities and sites that have organized themselves around Lusofonia. These include Associação Sons da Lusofonia (1996), the project Lusofonias: Culturas em Comunidade (2008), B. Leza's performance venue, and the documentary film *Lusofonia, a (R)evolução* (2006). Since 2008 the date May 5 has become the CPLP and Lusofonia day of commemoration with cultural events, always located in Lisbon.

In a recent interview, the Mozambican sociolinguist Gregório Firmino explained why Lusofonia is a tricky and often misinterpreted concept, especially when applied to a plural linguistic place like Mozambique. On the one hand, independence political parties, or "fronts" (*frentes*), needed a unifying language for traction. Firmino observes that "the independent Mozambique produced more Portuguese speakers than the colonial Mozambique" (quoted in Kaczorowski 2014). However, affirms Firmino, it is a linguistic error to state that all or even the majority of revolutionaries spoke Portuguese. Rather, in a tone reminiscent of Cabral's views on Portuguese cited above, speaking Portuguese acted as a symbol for talking back to the empire and mobilizing for its removal. The current movement in Portugal (and in Brazil) called Lusofonia is about possessing the Portuguese language and, by extension, its dominant cultural connotations.

Firmino's views on Portuguese and labels, such as Lusofonia, dovetail with the work of sociolinguists Alastair Pennycook and Samy Alim regarding English. Their central thesis is that languages are always simultaneously local and global in use. The phenomenological context, that is, the speech act, intertwines with the routes of contact, borrowing, and other fruits of encounters that produce the structures of vocabulary, syntax, and so on. In the end, Lusofonia is a market, and plural and interlinguistic perspectives on languages are difficult talking points to sell culture and identity.

For Vanspauwen, Lusofonia is a category foisted from above with little relevance to practicing musicians. It is mere marketing and at times is a distasteful reminder of the past and a proposed reality of unity and singularity that simply doesn't exist anymore. Antonio Pinto Ribeiro takes a similar stance: "Indeed, the most perverse expression of Lusofonia is the amnesia of the pre-colonial past with regard to African countries or East Timor and, in certain ways, [Lusofonia becomes] the repetition of the colonialist expression of the 'discovery' of these peoples, who only came to have history when the colonizers 'discovered' them. Lusofonia is, in the end, the final mark of an empire that doesn't exist any longer" (2013).[13]

Ribeiro argues further that the error of Lusofonia and all other Luso discourses is that they imply that Portuguese identity, while perhaps dynamically mixed, remains a singular entity. Anthropologist Timothy Sieber has shown that in the Boston area, musicians of Cape Verdean descent, who represent a wide range of styles, are consistent on this point as well. While it may be one response to the economic recession in Portugal and the austerity straitjacket of troika (Epifânio 2013), the concept of Lusophone is reductionist and drowns out the distinctive tonality of Kriolu and PALOP, more generally (Sieber 2005).

If Luso discourses are inclusive but flat, what does Kriolu offer in the way of a more robust sense of identity and citizenship? The recurring answer from Lisbon consultants is coded in stories about action, skills, and alternative social networks. One reason Luso umbrella terms are unsatisfactory for Cape Verdeans is because the terms circulate in a top-down manner. Political figures, scholars, and school-textbook authors make sweeping claims that the "Portuguese spirit" is a nostalgic one, a series of reflections on the moorings of sea and land encounters. So overwhelming and broad, Luso contains few accessible handles; it just spreads out. On the other hand, Kriolu is relevant at the individual level. As a coherent language, Kriolu contains a definable structure, but this does not prevent it from also demonstrating the "changing same" of Amiri Baraka's ([1963] 2000) analysis of "black music" and Lok C. D. Siu's (2005) interpretation of the migrant narrative in "Chinese-ness" in Central America. Kriolu offers an opportunity by eliciting the speaker/member to participate and perform belonging.

CHAPTER 2

## Kriolu Flexibility

Rapper Chullage prides himself on his Kriolu nickname meaning "stud" and "godfather." Chullage moved from the improvised neighborhood of Asilo 28 de Maio after it was demolished in 1989 to Arrentela, a *bairro social,* or housing project (discussed in chapter 4), on the south side of the Tagus River. Chullage departed the Red Eyes Gang and has consolidated his position as a respected elder of hip-hop in Portugal since the late 1990s. In June 2007, we met outside the small community center, Associação Khapaz, literally translated as association of the capable. Such concepts as capability and skill are particularly salient for hip-hoppers and conventionally disenfranchised social groups and, thus, function effectively as symbols of convergence. In fact, Chullage helped organize and finance the association with the aid of Programas Escolhas (the choices program), a state-sponsored organization whose mission is to improve the lives of immigrant and at-risk populations in particularly urban areas inside Portugal. Chullage is a tough and sweet type, eager to provoke.

> Yo, nigga, what have you done? Why are you up in here? See this [pointing to the association building], this is a space that Kriolu hip-hop created, where there was nothing before. You gotta make a place to speak before you can do anything. This is an island, but we're not alone. I'm studying sociology now, and a couple of the community center leaders are doing graduate degrees in health and social work. We're taking hip-hop to another level and making more spaces.

As suggested in chapter 1, the semiotics of *nigga* and *Kriolu* in contemporary Portugal are complex and contentious within the hip-hop community. Unlike Brazil and somewhat more akin to the United States, *nigga* and *niggaz* are terms used ubiquitously in Lisbon hip-hop, and for many of my interlocutors, the terms have been weakened as vessels of racial significance, historically or otherwise (see Raposo 2007). However, as LBC and Chullage explained to me, *nigga* can be used strategically, following American rap legend and martyr figure Tupac Shakur's acronym N.I.G.G.A. (Never ignorant about getting goals accomplished). In a 2012 recording, Chullage creates a new signification of the acronym, which translates as, "Black folks impose themselves in a gated ghetto [to form] self-esteem."

This eponymous song continues the sentiments expressed in a previous recording, "Times Change," both of which present the nigga as an empowered but conflicted protagonist. He is a product of migration and urbanization, but he knows only the here and now. The nigga's life occurs in the neighborhood streets, and Chullage depicts this life as a set of choices impacting positively and negatively the individual and the community. Still somewhat vague and open to interpretation, *nigga* does dovetail with Kriolu in the sense of labor history and a pragmatic politics. Returning to the conversation excerpt, it is this spirit of provocation that Chullage invokes the term in a challenge to my position and intention in his/their locale of Arrentela.

The stories of Karlos from earlier in the chapter and Chullage demonstrate that Kriolu affords a variety of ways to interrupt Luso discourses of inclusion. Karlos sees Kriolu as potentially one of the "new" European identities that has gained significant traction in youth and popular culture since the late 1950s (Hebdige 1987). Kriolu is, thus, a distinctive part of contemporary European cultural citizenship. Hip-hop's aggressive styles of ideological and commercial circulation are an excellent fit for Karlos's articulation of Kriolu. For Chullage, Kriolu is a strategic mode of provocation and persuasion toward a new Lisbon, which includes a shift in sociogeographical value. In essence, Chullage wants to attach Kriolu to institutions of culture, such as the Khapaz Association, and, thus, impose a Kriolu version of the social neighborhood on the Portuguese state as a recognized site of patrimony. A final example demonstrates a slightly different way some local hip-hoppers expand Kriolu in the hopes of creating community and staking claims in postcolonial Portugal.

Just as Kriolu is not synonymous with Kriol of Guinea-Bissau (Havik 2007; Lang 1996:54–55), Kriolu rap is by no means singular in practice. I met rappers Darkface and Biggie in July 2007 outside of Darkface's university classroom. Finals had begun, and Darkface seemed happy to take a break and stroll around the confines of the Universidade Lusófono (Lusophone University). Biggie, at the time of our conversation a member of the unemployed, was stressed about rising costs of living and the relative weak salaries in Portugal compared with the rest of the European Union (EU). Biggie reminded me, "You see, maybe Portugal is in the EU, but the PALOP aren't. We're just in Portugal." Darkface interrupted calmly.

> You have to understand. I was born in São Tomé e Príncipe and grew up in Angola. Our friend here Biggie comes from a family of folks from Guinea-Bissau and Angola. We are Creole, but we are also Portuguese. Better, we are more than Portuguese. What is great about rappers from PALOP is that we expand the influence of the Portuguese language. We stretch hip-hop tuga, and hip-hop evolves. Yes, we are Creole, but that's too limiting; we go beyond. We connect the PALOP reality, a not-quite-yet European membership, to the U.S., Brazil, and wherever there is hip-hop.

In the code words of "expand," "connect," and "go beyond," Darkface expresses what Homi Bhabha (1983) describes as the "articulation" of the postcolonial subject, a discursive positioning that resists an "originality" of place and essence.

Creole in the case of Darkface and Biggie is made manifest in an awareness of postcolonial mobility rather than language. Creole as a set of conditions approximates the milieu of stigma and cross-cultural camaraderie Raposo (2010) describes as an "affective community" in his work on the Red Eyes Gang of Arrentela, the stomping grounds of significant figures in this ethnography, Chullage and Jorginho. Kriolu becomes an obvious choice of the person positioned by structures of power and expressive of flexibility within popular and diasporic culture.

In a publication by the Portuguese state agency High Commission of Immigration and Intercultural Dialogue (ACIDI), anthropologists Carlos Elias Barbosa and Max Ruben Ramos used their interview with Sagas, a Kriolu rapper residing in Lisbon, as a launching pad to analyze general Cape Verdean experiences in Lisbon. Sagas's comments strike a similar chord to those of Darkface and Biggie: "I use crioulo not only for those who understand [the language] but also for the Portuguese. Crioulo brings a new scene to Portuguese hip-hop. I put the two things together in a natural way but also with a specific intention: to show, in a positive way, that this is crioulo. I want them to understand my culture just as I understand theirs" (in Barbosa and Ramos 2009:182). In a diplomatic but forceful gesture, Sagas implies a creative imposition of Crioulo onto "the Portuguese," a reaction to a similar pressure he has felt his entire life. Certainly, Sagas has had to "understand their" culture, why not they his? In their own ways, Sagas and Darkface articulate the extent to which Kriolu can interrupt Portuguese, linguistically and culturally through the medium of rap.

These rappers exemplify a range of experiences and personal agenda with relation to Kriolu and identity formation. Yet, they are all interested in pushing the idea of Portugal into a larger community, guided by hip-hop, in which Kriolu becomes a special mark of locality and/or diaspora but whose message is designed as common. Historically, such an effort has precedent. Scholars have demonstrated that the variants of K/Crioulo of Cape Verde enjoyed a long, involved exchange with the urban variants of Guinean *Kriol* since the sixteenth century (M. D. de O. Almada 1961; Baptista 2002; Havik 2007). In this manner, local rappers expand Kriolu beyond language and into a sphere of collective cultural experience.

## Kriolu Interruptions as a Reminder

Kriolu is a discourse rich with colonial history and contemporary pop cache. What is curious and what has taken center stage in this chapter are the manners in which Kriolu, a linguistic practice seemingly exemplary of Lusotropicalism and, indeed, historically a symbol of quasi-Portuguese status affording Cape Verdeans relative privilege during and after Portuguese colonialism, has become a vehicle for difference and discontent in the former metropole of Lisbon.

For Portuguese sociologist Fernando Luís Machado, the Luso-African is more than simply an immigrant of African descent residing in Portugal. The term also connotes settlement, a marker of African presence and spatial claims (F. L. Machado 1994). Similarly, anthropologist Jayne Ifekwunigwe has argued, "African diasporas in Europe can be configured not simply as political *spaces* but also as *processes* and *conditions*" (2010:315, italics in original). For their part, some local rappers have taken the turn to Kriolu as an opportunity to narrate the ambiguities of globalization, migration, and diaspora. They have provoked political reflection among listeners, media outlets, and state agencies just as they remind a large swath of Lisbon's residents of *other* places and times.

Lisbon has become the site where colonial and anticolonial temporalities are emplaced. The moments of enlightenment (*claridade*), Lusotropicalism, Kauberdianu, PALOP, EU, and nigga are all formative of Cape Verdean migrancy and contemporary Lisbon. These rappers contribute to an alternative history of Portugal, one uncomfortable with assimilation as a national treasure. Due to their keen awareness of location, rappers have emphasized the significance of migration experiences, residential daily life, and collective imaginations as an intervention into the Luso mythology. Kriolu interrupts Luso discourses because those categories emphasize mixture over difference and acculturation over the encounter. With that said, the idea of interruption differs from disruption in that the former kind of intervention remains engaged within a flow of talk, history, or power. Kriolu and Creole, more generally, follow this logic, and their development has emerged from relationships of intimacy and contingency within the processes of coloniality and indigenous locality.

Kriolu rappers show us that Creole is not an isolationist secession, but it can be an interruption, the more or less sustained moment of impeding a grand narrative of "modernity" and "inclusion," employed in order to remind us of the difference of race, colonialism, and, in this case, Cape Verdean belonging. The next two chapters focus more explicitly on the roles of language and space, glossed above as emplacement, in creolization as a formation of identity and condition of citizenship.

# CHAPTER 3

# Lisbon Rappers and the Labor of Location

> What we lose [in the "travel of writing"] is the security of the starting point, of the subject of departure; what we gain is an ethical relationship to the language in which we are subjects, and in which we subject each other.
>
> —Iain Chambers

> You are the only Portuguese guy in Cape Verde who learned how to speak our language, because these other folks think that Kriolu is a savage language. They are afraid that they will turn black. To speak Kriolu is to be a leper.
>
> —Djedje

Donaldo Macedo, a Cape Verdean linguist and man of letters employed at University of Massachusetts–Boston for decades, addresses the politics of language in a provocative dialogue between two characters in his play *Descarado* (Scoundrel), published in 1979. The conversation between Djedje, a Cape Verdean youth, and Artur, a Portuguese resident of Cape Verde, centers on the role of Kriolu in the construction of reality and the positioning of speakers as racialized subjects. What Iain Chambers describes in the epigraph and what the characters in *Descarado* as well as Kriolu rappers in Lisbon, such as Praga from the rap duo Nigga Poison (figure 5), put into practice is the risk of migrant language, a creative and political play of discourse and identity. To speak Kriolu is a challenge to the place of the speaker and the listener. Such practices constitute a scene.

Chapter 2 makes the case for Kriolu as a kind of interruption that has resulted in a certain politics of difference. Such differences are based in Creole histories

FIGURE 5. Praga, Kriolu rapper, during a Lisbon performance. Photo by author, 2009.

within Portugal–West Africa–Cape Verde encounters. What remains to be seen is how difference, a complex kind of "ethical relationship" embedded in Luso categories, is made material in language. In short, what does Cape Verdean Kriolu actually *do*? In her work on the *creolité* movement of Francophone Caribbean writers, Mary Gallagher describes their intention as a shift "away from a notion of displacement to a notion of a newly forged culture" (2007:227).

This chapter departs from two observations. The first, following Alastair Pennycook, is that the social context of language involves a "locality of perspective" (2010:4). The second, which follows on the first, is that such a perspective often informs an ideology of linguistic differentiation (Irvine and Gal 2000). In the case of Portugal, the ideological positioning of Kriolu is relative to its iterative differentiation from (and distinctiveness vis-à-vis) Portuguese.[1]

In the idiom of global hip-hop, "perspective," more often than not, means a position on the "real" as a complex performance of the *relationship* between local and global, rather than an either/or formulation. This relationship, involving processes of underscoring place (locality) and highlighting history (temporality), must emerge in rap language and circulate through recognizable media outlets in order for the expression (e.g., the song or statement) to be effective (Terkourafi 2010; Alim 2009). To be effective is to be "real," referring to the original raison d'être of hip-hop, which, paraphrasing hip-hop's reason for existence, is to represent lived experiences of marginalization in an honest (i.e., "true to self") and informed manner. In the case of Kriolu rap in Lisbon, situations of neighborhood hanging-out and studio recording are the principal sites where rappers do identity work, and the main message is one of distinction: to be or to speak Kriolu is not to be or to speak tuga, or Portuguese.

I argue that the local language practices evident in Kriolu rap illuminate an essential component of identity formation, namely, the ideological force of time-place articulation, or *chronotope*. As made clear by Mikhail Bakhtin, the primary figure who translated this concept of mathematical physics for the humanities, the significance of chronotope is not simply the articulation of time and space but the existence of a certain relationship between time and space that organizes experience (see Dent 2009:63). In Bakhtin's formulation of the chronotope concept, there is an emphasis on time in the search for the "generic significance" of literature (1981:84–85), but I foreground, instead, issues of space and place in order to examine processes of identity formation.

Following popular music scholars, such as Aaron A. Fox (2004) and Alexander Sebastian Dent (2009), I use the concept of chronotope to interpret local strategies of subjectivity. Just as "Brazilians sing the countryside into existence" and rural working-class Texans "evocatively grammaticize" time through songs of country "mem'ries" and "feelings" (Dent 2009:40; Fox 2004:82), some Lisbon rappers assert themselves by means of Kriolu. Kriolu rappers are not just ghetto-centric poets or diasporic griots nostalgic for African homelands. They sing the improvised neighborhoods and housing projects of Lisbon into existence, implying a density or a "flesh" (borrowing from Bakhtin) of time in their invocations of drama. Kriolu rappers use Kriolu as a provocation to Cape Verdeans and to non–Kriolu speakers alike to consider categorical alternatives—in particular, an alternative to tuga, that is, Portuguese—within the social and ideological dynamics of language in Portugal.

The concept of chronotope is useful in the Kriolu case because it allows a rich investigation into the tension of identity politics coded in a form of popular poetics, namely, rap music, not only by eliciting an appreciation of the space of identity formation as historically constituted but also by drawing attention to the linguistic and narrative evidence for such identity work. Not unlike Kathleen Stewart's (1996) exploration into the dialectics of West Virginia "hollers," coal camps, and other "ruins" of postindustrial America, interpreted as contested, emotive sites of signification about getting "pulled down," "letting go," and becoming "haunted," my investigation reveals the generative friction of places and remembering. Kriolu is a language and identity based on experiences of migration as well as certain kinds of expectations. Kriolu rappers rework notions of diaspora in terms of dis(em)placement as they wait for recognition from the state (in official forms, such as citizenship) and from cultural and educational institutions. At the same time, they also hope for recognition among rappers abroad, wherever hip-hoppers celebrate verbal skills and "real" life narratives.

As the adage goes, rap began as a treatise on who you are, where you're from, and the place to be. Rakim, the legendary U.S. rapper, extended hip-hop's notion of place to include "attitude" in his popular mantra from the late 1980s, "it's not where you're from but where you're at." Rappers and scholars have demonstrated in detail that the combination of life experience and local knowledge is a powerful resource for poetic and ideological articulation (Gilroy 1993; Rose 1994; Forman 2002; Fradique 2003; Maxwell 2003; Condry 2006; Pardue 2010). Where one "is at" is a matter of positionality and of stance. Recent work by linguistic anthropologists (such as Kiesling 2001; Goodwin 2007; Keane 2011) interested in the intersections between moral judgment and code recognition in everyday speech informs my notion that "being [at] kriolu" necessarily implies a conscious sense of place that is somehow different from tuga and that this position is true, legitimate, and valuable.

For example, when asked about his song "Gerason di Gosi" (The now generation), rapper Kromo responded: "Kriolu is a way, a manner [of being]. It is Kova M [his neighborhood of Cova da Moura]. It is about coping with the ghetto life stress. That's what the song is about. People feel that in the words and the way I speak the words" (personal communication, 2009). Alto da Cova da Moura is a large improvised neighborhood in the municipality of Amadora with a majority of residents who identify as Cape Verdean (Vaz 2011). According to local mythology and community documentation, Cova began with the end of Portuguese colonialism in 1974, represented by the implosion of the Portuguese military and the independence wars in Portugal's African colonies.[2] For four years thereafter, a gradual but consistent stream of day laborers, predominantly Africans and the white Portuguese who were forced to return to Portugal, the so-called *retornados* (returnees), sought out residence close to the automobile-accessory factory of Martins and Almeida and various construction sites, which contributed to the boom in social-neighborhood urbanization (discussed below). In 1978 the municipality finally recognized Alto da Cova da Moura officially as a legitimate neighborhood, albeit improvised.

A Kriolu stance, then, comprises locations of Lisbon, such as Kova M, and more specifically, the sentiments involved in making place or emplacement. In addition, a Kriolu stance represents particular, recognizable manners of self-presentation. Kromo's comments on coping speak to the truth value of Kriolu, a response to marginalization and daily anxiety. Rap music, in turn, acts as a vehicle to distribute a basic code of recognition, that is, Kriolu as experienced right now in Lisbon, expressed in a language of historical encounters.

## Kriolu Language Background

The unique quality of Kriolu is its structural and existential intimacy with Portuguese as language and as coloniality, thereby reminding the interlocutor that practices are actions with histories (Pennycook 2010; Winford 2003). Unlike in the cases of Kimbundo, Umbundo, Fula, Mandjak, and other speech communities under Portuguese dominion, Cape Verdean Creole registered with the Portuguese as a social fact of the colonial encounter and, indeed, a mark of Portuguese exceptionalism as stewards of civilization.

In terms of aesthetics and ideals of culture, Kriolu is a register of potential. For example, acclaimed Portuguese man of letters José Osório de Oliveira predicted in a 1928 speech that Cape Verdeans had the "virtues and the talent ... to create a literature that would express their Creole society, a new 'euro-tropical' message" (quoted in Gomes 1970:29). Cape Verdean intellectuals, such as poet Baltasar Lopes, also espoused Kriolu as a black inflection on an otherwise Portuguese essence: "The Creoles of that archipelago [Cape Verde] are nothing more than, in essence, than a Portuguese altered in the mouths of Blacks, whether it be phonetically, morphologically, semantically or syntactically" (1957:12). Enlightened writers, such as Lopes and Pedro Cardoso, helped establish Kriolu as a dialect that, in the words of Portuguese writer Edmundo Correia Lopes, "possesses the normal elements for the resolution of [typical] linguistic issues [that might arise in practice]" (1941:429). Portuguese officials and educators developed this paradigm of Kriolu as dialect and by extrapolation as a social fact of positive colonial encounters in various inclusive ways throughout the twentieth century. As the popular travel writer Augusto Casimiro contends in the opening words to his collection of essays *Ilhas Crioulas* (Creole islands), "to write about Cape Verde is a national obligation" (1935:2).

This history and ideological perspective help to explain why, to this day, Kriolu is not recognized as an official language in either Cape Verde or Portugal. In Cape Verde, there are still other political obstacles to the formal adoption of Kriolu. Most obvious are the lingering divisions, in regard to language and national identity, between the two dominant political parties, Partido Africano da Independência de Cabo Verde (African Independence Party of Cape Verde) (PAICV) and Movimento para Democracia (Democracy movement) (MPD), part of the shift to a multiparty political system in Cape Verde. The debate can be reduced to a combination of regionalism (many variants of Kriolu are spoken throughout the archipelago), economics (the cost of implementing language standardization), and ideological affiliations (the two parties are overwhelmingly defined by previous associations to pro-Portuguese and prorevolutionary forces dating back to the independence wars of the 1970s).

As a number of linguists have demonstrated, Kriolu is a language and not an argot of continental Portuguese (Baptista 2002; Duarte 2003). Advocates of Kriolu as an official language have argued that all languages contain variation and that this fact alone is not a legitimate argument against standardization—focal points of what is known in Cape Verde as the ALUPEK debate (see Note on Orthography). In demographic terms within Portugal, although persons from other PALOP countries speak Creole languages, these émigrés have not established language as a marker of identity with the same intensity as Cape Verdeans (Rodrigues 2011; Grassi 2009; see also Batalha 2004b). This is true not only in Lisbon but, to varying degrees, throughout the Cape Verdean diaspora (Gibau 2005; Batalha and Carling 2008). In my conversations with Cape Verdeans in Lisbon, Cape Verde, Dakar, and Boston, making Kriolu an official language has not been a point of consensus. But there is broad agreement that Kriolu is "natural," as several ethnographic statements in this book demonstrate, and Cape Verdeans insist on speaking Kriolu as a matter of pride.

## A Kriolu Alternative

*Kriolu* and *tuga* are relatively new terms in the Lisbon hip-hop scene, but their etymological and political histories are extensive. These terms point to the historical and cultural specificities of what Chambers calls the "conditions of dialogue" that, in this case, created Kriolu (1994:12). *Tuga* is shorthand for *Portuga*, or a person from Portugal; however, the terms have come to mean for Kriolu a "language of immigrants" and for tuga all things or persons produced in or from Portugal. Rapper LBC implies this newness: "In my view, what happened was that hip-hop got exported and imported all around the world, usually without its history, its culture. So, people appropriate characteristics and nationalize it. [They] negate the multiracial, multiethnic, and democratic part of it. They whiten it. The term *tuga* emerged around the year 2000 in this context" (personal communication, 2009).

Thus far, my discussion has hovered primarily at levels of background history, national ideology, and ethnographic sketches. Certain basic questions remain: How exactly do Kriolu rappers use language, and how might this provide insight into their identity work? Rap, as a form of extremely stylized speech, depends on a combination of enunciation techniques (occasionally referred to as "spitting skills") and creative paradigmatic substitution schemes. For example, in the song "Buggin' Out" (1991) from the U.S. group Tribe Called Quest, rapper Q-Tip introduces himself.

> The abstract poet incognito runs the cape
> Not the best not the worst and occasionally I curse
> To get my point across so bust the floss
> As I go in between the grit and the dirt
> Listen to the mission listen Miss as I do work.

In this excerpt, the rapper demonstrates his "abstract" style by performing interphrasal and suspended rhymes—*worst, curse,* and (much later) *work*—rather than more regular, straightforward rhymes at the ends of phrases aligned with musical beat patterns. Simultaneously, Q-Tip inserts alternative, imaginative vocabulary to convey ideas, such as "hero" or "master" and in the phrase "runs the cape," and to reflect on reality in the lyrical string "bust the floss as I go in between the grit and the dirt." In the contemporary Lisbon scene, the following excerpt from "N.I.G.G.A.S." (2012) by Kriolu rapper Chullage demonstrates similar properties.

> *Niggaz conscientiz e so sekaz—so fake nigga*
> *Nha rapa e dillaz e carjackaz—real nigga*
> *N ka konxi museu ne biblitekaz—kel a ka pa niggas*
> *Ma n konxi tudu diskotekaz—sima real nigga*
> *N ta txomaz di bonekaz*
> *Pés podi baxa kuekaz*
> *Largaz dipos dunz kekaz—sima real nigga*
>
> Conscious niggas so dry—just a fake nigga
> My raps and dealers and car jackers—real nigga
> I don't know any museum or library—not for niggas
> But I know all the discos—like a real nigga
> I call them dolls
> My feet can drop their drawers
> Drop them real quick after a fling—like a real nigga
> —(*Rapressão*)

Chullage uses tags, such as "real nigga" and "like a real nigga," as a repeated form to create a manifesto. In this respect, the song is a significant departure from "Buggin' Out," though Chullage does experiment with Kriolu adaptations of English words, for example, *dillaz* (dealers) and *carjackaz* (carjackers). The entire song is a reflection on various aspects of everyday life through the American English term *nigga*, used by both Portuguese and Kriolu rappers in the Lisbon scene.

With regard to rhetorical delivery, Chullage is effective stylistically in his drawing out of the word-final syllable -*kaz* throughout the entire excerpt. Sometimes a capella, sometimes competing with the full boom of bass samples, Chullage's performance combines style and content. Although Chullage does not specifically name places or times in these particular excerpts, he does imply a rough sketch of Lisbon cityscapes through scenes of larceny, entertainment, rape, culture, and education. These implications are the stuff of chronotopes and, I suggest, part of the knowledge base of "real" rappers and of Kriolu rap's attraction for listeners.

Chronotopes are more than devices of speech and narration to orient the interlocutor; they also key in participants to such things as the power relations involved in processes of identification. Kriolu elicits reflection on speakers' and nonspeakers' "ideas about language ... and how these articulate with various social phenomena" (Kroskrity 2000:5). As implied by rapper LBC above, the chronotopic dimension of Kriolu is a racial formation because Kriolu exposes the hegemonic erasure of race that tuga represents in its simplistic categorization of anything that occurs within the national territorial borders as "Portuguese."[3]

As noted earlier, *tuga* is a shortened form of *Portuga*, which itself derives from *português* (Portuguese). *Tuga* indexes two pertinent sociolinguistic moments in Portuguese modern history, both of which demonstrate the existential conflict made manifest in contemporary Kriolu rap. In the late nineteenth century, *tuga* emerged in the Portuguese lexicon during a moment of intense nationalism, as Portugal struggled to legitimate its colonial presence in Africa in the face of, particularly, British hegemony in southern Africa. In the 1960s, as decolonization wars began to rage in Guinea-Bissau, Angola, and Mozambique, local guerrilla forces began to use *tuga* as a call to arms in resistance to the "white" Portuguese military forces. *Tuga* emerged as a response to the term *turras*, a shortened colloquialism of *terroristas* (terrorists), intended to mark resistant Africans as savage, irrational maniacs. Such symbolic intimacy between tuga and coloniality with respect to space and race is important because it is this history that Kriolu rap recuperates and exposes for direct critique.

*Tuga* and *Kriolu* represent vested, competing positions within a language ideology in which Portuguese is portrayed as fostering and embracing intercultural encounter. The following example provides a glimpse into language politics in contemporary Lisbon. Kriolu rapper Kromo is an outspoken resident of the long-standing squatter neighborhood in Lisbon called Cova da Moura, or Kova M. The neighborhood has been stigmatized by the media as an illegal, drug-ridden dump filled with lazy African immigrants. Kromo's brash, evangelical Christian views on daily life and state violence come through in his rap songs as well as in his occasional appearances on Lisbon television news reports and variety shows.

His insistence on speaking Kriolu during one particular interview in 2009, after a police raid in Kova M, coincided with a spate of racist and xenophobic YouTube comments related to Kromo's viral hit "Freestyle." The video consists of Kromo improvising in Kriolu for more than seven minutes in the living room of his friend and occasional rap partner LBC. Most viewers (even, in some cases, those with no apparent linguistic competence in Kriolu) expressed praise for Kromo's rhetorical prowess, but several posts expressed rage at Kromo's direct assault on tuga and his cowardice of hiding behind his identity's façade. Over time, these posts, along with charges of "go back to Africa" and "Portugal is for Portuguese," have been drowned out by celebratory remarks about Kromo, Kova M, and Kriolu rap, more generally. Kromo's use of Kriolu, thus, elicited a vibrant and contentious exchange of ideas about language—or, as Donald Winford glossed as language ideology, the "deeply rooted set of beliefs about the way language is and is supposed to be" (2003:22).

The Kriolu scene exemplifies what Judith Butler (1990), in her writing on identity, calls a product of "sedimentation," defined as the process of establishing a structure in space and time through creative repetition. The concept of chronotope is useful as a way of providing an empirical basis for analysis of this social and performative process of making a scene and, by extension, (re)making selves and community.

Like hip-hoppers in other parts of the world, Portuguese hip-hoppers established a national genre in the 1990s. "Hip-hop tuga" emerged toward the end of the decade; the term currently, somewhat polemically, refers to hip-hop culture made in Portugal.[4] In response, Kriolu rappers employ the "ideology of the word" through a set of territorial claims by means of which they carve out alternative subject positions and linguistic-cultural communities in relation to tuga and, thus, dislodge conventional notions of what it is to be Portuguese at phenomenological and narrative levels (Morgan 2009).

## Working Inside Out

The milieu described above helped frame the following ethnographic research questions: Why do some local rappers sing in Kriolu rather than Portuguese, and how is their use of language effective in drawing attention to Cape Verdean projects of place-making and belonging? Following Pennycook, Samy H. Alim, and others, I suggest that Kriolu rappers are not just using an existing system of signification in a fresh, volatile context, that is, contemporary urban Portugal. Kriolu rappers have vested interests in gaining recognition as all of or a selection of the following cultural communities: hip-hoppers, educators, revolutionaries, global citizens,

Cape Verdeans, PALOP people, black folk, Portuguese, Africans, youth, and/or residents of Kova M and other predominantly immigrant neighborhoods. Their striving for recognition (re)creates the language called Kriolu.

A community of scholars involved in articulating the relationship between language and ideology has traced the sociopolitical efficacy of iteration to linguistic structures (Silverstein 1979; Kroskrity 2000; see also Rumsey 1990). Such structures manifest critical values intended by speakers, located in specific situations, in processes of social evaluation and justification (Woolard 1994). In the sociolinguistic scholarship regarding rap, the dominant ideologies have been versions of pan-Africanism and "ghettocentricity" (Kelley 1997; Forman 2002; see also Rivera 2003), or what Alim describes as the "strategic construction of a street conscious identity through language" (2003:45).

According to Alim (2003, 2004), the management of the copula, the linking verb between the subject and predicate of a sentence, is a key site of African American Language (AAL) that rappers explore and quantitatively hyperperform in order to emphasize blackness and a "street consciousness." As Alim and others have demonstrated, absence of the copula, as in "he runnin' scared now," is neither aleatory nor universally applied in all AAL syntax but is, rather, a strong mark of distinction as AAL continues to develop away from American English. A brief consideration of the linguistic contours of Kriolu rap is important to a critique of tuga as hegemonic, for they manifest a particular aesthetic that attracts local publics to consider matters of difference in place and belonging.

Kriolu is a distinct language, not simply a dialect composed of cool, hip ways to pronounce Portuguese words. Unlike Portuguese, Kriolu encodes temporality by means of a set of single-syllable particles, for example, *ta* and *sa*. The particle *ta* marks the verb (particularly a nonstative verb) as being in the present tense, and *sa* in conjunction with *ta* (*sa ta* + verb) indicates the present progressive. Other frequently occurring single-syllable elements in Kriolu include the function words *ka*, which indicates negation, and *ma*, which serves as a complementizer much like English *that* (as in "I told him *that* I couldn't understand his lyrics").

For the Kriolu rapper, structural elements of Kriolu such as these can provide the infrastructure for a flow of interphrasal rhymes. For example, in the song "Ka Ta Mesti Apresentason" (I don't need an introduction), Araphat, a rap partner of Karlos, uses "ka ta" as a rhythmic beginning. For the most part, Araphat creates rhymes on the many words that end in *-son*, equivalent to an English-speaking rapper punctuating lines with words ending in *-tion* (or, in Portuguese, *-são*). But it is "ka ta" that starts off many of Araphat's assertions; it allows for a flow with a built-in rhyme in ways that would not be possible in Portuguese or English.

# CHAPTER 3

*Ka ta txiga na ora*
*Não chega na hora*
*Ka ta sabi ma*
*Não sabe que*
*Ka ta fla-m ma*
*Não me fale que*

[You don't arrive on time
You don't know that
Don't tell me that]

The effect of ka, ta, and ma is mostly one of tempo. These ubiquitous elements of Kriolu serve as structural stepping stones that enable the rapper to skip fluently through a phrase.

The distinctive features of Kriolu (vis-à-vis Portuguese) include other aspects of its verb system. As the verbs are modified for tense, mood, and aspect by means of particles, such a ka, ma, sa, and ta, almost all verbs remain morphologically invariant in a form that generally resembles the third-person singular in Portuguese, for example, *fase, skrebe, sabe* (does, writes, knows). The significance of this lies in the poetics of rhetoric and the flow of rap music, as can be seen in the following excerpt from Karlos, given first in Kriolu, second in Portuguese, and last in English to show some of the linguistic elements in operation.

*Dja n pasa fome*
*Já passei fome*
I've already gone without food

*Dja n pasa pa tudu ki un pobre ta pasa*
*Já passei por tudo que um pobre passa*
I've already been through all that a poor man goes through

*Dja n pasa na te inda n sa ta pasa ma . . .*
*Já passei por tudo e continuo passando mas . . .*
I've been through it all, I keep going, but . . .

In the case of this song, "Kotidianu" (Everyday life), the issue is not that Karlos highlights the Kriolu elements *sa, ta,* and *ma* in his rhyme schemes; rather, what is of interest is the fact that they function as a guide in rhythmic meter. The emphasis on the verb *pasa* (to pass by, to experience) is certainly important semantically to Karlos's message as he focuses on the kinds of past and present daily-life experiences suggested by the Kriolu term *djuguta* (daily struggle), which appears later in the lyrics. But *pasa* is also effective sonically and rhythmically in relation to *sa, ta*, and *ma*. In Portuguese, this kind of rhyme scheme would not work at all, for the inflectional marking of verb tense would transform the verb into *passei*, thus altering not only the continuity of the /a/ sound but also the rhythm of rhetorical accent, as the emphasis would shift to the last syllable. Again, as noted above in regard to Alim's observations about U.S. rappers' use of certain features of AAL syntax (2003, 2004, 2009), Kriolu rappers have not invented a new Kriolu, nor do they use the language in ways that are markedly different from the usage of other Cape Verdeans. Rather, their milieu of stigma, marginal urban living, and postcolonial ambiguity has fostered "sedimentation" of particular attributes of Kriolu's linguistic structure and an aesthetic distinction in rappers' flow.

Kriolu rappers in Lisbon express Kriolu as a chronotope that links Lisbon spaces to postcoloniality, asserting Creole identity as part of Portugal and, by extension, Europe. This is politically significant, as Kriolu is rooted in a place, Cape Verde, that is not part of tuga and, in fact, has had a conflicted relationship with it. But rappers insist that Kriolu should express local experiences as well as global sentiments of community through hip-hop. Kriolu rappers draw attention to this complicated experience of difference and place through their lyrics as well as through the sounds that they choose to accompany their lyrics in collaboration with local DJs and producers.

Few Kriolu rappers employ any of the wide variety of Cape Verdean musical genres, such as *batuko, coladera, funaná, morna,* or *tabanka*, in their beat mixes.[5] The absence of these musical forms is curious, considering that owing to the international success of artists such as Cesária Évora and, more recently, Sara Tavares, Lura, Mayra Andrade, and Paulino Vieira, these genres have become virtually synonymous with Cape Verdean culture within a logic of multiculturalism based on world music circulation. LBC describes this apparent contradiction.

> Sometimes people, normally tugas, ask me why I don't sample, you know, more Cape Verdean sounding music. And, I say that I like listening to mornas and coladeras and dancing to funaná. We always swing by my mom's café here in Cova da Moura on Friday and Saturday night to check out the funaná. But, I think, and a lot of us believe, that rap needs a different kind of drama. I mean, mornas are very dramatic; they are often sad and nostalgic, very emotional. I am dramatic and I like to choose the beats of rappers like 2Pac [Tupac Shakur]. He understood drama. But, this doesn't make my music American or less Cape Verdean. In fact, it is not just Cape Verdean; it is immigrant music; it is a particular kind of resistance music, and Kriolu is essential to that. Kriolu links us to Cape Verde, but the content is about a drama here or maybe better said "not quite here." (personal communication, 2011)

## CHAPTER 3

The great majority of Kriolu rappers in Lisbon were either born in the Lisbon area or immigrated with a family member when they were children. As LBC implies, Kriolu is part of daily socialization, and it does, in fact, link local youth to Cape Verde or an idea of Cape Verde. However, Lisbon Kriolu reality narratives cannot simply stop there; they are not a "back to Cape Verde" mantra in complete opposition to Lisbon or Portugal as a whole. Similar to the challenge Native American country-music performers have in proving country authenticity (Samuels 2009), Kriolu rappers struggle to expand the notion of Cape Verdean music to include rap. Whereas for Native Americans, the rub is lodged in the popular imagination that country music, in the popular imagination, is "white" and in the Kriolu case, it is assumed that diasporic obligations to perform signature musical genres of Cape Verde will direct youth in their identity formation. Yet, rap offers other diasporic parameters, that is, the concept of "hip-hop nation" espoused by rappers and hip-hop activists around the world. In addition, as LBC, Karlos, and Kromo imply, diaspora is a lived experience grounded in the spatial realities of Lisbon's marginal neighborhoods, such as Cova da Moura, Arrentela, and Oeiras. LBC concludes that Kriolu mediates an experience of "drama," which is not totally "there" in Cape Verde nor entirely "here" in Portugal.

The structural features of Kriolu as used by rappers of Cape Verdean descent in Lisbon suggest that Kriolu rap is an act of dis(em)placement, the process by which people manage migrancy and the significant attributions they give to space. Cape Verdean Kriolu has emerged as one idiom with which youth work to reclaim control over space or what Caroline B. Bretell and Deborah Reed-Danahay describe as the "everyday practices of a cultural landscape" (2010:38–48).

The final section of this chapter focuses my analysis on two contrasting examples of Kriolu rap and highlight the role of place in each at the semantic and sociopolitical level. In the first excerpt examined below, LBC joins with his occasional rap partner Hezbollah in a freedom song for Palestine, "Liberta Palestina" (Free Palestine). This song demonstrates the occasional theme of Kriolu as a medium of connection—one that, in this case, connects the everyday reality of marginalization to "new world orders" of oppression through metaphors of movement, forced migration, and conflict. The second excerpt is from Chullage's "Nu Bai" (Let's go), and it shares the urgent tone and strong attitude of the first, but it links Kriolu to a more common Cape Verdean reflection on place, one concerned with the struggles of migrancy in Lisbon.

## LBC/Soldjah and Hezbollah's "Liberta Palestina"

Since 2006, with the success of "Yah!" the electronic music group Buraka Som Sistema (Buraka sound system) has engineered a remarkably successful commercial career by articulating electronic sound mixes, Angolan-based *kuduro* music/dance aesthetics, and local Lisbon place references. Well within the entertainment package of global pop, Buraka has pronounced their message of fun and "ghettotech" consciousness to the world. LBC and his Kriolu partners are also interested in such expansion through their rap, but, in their case, the message is overtly political. Just as the group Buraka is an homage to the district Buraca in the city of Amadora, the significance of LBC/Soldjah is chronotopic in nature.

LBC, the man behind the acronym for learning black connection, lives in the neighborhood of Cova da Moura (Kova M), part of the municipality of Amadora, adjacent to Lisbon within the metro area. Kova M lies on the train line Linha Sintra, a trajectory that takes passengers from the grandiose, baroque train station in Rossio to the equally impressive architectural feat of the medieval castles of Sintra. For the tourist, this trajectory links one center of "civilization," the colonial downtown establishment of Rossio, to an overarching symbol of the struggle for "civilization," marked by the military and ideological conflict between Christianity and Islam. Pragmatically, the terrain in between exists as a series of working-class districts inhabited by thousands of immigrants from not only former African colonies but more recently from Eastern Europe and Brazil. Kova M along with the territories around the train stops of Reboleira and Amadora are part of a sociogeographical mindset, also referred to as "Linha Sintra" (the Lisbon-Sintra line) that constitutes a Kriolu time-space—one that, among Lisbon hip-hoppers, evokes fresh "reality" and highly skilled rappers.

As we hung out in the living room of his apartment in the heart of Kova M, LBC intimated that he was in a moment of transition. He was trying out a new moniker, Minao Soldjah. While it certainly doesn't roll off the tongue like a brief acronym, Minao Soldjah reflects central elements of his personality and helps contextualize the song "Liberta Palestina." *Minao* is an invented composite word, derived from the phrase *ami nau* (not for me) in ordinary Kriolu. *Soldjah* is a different case of linguistic invention. In a move common within global hip-hop, LBC borrowed *soldier* from English in an effort to align himself with certain U.S. rappers. Regardless of where they actually live, Cape Verdeans have a distinct connection to the United States, or *Merka*; the diasporic community in the United States, especially in the metro areas of Boston and Providence, is the largest and has the longest history (Halter 1993). Virtually every person of Cape Verdean descent with whom I spoke, either in Lisbon or in Cape Verde itself, had at least one relative in the United States.

In addition, *soldjah* contains another curious element, the phoneme *dja*, which is indicative of affecting presence of Kriolu. As noted above, *dja* is a hard sound relative to the Portuguese *já*. In the case of *soldjah*, *dja* approximates the sound of the English phoneme *die* within *soldier*, especially in a dialect of New York City or other locales where terminal *r*'s frequently go unaspirated. The jab of *dja* is a standard rhetorical tool, used as rhythmic punch tone in U.S. as well as Kriolu raps.

This blending of linguistic, geographic, and ideological components within a proper name came to make sense to me as I reflected that early evening in Soldjah's apartment. The calls from pedestrians, the screeching noises from passing cars, the music blasting from open windows, and the sounds of kids on the corner seemingly all converged on the five-point intersection outside Soldjah's apartment. Soldjah is an oppositional activist; he became energized and angered by the ubiquitous commotion of his surroundings. "Not for me" is a critical stance on the everyday, and "Liberta Palestina" is Soldjah's attempt to export his oppositionality abroad and to advance a cause that he sees as just by means of a symbolic code that he finds both natural and combative: Kriolu.

LBC/Minao Soldjah and Hezbollah identify with what in Portugal is called "intervention" rap. This school of rap has parallels throughout global hip-hop. The most basic creative and ideological division, in general, is between those who understand hip-hop as essentially entertainment and those who believe it to be fundamentally about social critique and change. The latter philosophy, based in the assumption that the potential for change is a universal trait of human societies, characterizes the interventionist school.

Along with Soldjah, Hezbollah is a member of a hip-hop posse or organization called *Nos k nasi omi k ta mori om* (We who are born men die as men) and identifies as an atheist and human-rights activist. Both assured me that the moniker Hezbollah has no direct relation to the Shi'ite Muslim group based in Lebanon or to Islam, in general; rather, they were drawn to the "warrior" connotation of the word. While Hezbollah insisted in other conversations that his name had nothing to do with the geopolitics of the Middle East, I believe that this nickname along with the Palestine references made by LBC, Hezbollah, and other radical and relatively bookish Kriolu rappers do, in fact, assert an affiliation between Kriolu identity politics and anti-Zionist activists.

For example, during a visit to Lisbon in 2013, I accompanied a group of Kriolu rappers through the metropolitan downtown after a vibrant debate about Marcus Garvey, Afro-centricity, and Luso-African experiences in contemporary Lisbon (referred to in chapter 1). We passed the Rossio plaza, a center of tourist activity and public national memory, filled with bustling commerce and historical monuments. Curiously, in the spot where Luso-Africans used to gather and discuss the fate of their home countries during the independence struggles of the 1960s and 1970s and where many survivors of that generation continue to gather to reminisce and show their ethnic customs of dress there stands a small monument. It marks where the dramatic torturing and slaughtering of hundreds of Jews took place as part of the Inquisition in 1506. I confessed that I had passed this monument dozens of times and never noticed its significance. One particularly combative and articulate rapper immediately responded that while the massacre of the Jews was a horrible act, at least they have a home. He went on to say, "They were given Israel with all this protection and privilege. Why? There are so many with just as much claim to territory but with no home. Diaspora can be a bit like that. I feel that way."

Kriolu as an identity of encounter and difference, thus, can be a medium of imaginary alliances with other displaced groups who publicly try to stake claims on territory and ownership of local histories. With that said, it is clear that the adoption of Hezbollah or favorable references to Palestine are in no way calls to arms. Kriolu rappers are discursive activists, not underground militia men, and rhetorical soldiers, not military troops.

"Liberta Palestina" was recorded in a local home studio in 2008. It exemplifies a combination of sound engineering and rap narrative in the service of drama, a repeatedly stated objective of Soldjah during our conversations. The group achieves drama musically by employing a sequence of modulating cycles and discursively by linking death and violence to state ideologies rather than military actions. The song itself consists of an instrumental opening and three verses, divided by a repeated refrain. The listener feels the marriage of Kriolu linguistic features to rap aesthetics, particularly, when Soldjah rhymes. Influenced by the legendary Tupac Shakur, Soldjah has borrowed one of his hero's vocal styles. Instead of ending certain key verses with a return to the tonic pitch, a typical resolution on the rhyming word, Soldjah, like Tupac, unexpectedly leaves his voice unresolved at the end of the phrase. This suspension of melodic resolution, he explained to me about his rap, mirrors a suspension of commonsense associations between globalization and citizenship. In an interview via Skype in 2010, LBC/Soldjah summarized his attempts to use Kriolu language to link ideology and spatial territory: "I try to convey a global perspective of this capitalist, racist, and imperialist system."

"Liberta Palestina" is not a narrative in the conventional sense of a story with distinct characters and an overarching, cohesive message. Rather, it is a series of indictments regarding contemporary cases of human-rights violations and genocides, which are loosely but assertively juxtaposed with the horrors of Iberian colonialism and U.S. imperialism. The translated lyrical content emerges from an attempt to represent both the powerful and the powerless. The first line has a drop on the last syllable; the next three lines have repeat intonation.

It's a satanic and Mephistopheles consideration [*mefistoféliku*].
Of an ill and malign government [*maléfiku*].
They are hideous and sadistic [*sádiku*].
To make the world a stage of hate and panic [*pániku*].

Similar to my previous analysis regarding Kriolu semiotics and potential rap ideological ruptures, I do not argue that what Soldjah iterates is an anomaly within the Kriolu-speaking community. Rather, I posit that the efficacy of his style emerges from a combination of a linguistic or ideological "sedimentation" (aspects of pronunciation and grammar) and an emboldened and activist social group (local rappers' discomfort with categories, such as tuga). In the lines above, the accented, glissando drop in tone on the terminal syllable is effective, in part, because the prior consonants of *l*, *f*, *d*, and *n* are particularly strong in Kriolu. They stop the air and the sound flow of the word and separate the syllables in a noticeable fashion. Such combinations of vocal intonations occur at moments of the song when the musical tracks are relatively lower in volume, thus implying a space of attention. Soldjah continues.

> Mankind's behavior has reached a point; it's like an apocalypse
> The residue of arms has reached a point of an eclipse....
> Is it true that the U.S. promotes liberty? Issues of dignity, bought? Sold!
> Where is our sentiment of solidarity?
> Freedom has to come to Palestine, has to come to the other
> He is suffering....

The David-versus-Goliath metaphors of the rhetoric are matched by hyperbolic features of the sound structure. The song's refrain initially contrasts with the solo rap of each verse; however, as the verse proceeds and the musical sequence gains momentum, the solo voice begins to echo, thereby producing a sense of collectivity. In my conversations with Soldjah, he intimated that in the studio, Machine, a local rapper and sound engineer residing in the adjacent Reboleira neighborhood, had suggested using the echo effect because it suggested multiplicity, voices of a crowd in unison, in keeping with the song's theme of revolution.

## Chullage's "Nu Bai"

In contrast to LBC and Hezbollah, Nuno Santos, also known as Chullage, takes a more domestic path in the song "Nu Bai" (Let's go). As mentioned in the introduction, Chullage with this song captures the energy of urban youth in the early 2000s and helps to focus attention on key contemporary problems of identity and belonging.

Chullage and Soldjah know each other's work and are mutually respectful colleagues. Both are deeply invested in connecting hip-hop to social movements concerned with education and citizenship throughout the Lisbon area. While both rappers are Kriolu activists, Chullage is a more experienced rapper and has achieved a pop charisma through his variety of musical styles and public presence. Based on anecdotal evidence during my fieldwork, along with quantitative evidence from music sales and YouTube video hits, it is clear that Chullage is more widely heard than Soldjah. Kriolu rappers as well as dozens of young tuga hip-hop fans and participants cited "Nu Bai" as a critical moment in Lisbon rap history and the overall hip-hop scene.

Chullage exudes social consciousness. I first met him in 2007 in a small playground park at the center of his current neighborhood, Arrentela, located on the southern margin (*margem sul*) of the Tagus River, across from Lisbon proper. I had been in Portugal for a scant week and was slowly adapting to what seemed to me the uneven fits and spurts of the sounds of continental Portuguese, a far cry from the flowing diction of the Brazilian variety with which I was more familiar. I was unprepared linguistically for the likes of Chullage. As I struggled to follow his explanations of the neighborhood cultural center that he helped orchestrate, as well as the social problems of unemployment, drug trafficking, and police abuse, I found myself writing nothing and listening to everything. His tone was didactic and demanding as he provoked me to articulate my interests. Chullage's provocation was not only in content; I realized later that he had code-switched from Portuguese to Kriolu.

For Chullage, in contrast to Soldjah, Kriolu-as-chronotope features an urgency that is ultimately directed inward to the neighborhoods of contemporary Lisbon. His Kriolu works as introspection on the here and now. Unlike Soldjah, Chullage was born in Lisbon and grew up in the now-defunct, improvised neighborhood of Asilo 28 de Maio. In live performance and in the studio, Chullage's mouth widens as he shouts his Kriolu at the listener, not in rounded strophes but in purposefully unwieldy loads. Chullage overwhelms with his delivery style, and the listener struggles to catch up.

The song "Nu Bai" consists of several rap verses from invited Kriolu rappers, all of whom connect individual experience and identity to ponderings of place and belonging. Musically, the song begins with a sample of the ebb and flow of the wind, perhaps a Cape Verdean breeze, but more likely a gust signaling the sunset over Lisbon; an oncoming darkness sets on Chullage's current social neighborhood of predominantly Cape Verdean–descent residents. Discussed in greater detail in chapter 4, the social neighborhood emerged, in large part, during the 1970s as Lisbon attempted to provide for, and to regulate, tens of thousands of immigrants

CHAPTER 3

as well as white "Portuguese" families who were retornados from former African colonies that were becoming independent nation-states.[6]

Chullage locates the listener immediately by means of the first rhetorical phrase, strategically produced without a musical background to emphasize its effect.

> Cape Verde, let's go.
> But, yeah,
> Now, we're here in Portugal. Let's go.
> They [Cape Verdeans] come and go. Chullage.

The protagonists of this rap narrative are, first and foremost, displaced storytellers. As the sound loop kicks in, it becomes evident that the flute sample is not from an acoustic instrument; it is a synthesized simulation. Throughout nine minutes of hardcore rap rhetoric, Chullage and his Kriolu partners expand on the notion that their precarious reality is a tension between place and simulation. The task of articulation and narration involves both the social fact that many were "born in the *txada* [open fields of Cape Verde], grew up in the alley [in the Lisbon periphery]" with the ideological desire "to represent the dreds [not only Rastafari but, metonymically, people of African heritage] throughout Europe," according to Jorginho, one of Chullage's guest rappers ("Nu Bai").

In "Nu Bai," Kriolu is not a childhood memory or a fun-loving party vacation, as one might infer from Boss AC, a more commercially successful Lisbon rapper of Cape Verdean heritage, and his 2005 hit song "Sabim." For Chullage and his crew, Portugal is a set of material conditions but not a favorable cultural heritage. Lisbon and, more specifically, the social neighborhoods are a pit of despair and a potential launch pad of distinction. Kriolu is a call to action: Nu bai.

## Kriolu Back Talk

Within hip-hop culture, rappers, in general, pride themselves on being most adept at rhetorically honoring the ideological commitment to represent "reality." Such pride emerges in both an attitude of determination and persuasion as well as a flair for the aesthetic neologism and vocal style. One of the most important themes in rap's penetration into global popular culture has been the dynamic articulation of time-place. All around the world, rappers have strategically used their rhetorical skills to legitimize local rap and, by extension, hip-hop as territorial—a scene. In this manner, rap music provides a strong example of the "sociolinguistics of globalization" (Blommaert 2003; Alim 2009). More than an aphorism, this phrase underlines the primacy of language as a set of performed and circulated practices that are chronotopic in nature, not only because ideas of time and place are present together but, more important, because this relationship strikes a chord with listeners and provokes performers to be creative wordsmiths. In the case of Kriolu in Lisbon, such signification is part of identity work within the milieu of Portuguese nationalism and the contemporary panic around European citizenship.

In Portugal, rappers achieved what appeared to be a solid tuga chronotope through hip-hop recordings and public recognition in the mid-1990s. Participants emphasized a solidarity built on cosmopolitan youth culture and shared urban experiences. The category *tuga* became problematic for some local rappers, however, because it is saturated with histories of a colonial Portugal desperate for profits and an emerging milieu of African independence.

Emergent from these conflicted and conflicting histories is Kriolu, an early product of Portuguese colonialism and West African movements of people, goods, and languages, the speakers of which have established an independent nation-state in Cape Verde as well as several residential communities in the Lisbon metro area. I have argued that Kriolu rappers, in their expressions of time-place, critically assess the category *tuga* and, thus, interrogate what it means to be Portuguese. Furthermore, local rappers' efficacy in provoking reflection derives, in part, from structural attributes of the Kriolu language.

In terms of position or stance, rappers who have linguistic competence in Kriolu frequently choose to rap in Kriolu for reasons of congruence between code and audience and, more interesting, between code and political-aesthetic perspective. Hip-hop occurs with little conventional publicity in local neighborhood events where many of the residents are of Cape Verdean and/or PALOP heritage, so it follows that rappers would be most effective through use of local parlance. Kriolu works ideologically to combine locality with a critical edge, one that is often missing from rap in Portuguese. As is true of many Creole cultural-linguistic formations, the very emergence of Kriolu involved a negotiation of crossover and difference. Being/speaking Kriolu has been, and continues to be, both natural and bold—and such a stance or evaluative position on reality is the essence of underground hip-hop.

Kriolu lends itself to two operative chronotopes: one of extreme locality, with a focus on the present, and another of diasporic expansion, expressive of historical roots and future claims. Regarding the latter, Kriolu rappers' articulation of diaspora often detours from the conventional tropes of nostalgic recognition of past serial emigration to several European and American locales and a longing to return to the mother archipelago. As rapper LBC/Soldjah demonstrates, Kriolu can represent a wide-ranging diaspora of marginalized and displaced youth who are critical of imperialist, corporate values.

Kriolu creates meaning through specific chronotopes in, for example, Kromo's provocative improvisational YouTube video and Chullage's song "Nu Bai." Both performances link Kriolu language and experiences to moment-places of contemporary Lisbon neighborhoods and reality, as well as to the moment-place of migration, especially in the case of Chullage. In the case of LBC/Soldjah and Hezbollah, Kriolu serves as malleable material from which the two create drama while referencing the particular delivery style of Tupac Shakur. In all of these examples, the Kriolu language is a tool to foster ethnic, racial, and class allegiances. LBC ultimately reminds the listener, "The spaces are linked. Kova M is like Palestine is like Praia, and so many other places. I am a soldier of the Third World, inside Europe, doing outreach" (personal communication, 2011).

The case of Kriolu has implications for the current milieu of citizenship in Western Europe. High-profile cases involving the public visibility of the veil in France and violent racial and ethnic riots in suburban England have contributed to a crisis in identity politics that has challenged the legitimacy of migrant experiences as truly French, British, Portuguese, and so on. Thoughtful dialogue and legislation regarding the dynamics of postcoloniality, reformulations of national identities, and recognized public spheres have been put on hold due to the current economic recession. After a period of celebration and sponsorship from the mid-1990s to 2007, European policy makers have become equivocal and occasionally rejected projects organized around multiculturalism and interculturality.[7] Such posturing has flattened the complexity of what Robert Stam and Ella Shohat call the "multichronotopic frame" (2011:20) or what Terry Eagleton terms the "geopolitical hybridity" of identity formations (2000:79).

Local rappers are adamant about inserting Kriolu into the Lisbon scene as part of the global linguistic flow of hip-hop, a necessarily interdependent relationship between the global and the local. The global and local are not established entities of time and place but are emergent from expressive practices. In the case of Kriolu rap in Lisbon, the experiential frame is postcoloniality, a set of "dramas," to use LBC's term, that are shared not only by Cape Verdeans and other PALOP groups in Portugal but also by a range of other contemporary European residents. Focused attention to Kriolu-as-chronotope allows an empirically based investigation into the discursive stuff of identity formation as local rappers put Kriolu words and experiences into the public domain in order to provoke a reconsideration of membership and belonging. As the next chapter shows, the Kriolu scene is not simply aesthetic and potentially ideological. Kriolu rappers join other Cape Verdeans and PALOP youth in using language as material evidence in the current debates over housing in Lisbon.

CHAPTER 4

# Spatial Politics of Kriolu Presence in Lisbon

> You can imagine all sorts of things to yourself; you can guess at the outline of the unseen landscape, the fields, orchards, the towns of white stone, the churches and squares cooling after the heat that lasted all day; you can try and come to terms with the perverse abundance of matter, the pornographic immodesty of history, which is lying on its back beyond every curve and over every hill; but ultimately it all turns out to be futile, because we remain alone with the space, which is the oldest of all things.
>
> —Andrzej Stasiuk, *Fado*

The acclaimed Polish writer Andrzej Stasiuk begins *Fado*, a wandering and wondering book, with a thought piece on traveling. Although Stasiuk never actually discusses Portugal, despite the title's reference to the Portuguese national music tradition, he implies an affinity with other "marginal" places of Europe. At the end of the day, Stasiuk muses that there is always the physical space of existence, which never completely washes away. Michel Foucault made a comparable point in his reflective text on space and place: "our epoch is one in which space takes for us the form of relations among sites" (1984:46).[1] Space and geography continue to be an essential orientation through which we understand, represent, and make claims on history, ideology, and identity. Space, then, is an irreducible dimension of presence.

This chapter tracks Kriolu presence in Lisbon to argue that there is a "Creole citizenship" emerging in Lisbon. *Kriolu presence* refers to the various manifestations of Cape Verde and Cape Verdeans in the metropole. This formation is one significant influence in the sentiment and management of what it means to be Portuguese and, by extension, European. Certainly, Cape Verdean presence is historical and linguistic in nature, as chapters 1 and 3 show, respectively. This presence is also part of a grounded politics, a struggle for recognition and enfranchisement based in the everyday realities of improvised infrastructure, state campaigns of relocation, and dynamic views on belonging.

Figure 6 is an example of current housing politics in urban Portugal, which has pitted predominantly immigrant communities, especially so-called Luso-African groups, against state agencies. The elevated levels of unemployment, since 2009 with sharper intensity during 2012 and 2013, due to the economic recession in Europe have exacerbated the tension. Currently, unemployment has stabilized at approximately 15 percent, and the percentage hovers around 35 percent among youth (ages 16–25) ("Portugal Youth"; "Unemployment Rate"). Kriolu addresses the multilayered experience of place involved in housing categories, such as social and improvised, represented in figure 6, the Prior Velho neighborhood, and Quinta da Serra neighborhood. I took this photograph in November 2009. Since then, Quinta da Serra has been demolished. To understand the significance of migration and housing, we need to appreciate the processes of not just displacement but also "emplacement" (Siu 2005), the set of agentic practices necessary to attribute meaning to spaces as part of occupation and settlement.

Although the case of Cape Verde youth in Lisbon is particular on many levels, this chapter's analytical focus on social practices as constitutive of space and accompanying identification has potential for general application. My interpretation of space and place serves as one more component in the general argument that to analyze citizenship requires a combination of lived experiences and political policies. Cape Verdean-ness, or Kriolu, as an archetype of the colonial encounter and postcolonial migrant recuperates Creole as a viable model for contemporary citizenship, especially in the highly flexible, multicultural world of Western Europe.

## Spatial Scales

If identity and, by extension, citizenship are spatialized, how does one differentiate the various reference points of affinity? In other words, what are the operative scales of space involved in Kriolu presences in Lisbon? Cape Verdeans share a basic challenge of spatial scales with other communities rooted in archipelagos and routed globally to continental land masses. Cape Verdeans are essentially diasporic, and it is commonplace for family members to be dispersed across Europe, Western African, and/or the Americas. As an initial entrée, Cape Verdeans often must entertain the uncomfortable simultaneity of two notions of space,

FIGURE 6. The division between the social housing neighborhood Prior Velho (left) and the improvised neighborhood of Quinta da Serra (right). Photo by author, November 2009.

*espaco-ilha* (island-space), in contrast to *espaço-continente* (continent-space). According to Ana de Saint-Maurice, such distinctions in scale represent an "unequal development of space with a tension in how to occupy space within one society" (1997:92–93). Kriolu rapper Jorginho in his participation on Chullage's iconic song "Nu Bai" alludes to this spatial relationship when he juxtaposes the island-space of *txada*, the open field ubiquitous in the piecemeal urbanization so visible in the Cape Verdean cities of Santiago, Tarrafal, Mindelo, and the *beku*, the alleyways of peripheral neighborhoods in European cities, such as Lisbon.

When Cape Verdeans move from categories of Luso-African migrants to European residents, they face the daunting but creatively exciting challenge of emplacement. Cape Verdeans, thus, begin to construct a certain kind of continent-space. But which continent? Rapper and documentary filmmaker Uncle C, when recounting his migration trajectories, once reflected, "Yeah, I'm Cape Verdean. For sure, but I have to say that I came in contact with hip-hop on the Azores and, well, with the military base.... Sometimes, I think of myself also as American" (personal communication, 2009). Uncle C is referring to the U.S. military base Lajes Field, established in 1953 on Lajes Island. This is the so-called Terceira Ilha

## CHAPTER 4

(Third island) of the Azores, another archipelago, which constitutes part of Macronesia and is located roughly fifteen hundred miles to the north of Cape Verde. Uncle C emigrated with his older sister from Santiago to the Azores when they were teenagers. A male cousin, a U.S. citizen, was stationed at the base. In one of our first conversations, Uncle C enjoyed remembering how as a teenager he used to sneak into the barracks and hear different kinds of music, including, on one occasion, the sounds of legendary U.S. rappers Run DMC and LL Cool J. Clearly, these episodes influenced Uncle C significantly to the point that although he has never been to the continental United States and speaks little English, he feels a belonging to America via hip-hop culture. In so doing, albeit imaginatively, Uncle C periodically creates an alternative continent-space.

Cape Verdeans are remarkably heterogeneous along a range of indices. Not unlike Mauritius, another Creole place and formation, Cape Verde "has been a profoundly cosmopolitan place ... and a profoundly parochial one" (Vaughan 2005:2). Factors such as the variability in European and African contact, diasporic trajectories, and the historical difficulties in communication and travel between the islands have shaped Cape Verdean Kriolu/Crioulo into a language of multiple dialects and an identity composed of multiple racial inflections.

However, the projects of "making home" and diasporic belonging serve as common ground. In her work on Chinese-ness in Panama, anthropologist Lok C. D. Siu describes the "changing same" of the migration narrative as variable along lines of class, gender, and geopolitical history and, yet, still formative of "diasporic Chinese consciousness" (2005:88). Similarly, Cape Verdean-ness, that concept indexed in the phrase *ami é kriolu* (I am Kriolu), consists of a migration narrative, often serial in practice involving multiple destinations, and diversifies by class and political affiliation, race, gender, and island origin within Cape Verde. For example, during the decolonization wars throughout Lusophone Africa from 1961 to 1975, those Cape Verdeans who identified with Amílcar Cabral's African Party for the Independence of Guinea-Bissau and Cape Verde (PAIGCV), a party based in Marxist political economic theory of mass distribution of wealth and land as well as a cultural nationalism underscoring the importance of Kriolu, have a significantly different notion of Cape Verdean identity than those who fled the archipelago. The latter opted for the safety and opportunities of the Portuguese metropole or became Cape Verdean conscripts in the Portuguese military abroad on the African continent or even Asian posts, such as Goa and Macau (Lobban and Halter 1988). This small sample of Cape Verdean heterogeneity helps one understand how and why Cape Verdeans in contemporary times differ on whether they identify as African or European or both or neither, since such general identity terms code histories and experiences of race, class, and island affinity (Carling 2002; Åkesson 2004).

## Scenes, Topos, and Emplacement

The story of Cape Verdeans in Lisbon is one of scenes, a creative link between physical space and expressive culture that shapes identity. In an interview about his first Kriolu rap group, TWA (Third World Answer), Jorginho describes the relationship in linguistic terms: "we have been able to translate Portuguese into Kriolu, and in this manner we construct a scene here in Miraflores [members were relocated after the demolition of the improvised neighborhood Pedreira dos Hungaros in the late 1990s].... In Kriolu I know [how to express myself], and I feel the words, while if I rap in Portuguese, I know, but I don't feel it so much" (personal communication, 2011).

Groups of youth residing in Lisbon of Cape Verdean descent use Kriolu to empower themselves psychologically, economically, and politically by connecting their hybrid native tongue to space (local neighborhood, Lisbon periphery, Cape Verdean diaspora, Cape Verde itself, Africa, Europe, generalized migrant communities) and time (Portuguese colonialism, sixteenth-century West African migrations, twentieth-century decolonization, late twentieth-century personal narratives of family migration). Such space-time couplings are chronotopic, as Kriolu speakers generate new meanings out of these combinations. The semiotic work of Kova M dwellers is also heterotopic, as Foucault describes, in that the space of a pile of rubble gathered near the impromptu corner at the top of the hill is a juxtaposition "in a single real place several spaces; several sites that are in themselves incompatible" (1984:25) (figure 7). In the cases presented here, it is Kriolu that provides a thread of cohesion to otherwise conflicting or "deviant" articulations of space (Foucault, 1984:25) (figure 8).

The pile of rubble in figure 7 signifies state projects of relocation, unfinished local development, leisure spaces for youth social networking, marks of marginality in the Lisbon public sector, and references for pop culture, such as rap and graffiti art. Some of these meanings contribute to conventional notions of peripheral improvised neighborhoods, while others amplify alternative perspectives on space and society. The whole is more than the sum of its parts, and these tactics help create distinction (identity) and are born from the intimacy of Portuguese colonialism (Creole). In short, this is the topos of a particular Kriolu formation in Lisbon.

In September 2009 I visited Dani, a local leader of an affiliate of the international hip-hop organization Zulu Nation, at what served as its headquarters in Portugal. I soon realized that this place was very different from the Zulu Nation centers with which I was familiar in New York City and São Paulo. Dani had prefaced her invitation with the confession that the local affiliate of the global hip-hop organization was just beginning and had no funds to speak of: "We [she and her

FIGURE 7. Scenes of demolition on the way to Quinta da Lage. Photo by author, 2009.

FIGURE 8. Hip-hop street dancer B-boy Zé Macaco leading a workshop on hip-hop dance. Photo by author, 2009.

son] just applied for a grant, and we hope to get some backing from ACIDI." In 2010 they succeeded on both accounts, financial and official recognition by the state agency related to immigration and intercultural communication.

For the time being, anybody interested in the cause would meet on Saturday afternoons in an abandoned one-story building in what used to be the middle of a thriving neighborhood called Quinta da Lage. Dani's directions to me were, after departing from the Amadora subway stop, to take a series of lefts and rights, using piles of rubble and worn-in paths amongst the weeds as landmarks. As I entered a relatively dense cluster of residences, I turned around and took a photograph, received a text checking on my whereabouts, and hurried to the meeting place. Dani promptly introduced me to Fema D and Marilene, who were practicing for an upcoming performance. The two young women were from Chelas and Damaia, two planned, social neighborhoods. They told me that over the past months, they had become acquainted with many of the children and some families in Quinta da Lage: "It took a while for people to recognize and trust us. We're all basically in the same boat. When I was a kid, our family had to move from a neighborhood like this and into the social neighborhood, Chelas, where I live now. We came to an understanding, and we started to share stories, candies, say 'hi' . . . that sort of thing." Marilene confirmed Fema D's portrayal of the insider/outsider relationship as calm, normal, and everyday.

After practice Dani led a small group of us around the neighborhood and introduced us to a few families. I realized in a dramatic way that the two young women rappers had understated the relationship and downplayed the role of Kriolu, rap, and neighborhood in this tense and violent place. Everyone understandably had been shy but very cordial. Then we called on França, a transgender mother of two, living in what appeared to be a domicile without a fixed door. She was at her wits end, crying, communicating in bursts of Kriolu and wails of emotion. França's teenage son had been murdered two days earlier. She ultimately blamed the police as she recounted a litany of stories involving harassment due to the family's illegal residency and residence. Quinta da Lage was an improvised neighborhood—half there, half demolished—a liminal place and a target for violence and stigma. As França pleaded with Dani to stay and apologized for her state of mind, I struggled to make out what exactly was being said. A few of us hugged França, but due to my poor Kriolu language skills, my empathy remained vague. I couldn't articulate anything other than sadness.

It wouldn't be until 2011 that I began to understand the heterotopic dimensions of that dramatic scene. França, Dani, Fema D, Marilene, other young hip-hoppers practicing, surrounding neighbors, and I, the wandering anthropologist in the early stages of a new research project, had imbued the abandoned building in the

CHAPTER 4

center of Quinta da Laje with different, competing, and, in certain circumstances, incompatible meanings. It was a space of leisure, a space of new social relationships, a space of problematic state policies, a space of desired state investment, a space of renewal, and, for França, a space of horrifying death. Her son had been murdered very close to the building. Despite it all, the estrangement and miscommunications, there was no personal ill will among us. What I failed to understand that I found present in lyrical scraps from my field notes was a set of Kriolu words and memories of what I would learn comprised Kriolu manners of speech. Emphases on little words, such as *li* (here), in pronunciation as a call for reflection in place complemented actors' elaborations on deep concepts, including *xinti* (feel), *nkontra* (meet), and *manda boka* (joust verbally, have a "beef" with someone).

Kriolu is an empowering medium through which competent speakers bring together notions of identity and culture to stake out claims on territory. Such a presence (recall chapter 1) is historical; it is also a political act with ties to other immigrant practices of emplacement in Europe. Unlike the situation of Libyans in Italy, Moroccans in France, or Sunni Muslims in England, who place themselves in (sub)urban neighborhoods, Cape Verdeans have been historically not an "other" but a central part of Lusotropicalism, the Portuguese ideology that holds racial mixture and colonial understanding as central to Portuguese identity both at home and abroad. As demonstrated in chapter 2, my findings support the claim that the strategic turn to difference among local rappers in Lisbon hinges on an invigorated articulation of Kriolu.

Due to the unique relationship between Portugal and Cape Verde, neighborhoods such as Kova M have become the sites and the products of emplacement, referring to the heterogeneous routes of migrant displacement (Anderson and Lee 2005) and what Kirin Narayan describes as "the process of staking out space rather than any specific moment of fixed arrival" (2010:485; see also Bammer 1994; Siu 2005). In this chapter, I bring my analysis of emplacement to the level of the street, the concrete block, and refashioned alleyway. In particular, through an analysis of two neighborhoods, one a public housing project and the other an autoconstructed residential complex, I show that Kriolu identity is a combination of linguistic practices that not only have symbolic value but also remake the material realities of urban living. The evidence from these two neighborhoods reveals that Kriolu agency is dynamic but, ultimately, limited in its effectiveness due to state-sponsored notions of community architecture and citizenship. While the case of Cape Verde emplacement in Lisbon is particular on many levels, I argue that an analytical focus on spatiolinguistic practices has potential for general application in the scholarship on migrant agency and cultural citizenship (Rosaldo 1994). What was once a symbol of transition and Lusotropicalism in the heart of the Portuguese empire in Africa is now a heterogeneous practice of racial and diasporic pride inside Europe.

## European Emplacement and Citizenship

The relationship between space and identification has been a frequent and productive topic of scholarship and public policy. In the European context, scholars have approached the issue of immigration and city space in terms of collective action and sociopolitical agency (Bousetta 1997; A. Horta 2008; Sardinha 2010; Suárez-Navaz 2004). Since the late 2000s, social-media sites, such as Facebook and Habita, a focused website related to housing politics in Lisbon, have become remarkably active as archives of formal documents and mouthpieces for collective organizing and personal testimonies. In Portugal, as Anna Paula Beja Horta explains, such grassroots politics around space and identity is relatively new not only due to the logistics of technology but also because terms such as *multiculturalism, interculturality*, and *ethnic minorities* (often glossed as *Lusofonia*) emerged only at the end of the twentieth century (2008).

Kriolu as emplacement necessarily involves histories of labor and race. Local Lisbon rapper Ghoya, described later in this chapter, explains this relationship in plain terms: "What is left over is immigrants and poor whites, those who were already disenfranchised [*excluidos*]. We are losing space. We don't take it for granted" (personal communication, 2009). Similar to its neighbor Spain, Portugal's transition to a recognized multicultural nation-state and a "labor importer" is relatively recent (Cornelius 1994; Saint-Maurice 1997). Two major periods of migration occurred in the 1960s, as the Salazar regime granted labor permits, especially to Cape Verdeans, to replace Portuguese nationals who had left for Angola and Mozambique in efforts to maintain Portugal's African colonies. After 1986, when Portugal entered the European Union, a more diverse wave of migrants entered Lisbon, with a strong Cape Verdean presence but also including Brazilians and, more recently, various East European nationals.

That contemporary European citizenship involves a tense relationship between inclusion and racial differentiation is also not unique to Portugal. As Liliana Suárez-Navaz (2004) and Mikaela Rogozen-Soltar (2012) explain, the rapprochement of Spain with Europe in the 1980s transformed what had been previously a general alliance along class lines between working-class Andalusians and African immigrants into a racialized difference marking the latter as a suspicious group of "foreigners" and "illegals," thereby constituting Andalusia as a "Mediterranean border" between Europe and Africa, as well as between democratic modernity and dangerous traditionalism.

However, unlike the situation in southern Spain, the move toward a "naturalization of difference" in public practices of hegemony, such as documentation regulation and behavior, has been rearticulated to a certain degree by Kriolu negritude and local neighborhood politics (Suárez-Navaz 2004:7). This is despite the fact that xenophobic racism in Portugal carries significant heft in Portuguese politics, as represented in national parties of the center-right populist Centro Democrático e Social–Partido Popular (Social Democrat–People's Party) (CDS-PP) and in social media venues, such as YouTube and Facebook commentary. Whereas in Spain, Senegalese migrants employ the qualifier of "Muslim" to place themselves legitimately in Andalusia as part of regional histories and, indeed, "migrant" to take part in the "Andalusian collective memory" (Suárez-Navaz 2004:81), Cape Verdean youth purposefully mark themselves as Kriolu and, thus, not as part of Lusotropicalist history of hybridity and quasi-Portuguese status but as transnational African residents who shape the present Lisbon.

## Scenes and Neighborhoods

Space is central to notions of value and power. In her oft-cited ethnography of hip-hop culture, Tricia Rose (1994) links the power of rap music to black youth's response to and reshaping of the "postindustrial city" in the late 1970s. More germane to Creole emplacement, anthropologists Michel S. Laguerre and Gina Sánchez Gibau have made the case that Haitian and Cape Verdean diasporic communities in New York City and Boston, respectively, have forged identity through the "materiality" of the neighborhood exemplified by the corner store (Laguerre 1998; Gibau 2005). For example, residents not only refer to the store as part of community but also through cultural practices, such as language and visual art, residents infuse the abstract concept of identity into the concrete material of the locale. Thus, migration and diasporic cultures materialize and become part of the urban landscape.

In the scholarship on rap music and territoriality, Murray Forman has argued that rappers are experts in analyzing and popularizing the "spatial partitioning of race and the experiences of being young and black in America" (2002:202). Rappers bolster their claims to authority and legitimacy by transforming vague notions of ghetto into sharp identity tales of the "hood." Yet, if we take the basic message of Paul Gilroy's *Black Modernity* (1993) to heart, we must agree that identity is always a translocal articulation (see also Pennycook 2010). To this end, the following lyrical excerpt from rapper LBC demonstrates that the reckoning of Lisbon neighborhoods and sociocultural identification often involves other places and the curious, diasporic vehicle of Cape Verdean Kriolu. In the song translated below, MINAO in Portuguese translates to "black anti-oppression mental intellect." LBC raps,

> What is that about real thugs and real gangstas in training who leave their
>     kids and women hungry in the ghetto?
> When I arrived from Eugenio Lima in Kova M, I learned a lot of things.
> A badiu soldier right here
> M.I.N.A.O. soldier is here to defend
> all those that the state oppresses.
> Fuck a nigga who isn't with my ideas
> who doesn't know about Carlos Veiga.
> He barely maintains his legitimacy.
> He was down with the guy who killed Renato Cardoso.
> Enough, nigga.
> I became a soldier here
> We must have a new kind of spirit.
>
> [*Refrain*]
> M.I.N.A.O.
> It's all about preparing people for a world revolution.
> —(M.I.N.A.O. 2009)

In this excerpt, LBC (learning black connection) locates his "learning" in the Cape Verdean diaspora. It is when he moved from the impoverished neighborhood of Eugenio Lima in the Cape Verdean capital, Praia, to Kova M that LBC began to reflect on Kriolu. In other sections of the song, LBC covers police brutality and racial profiling in the Lisbon periphery on his way back to references to Carlos Veiga and Renato Cardoso, two opposing political figures within the same party during Cape Verde's transition from a Marxist-style, one-party system to a multiparty, neoliberal system during the 1990s.

LBC identifies the problem of postcolonial emplacement as not only a challenge of physical diaspora but also of language. The latter is signaled in the term *badiu* (*vadio* in Portuguese; vagabond or scoundrel in English). Unlike the Cape Verdeans in past generations of migration, most young Cape Verdeans in Lisbon are badiu, meaning poor, working-class individuals. Initially, most were young men from the rural towns and later Praia, on the island of Santiago, considered to be the most "African" island by Cape Verdeans and foreigners alike. Recalling Brazilian scholar Gilberto Freyre's 1952 visit to Santiago, sponsored by the Portuguese state, we are reminded of his impressions of the island as "so negroid: a sign that, unlike what has successfully been happening in Brazil, this place has maintained the African elements of origin" (1953a:290). Just as Philippe Bourgois (2003) describes the impact of the *jíbaro*, a symbol of Puerto Rican rural masculinity, on the East Harlem landscape of New York City in the 1980s, the Cape Verdean badiu has influenced the milieu of masculinity and youth in the improvised and social housing in contemporary Lisbon.

As an expression of diaspora, postcoloniality, gender, class, language, and race, *badiu* is a key word in the "social imaginary" of certain peripheral spaces in Lisbon. LBC most directly relates *badiu* to his personal identity, "a badiu soldier," an identity marker that requires space to be meaningful. In his lyrics LBC qualifies *badiu* with two deictic expressions: "right here" and "arriving from Eugenio Lima." While the former refers to his current presence in Kova M, the latter refers to migration from the Cape Verdean island of Santiago and an improvised neighborhood in Praia. This brief example of *badiu* demonstrates that emplacement involves a range of spatial references. Such heterogeneity complicates the straightforward notion of place as an easily demarcated locale rooted in autochthonous or even unidirectional diasporic practices.

In popular culture, the term used by practitioners and scholars that best characterizes the creative and competitive dimensions of locality is the *scene* (Connell and Gibson 2003; Krims 2007; Straw 1991). Scholars of ethnomusicology have argued cogently that the concept of scene is a primary nexus point that connects aesthetics, in this case, of sound, with sociality, ethos, and a deep sense of history (Krims 2007; Straw 1991). Furthermore, the scene necessarily involves spatial differentiation, as in the Seattle scene of grunge, the San Francisco Bay Area scene of hyphy, or the London scene of grime. Of course, scenes, like any other category, are abstractions and, thus, are not comprehensive or deterministic. However, they can be heuristically useful insofar as they demonstrate a tendency or a source of social agency. For ethnomusicologist Frederick Moehn (2012), in his analysis of a musical shift in Rio de Janeiro, Brazil, the emergent scene revealed a nexus of alternative middle-class concerns during the neoliberal boom of the 1990s, which revolved around the polemic of being labeled as myopic folklorists or sellout global imitators. I focus on a different intersection point of the local-global, namely, the collective properties and spatial dimensions of Kriolu rap scenes as constitutive of Cape Verdean identification in a milieu of urban renewal.

Kriolu rap as a scene distinct from Portuguese rap (*rap tuga*) or Cape Verdean rap (*rap kauberdianu*) depends on participants' belief and assertion of their identities as essentially linked to inhabited space. While tuga and Cape Verdean rap refer to straightforward geographic parameters, that is, rap produced in Portugal and Cape Verde, Kriolu rap, since it has no obvious "home," represents a claim for space inside an already delineated cultural territory. As a Creole language and identity, Kriolu includes vocabularies and styles mediated by the encounter as well as differentiates through a diasporic pride.

The Kriolu scene uses the popular, in this case, rap music, which draws attention through the aesthetics of rhetoric and facilitates circulation in public presentations and information technology. Similar to the music scene in Austin, Texas, during the 1990s or the hip-hop scene in Newcastle, England (Shank 1994; Bennett 2000), the Kriolu rap scene and, by extension, Kriolu emplacement in Lisbon rely on landmarks of consumption or participation, broadly defined. For Kriolu, the efficacy of the scene depends less on commercial spaces of clubs and stores and more on the relative penetration into neighborhood community centers and the social ubiquity of streets. In this respect, Kriolu scenes contribute to the meaning of urbanization processes, such as the transformation of improvised into social neighborhoods.

The social neighborhood is a standardized design, featuring clustered apartment buildings around a central plaza with accessible streets of commerce, which provide basic services of groceries, baked goods, cafés, popular restaurants, clothing, hardware, and household items. After the 1881 *Inquerito Industrial* (industrial study), a state evaluative report on national industries, city administrations began to consider more seriously the geography of labor. The challenge was how to manage urban space to maximize labor efficiency. State urbanization agencies responded in two ways: *patios* and *vilas* (patios and towns). The former is annexes and ad hoc construction for laborers behind the houses of elite, urban property owners; the latter is small, enclosed residential communities that emerged around industrial developments. Subsequently, real estate developers proposed to standardize the patio phenomenon and codify it as the vila, thereby creating more spatial segmentation and differentiation (Pereira 1994).

Social neighborhoods, first established in 1918, essentially are vilas on a larger scale (Figure 9). Just south of Alvalade sits Arco do Cego, the first acknowledged social neighborhood, again, a result of cutting low-quality figures. After World War II, migrants from the countryside met significant groups of Cape Verdeans and, to a lesser extent, Angolans and Mozambicans and remade the Lisbon areas of Loures, Seixal, and Amadora into large residential municipalities with significant pockets of improvised settlements. In the 1950s Prime Minister Antonio Salazar began to address housing through a reinvestment in social neighborhoods to combat the surge of "clandestine neighborhoods" (small, supposedly hidden areas) and informality outside of the municipality proper (Eaton 1993; Cardoso and Perista 1994). Figure 9 shows one such postwar social neighborhood, Alvalade. Intended as a middle-class enclave, Alvalade became the site of the impres-

CHAPTER 4

FIGURE 9. Alvalade, an example of the popularization of the social housing project during the 1950s, now is a residential area of the relatively affluent in Lisbon. Photo by author, 2013.

sive stadium dedicated to the Sporting soccer club. Incidentally, the reputation of *betinho* (literally, a team of "little Roberts," a gesture to the middle class and relatively white makeup of the team) has stuck with the team historically.

The implementation of subsequent laws under the Salazar administration around residential property contributed to a stigma levied against those in autoconstructed communities. During the 1960s and 1970s, the bifurcation of socialimprovised intensified, and the consequent stigma of informality connected to the latter increased leading up to and following the implosion of the fascist regime and the concurrent independence movements in Lusophone Africa (A. Horta 2001).

Since the 1980s, neighborhoods, such as Alvalade, Roma, and Arco do Cego, that once were vilas and social neighborhoods became simply *bairros* (neighborhoods), unmarked entities of social geography. During the same period, the Lisbon landscape gradually changed for the underemployed working classes from a mixture of the social and autoconstructed to almost exclusively social neighborhoods. Damaia, the residence of rapper Marilene and featured in figure 10, exemplifies the contemporary meaning of social neighborhood.

FIGURE 10. Damaia, another social housing project. Photo by author, 2009.

It is important to underscore that the relationship between social and improvised housing in Lisbon is not Manichean with the former as a cold, rigid, drone village and the latter as an innovative cultural hub. For example, some Cape Verdean rappers, such as Chullage, have used the official recognition of his social neighborhood, Arrentela, by the Lisbon city administration to gain funding and other resources so that he and others in the area could transform the bottom floor of one of the housing-project buildings into a hip-hop cultural center and internet café called Khapaz, a purposeful misspelling of the Portuguese word *capaz* (capable).

Occasionally, community groups negotiate with local graffiti artists to give improvised neighborhoods, such as Bairro de Santa Filomena (BSF) (figure 11), a look representative of its residents. However, some residents, such as Gil, born in São Tomé e Príncipe of Cape Verdean parents and who lived in BSF (as of August 2013, 90 percent of BSF had been demolished), felt lost, defeated, and often not a part of any scene in Lisbon. Speaking with me in 2011, Gil explained,

> When I was a kid, BSF was more alive. There were more people here, more community vibe. The thing is they don't just demolish our places in a day or so. No, it takes years. So, our BSF breaks up. Some people leave, some stay. You know,

## CHAPTER 4

FIGURE 11. Mural project on residential buildings in neighborhood Bairro de Santa Filomena (BSF). Photo by Utopia. Reprinted by permission from Utopia and Cursino Furtado.

like divide and conquer. It's hard to live here now. Random people move in and out. There's no collective spirit anymore.... It's a struggle but, as a rapper, I try to bring a little BSF reality to the overall Kriolu thing going on in Amadora.

The "they" in Gil's story is often a coordinated team of state and commercial employees whose goal is to appropriate the public land and develop it in a strategic manner in accordance with the dynamics of the market, usually middle-class apartment complexes, commercial space, or, occasionally, luxurious apartments (e.g., Parque das Nações). The temporality of the intra-urban migration, expressed by Gil as "it takes years," fragments the improvised neighborhoods and exposes the infrastructure to alternative, stigmatized socioeconomic activities, such as drug trafficking and prostitution. Both of these result in violence and add greater stigma to the residential area. Gil contrasted this temporality of gradual, sometimes painful transition with a nostalgia of the early years of BSF. The bygone "community vibe" itself followed a much-faster yet more distant interurban migration, predominantly from Praia or Tarrafal, Cape Verde, to Lisbon. As temporalities of experience collide for BSF residents in their identification with place, youth like Gil find a potential vehicle in Kriolu and the sociolinguistic practice of rap. He tried to articulate his local knowledge to a wider scene, the "overall Kriolu thing going on in Amadora," the municipality adjacent to Lisbon that includes BSF and the two residential foci of this chapter, Boba and Cova da Moura.

## Kriolu Attempts at Neighborhood Formation: Boba and Kova M

The neighborhoods of Cova da Moura and Boba demonstrate a contrast in terms of the relationships among language, space, identity, and urban policy. I visited Cova twelve times and Boba six times between 2007 and 2013. Visits ranged from an hour to eight hours, depending on the day of the week and the time of day of the visit. While Kova M is (in)famous as Lisbon's largest improvised neighborhood, predominantly of residents of Cape Verdean descent, Boba is a smaller and more recent state project. Interesting, many of the most well-known and respected Kriolu rappers have emerged from the milieu of a multilayered transition—from Cape Verde to Lisbon to improvised to social neighborhood. This is the case of Ghoya, who along with his rapping partner, Boss, represents the problems of current relocation projects and the significance of Kriolu as a neighborhood signature.

Ghoya moved to the social neighborhood of Casal da Boba in the municipality of Amadora in 2001 when he was fifteen years old (figure 12). He had lived previously in Benfica municipality in the improvised neighborhood of Fontaínhas.[2] The demolition of Fontaínhas was part of PER (Special Program of Relocation), a project initiated in 1993 and sponsored by the Portuguese state and European Union agencies to eradicate the corrugated metal shanties (*bairro de lata*) from Portugal's main cities of Lisbon and Oporto by the year 2000. Many of the residents from the Fontaínhas demolition ended up in Boba (note the reference to "Fontaínha" in figure 12). The main goal of PER is to relocate approximately 130,000 people who were living in unregulated, nonstandard, poorly serviced communities to places with infrastructure in the most efficient, cost-effective manner possible.

In October 2009 during our conversation in Boba, Ghoya described the relocation process after the demolition of Fontaínhas.

> The experience here has been shit. You see these buildings? They're less than ten years old, and you can see how they're crumbling. I mean, they didn't invest much in this. That's obvious. I'm old enough to remember Fontaínha and that was tough, but we made that. People put that on the map. . . . The housing officials think that now it's all solved just because they made these white, cement boxes and call it new and then publish in the media that we are "new"—meaning included folks. It's not true; there's no recognition. That's why you find young folks like me, Boss, and dozens of others out here yelling and screaming. We're not interested in just asking for some help at the door. We're going to bust down the door so we can get some rights to make this place into our own.

## CHAPTER 4

FIGURE 12. Casal da Boba in the municipality of Amadora. Photo by author, 2009.

According to Ghoya, the problem with Boba and the social neighborhood, more generally, is the assumed connection between spatial management, that is, urbanization, and a collective sentiment about the city, that is, urbanism. The idea that standardized housing of poor material quality represents inclusion into modern Portuguese society appears to Ghoya as a farce. Perhaps, what is most distasteful, as Ghoya interjected, "It's not true," is that such investment by the state and real estate contractors has changed the migrant community, approximately 60 percent of Boba was Cape Verdean in 2007, into "new" residents. Rather, in his claim that Boba fails to represent any substantive recognition by the state, Ghoya maintains that the social neighborhood has not addressed "spatial segmentation" or the "landscapes of inequality" embedded in neoliberal urbanization projects, such as PER (Suárez-Navaz 2004). The demolition of Fontaínhas and demographic transition of several hundred to Boba are facts of imposition. However, language both at the stylistic level of rap lyrics and the ubiquitous level of public chatter remains a social practice from which residents like Ghoya work to reconfigure Boba and, thus, "make this place into our own."

Kriolu is a linguistic practice that creates locality through social participation, that is, a "speech community," and a more literal connection of the discursive to the material of the city. In the case of moving from Fontaínhas to Boba, what was once done in the *becos* (labyrinth) of alleyways within shantytown living is carried out around the cement soccer court and in the nondescript cement courtyards between the residential buildings. Ghoya explains, "We start from the street. This is where we make ourselves. OK, it looks different here in Boba than in Fontaínha or wherever, but we make it work. That's one of the powers of Kriolu. We link Kriolu with rap to speak" (personal communication, 2009). Otávio Raposo, in his work with Red Eyes Gang, a group active in the early 2000s in the social neighborhood of Arrentela, makes a similar observation about the transformative properties of Kriolu with respect to the local environment.[3]

> The way the Red Eyes Gang appropriate Creole is an example of the dynamic reinvention of their parents' cultural heritage. Besides giving it their own characteristics, they withdrew it from the almost exclusive domain of the family, turning it into an urban language, of the street, and one that symbolizes belonging to a group of peers. It is the internal and daily language of the Red Eyes Gang, establishing itself as an instrument of transgression of the fundamental principles of the formal language of adults and school, besides serving as performative material to their cultural practices. (personal communication 2010)

The question is: how specifically does Kriolu reconstitute "street," if at all? In our conversations, Ghoya repeatedly employed "drama" in response to such queries, but it wasn't until I heard several of his recordings and discussed these songs with Kriolu rappers around Lisbon that I was able to grasp a deeper sense of the operative imaginary. The Kriolu words for *street* and *drama* do not depart from those of Portuguese, *rua* and *drama*, respectively. Rather, it is in the narrative where Kriolu distinguishes itself as an emphatic and aesthetic practice.

For example, in Ghoya's songs "Life Is like That: Today It's You, Tomorrow It'll Be Me" and "The Other Side of the Law," there is a frequent use of the first person objective case ("me") connected to the verb. This is a typical Kriolu verb-object construction that doesn't exist in Portuguese or in English for that matter. Ghoya places himself immediately in the songs as under stress or under an imposition: *es kritikam* (they criticized me). Other examples include: *es dam* (they gave me) and *es mandam* (they told me or demanded from me). The phoneme of *m* when connected to the verb changes the rhetorical stress from the conventional penultimate syllable *kritika* to the last syllable in *kritikam* thereby creating the highlighted morpheme of *me*. Moreover, Ghoya and others often create emphasis, authority, and rhythmic tempo by using regularly *djam bai*, a phrase ranging in meaning from "I'm outta here" or "I'm off" to "I'm going to do [something]," depending on subsequent text. The significance here beyond the *m* is the urgency and accentuation of *dja*, the idea being that "my actions will take place right now."

## CHAPTER 4

The aesthetic features of *kritikam* and *djam bai* are part of a Kriolu sound, and due to the success of rappers such as Ghoya, LBC, Chullage, and others, such sonorous qualities serve to reconstitute the "Lisbon sound" within popular music scenes (Connell and Gibson 2003:90–116).[4] These rhetorical stress points give a punchy quality to the sound of Kriolu rap and enable the rapper to achieve the narrative goal of authority by way of a crisis in the form of "something is happening to me."

Ghoya's musings on imposition is a drama often accompanied by sound mixes featuring synthesizers with sequences of high-pitched string instruments articulated in high reverberation. For Ghoya it is the "false nigga" and the "system" that work against him and, by extension, all his "people" of Boba and the "real" Kriolu rap scene. How is "reality" reconstituted? For Ghoya, sometimes it is not possible, and his "feelings of rage and pain [related to police brutality, unemployment, jealousy] go to prison, to the casket," but if it is to happen, it is through the "sentiments of place" ("Other Side of the Law"). Ghoya raps in "Vida é assi" (2009),

> What we niggas have in common is suffering and solitude.
> Recover that nigga in this place right now.
> The other side is a movement that hasn't fallen.
> These are our suburbs and streets.
> Disillusion is enemy number one.

Somewhat vague in his attempt to address suffering, Ghoya does locate it in a way that is both specific to the urban margins of Lisbon and general enough to include anyone with sentiments of marginality. Based on fieldwork conversations with local rappers in Praia, I can affirm that Ghoya's stories have reached audiences not only back "home" in Cape Verde but also in other diasporic locales of Rotterdam and Paris, thereby suggesting a transnational dimension to Ghoya's descriptions of his struggles in Boba and Lisbon, more generally.

Certainly, Kriolu is about being Cape Verdean, as for the past five hundred years, residents have spoken Kriolu in public and privates spaces without any official recognition by the Portuguese colonial administration or, later, the independent Cape Verdean state. Yet, in the case of Ghoya and others, discussed below, Kriolu is not necessarily about the place of Cape Verde. Kriolu, as a symbolic system, affords a structured way of routinizing imagination, a "fantasy" of community inside a society that historically has recognized Cape Verdeans and the Kriolu language as productive intermediaries on the way to become Portuguese in the late stages of empire as well as in the current milieu of citizenship in the "New Europe" (Weiss 2002).

If Kriolu is a kind of "social imaginary," a routinized medium of "worlding" or reality shaping, have Boba residents translated the spoken language into an identifying landmark? While in Boba, Kriolu and the more general experience of migration have yet to grow beyond a daily tenor of difference in relation to the concrete boxes of apartment residence, the case of Cova da Moura provides an alternative model of neighborhood space and identity.

## Kova M

Alto da Cova da Moura, or Kova M, is a large, mostly improvised neighborhood in the municipality of Amadora, two miles south of Boba. Given Kova M's relative unofficial status, demographic information on its population varies significantly. While government numbers report six thousand people (ACIDI 2010), and independent sources cite ten thousand residents (Vaz 2011), what is generally agreed upon is that, similar to Boba, Cape Verdeans make up roughly 60 percent of Kova M. In contrast to the story involving Fontaínhas and Boba, Lisbon officials decided to spare Kova M from the PER demolition and urban renewal plan, in part due to the dynamics of local patronage (Horta 2001). Figure 13 shows the main entrance to Cova, the entrance closest to the train station.

Similar to Boba, in Kova M, youth are also present in great numbers and want to link talk to neighborhood landmarks. This is what youth call making *cenas* (scenes). Two different types of "scenes" are, first, institutional, exemplified in the landmark of Moinho da Juventude (mill of youth) (figure 14). The second scene highlights nighttime strolling and car cruising around the neighborhood. *Moinho* translated as *mill* is a connection to a traditional part of the Cape Verdean economy. However, perhaps, the best translation of *moinho* in this case is to draw from the colloquial phrase "to take the water to the mill," meaning to get the job done. The connotation here is more about achievement; therefore, one might understand Moinho da Juventude as an organization of youth achievement. Moinho da Juventude began in the 1984 as a grassroots project to improve living conditions and health care as well as provide day care and professionalization workshops for Cova da Moura residents. It employs approximately ninety people and is categorized as a nonprofit organization.

Moinho, which sits atop the Kova M hill, was founded by and continues to be managed by mostly Cape Verdean women. Many of these women express a longer view of history with life experiences of transnational and domestic migration dating back to the late 1970s. Their stories of domestic labor and daily struggles on the Kova M hill reminded me of an observation made by the British historian Basil Davidson. In a discussion of the slave rebellions in Cape Verde preceding the more formalized movements for independence in the mid-twentieth century, Davidson makes a comment on space: "Slaves seized their freedom, especially on the big island of Santiago, where, even now, the layout of solitary homesteads far

FIGURE 13. The main entrance into Kova M. Photo by author, 2009.

FIGURE 14. Moinho da Juventude in Kova M. Photo by author, 2009.

up the mountainsides or niched in high and pathless gullies still bears witness to the freedom that was seized" (1989:14). Although Davidson committed some historical errors related to plantations, such as comparing Cape Verde to Jamaica, his method of reading social history into the land is a productive one and worth application to the Kova M hillside.

As children ran by the Moinho buildings, Heidir, aspiring rapper, sound engineer, and veteran community activist, revealed his connection to the center. Before we met in 2009, Heidir had been in prison for over two years for drug trafficking; his brother, sentenced to five years, was in the same building. While in prison, they wrote pages of lyrics, and soon after he returned to Kova M, Heidir spent as much time as possible in the new confines of the Moinho recording studio. He saw it as a "platform to make a scene." We arrived at the recording studio, Heidir inserted his USB pen drive into the computer, cued up the control board, and made the desired adjustments for bass and volume. He signaled for me to sit beside him and soak up the sounds and lyrics. We listened without looking at or speaking to each other during the seven-minute song. It was intense; Heidir never once looked at me. While he mouthed his lines and bobbed his head to the pounding downbeat of the bass drum, I stared at the lone microphone in the insulated recording room. I thought about amplification and platforms. Later, Heidir talked about his song.

> You see. That [the song] right there is drama. It is real experience. It is straight up Kova M. You know, outside of the neighborhood there are few options for us. Few people really move away because we end up finding something in our immediate surroundings that we connect with and make into something ... a living. For me and many others, it was drugs. But that is a dead end. Cova da Moura has more scenes. That's a good thing. For me, rap and, even more to the point, Kriolu rap, is a good scene. There are two types of songs for me—drama and party. Drama, like the song I did with my brother right there, is real; it's about learning. It's fact. It's not about celebrating violence. It's just fact. Party is about celebrating Kova M; it's about pleasure and the spots.

The landmark status of the Kova M studio is not a secret. Many Lisbon-based Kriolu rappers record in Kova M, and, increasingly, more tuga rappers are embracing Kova M as a respected point in the hip-hop scene. In addition, directors of state cultural agencies, such as Programas Escolhas, an organization that works with immigrant youth with issues of citizenship, education, and employment, have sponsored sound-engineering workshops and rap contests linked to Kova M.[5] The colloquial reference of *Kova M* is instructive in this context because its proponents, rappers, such as Heidir and LBC, purposefully inject Kriolu language politics into the spatial politics of scene making.

## CHAPTER 4

The letter *k* does not officially exist in the Portuguese language, but it appears usually as a reference to English and, by extension, the global cache of the United States and American culture. While, certainly, Kriolu rappers are influenced by U.S. rappers' use of English, in this case, as well as with Khapaz, the cultural center, the *k* refers to a difference from *tuga* and *Portugal*. It is not crioulo; it is Kriolu. It is not Cova da Moura but Kova M. Kriolu rappers through orthography, pronunciation, and recording-studio hype have coupled language and space together and proposed it as a neighborhood value and an implicit obligation for others to learn or, at least, engage with Kriolu on its own terms.

Kriolu emplacement is not only a formal endeavor but also an everyday part of locality. My emerging friendships with Heidir and LBC garnered a series of weekend evening invitations. On one particular Saturday night, I arrived in Kova M unannounced. I decided to climb the main road (see figure 13) and not take my chances navigating the labyrinth of alleyways Heidir and LBC had shown me in prior visits. After the first fifty yards, I heard nothing but Kriolu. Children of all ages, young adults, and a few elderly folks were out in the streets. People were hanging out, sitting on steps, visiting friends, and making plans.

The evening's next scene was at the café owned by LBC's mother. Dona Anastácia welcomed me and told me to stay, as a funaná band would shortly begin to play. (Funaná, a Cape Verdean dance music typical of the island of Santiago that until independence was considered too "African" and "backward" for national identification, is now one of the most popular genres of cultural consumption both inside the archipelago and abroad.) Young men had already occupied the tile-covered balcony. They were drinking sodas, playing cards, and talking soccer. Instead of music stores or conventional entertainment clubs, Kriolu scenes in Lisbon root themselves during the nighttime hours in cafés like this one.

Alyson, a twenty-year-old rapper and recent immigrant from Santiago, impressed the men with his stories of Praia and the rough nature of living through droughts, dengue fever, and constant power outages. He battled rhetorically with the tales of money and labor from another rapper, Simão, who was in town from the popular Cape Verdean diasporic community of Rotterdam, Holland, to visit his mother and sister. The small crowd egged them on and eventually drowned out Alyson and Simão with "now, you all are here—the heart of Kriolu in Portugal. This is Kova M. Yeah!" As dozens of young men shouted, "*Kel li, Kova M*" (It's [going on] here [in] Kova M), others added, in English, "Black lyrics, soldiers soldiers, ghetto life." The juxtaposition of Kriolu and English, when approached from the perspective of practice, is less about the use of a stable entity called English or Kriolu and more about social practices of interest and persuasion, in this case celebrating the centrality of Kova M in reality knowledge based on experiences of blackness, masculinity, poverty, and violence.

As one can imagine from this chapter's photographs of improvised neighborhoods, Kova M is not an easy place to drive, with streets so narrow that cars can barely get by all the people who are seemingly always outside. However, car travel is actually important in Kova M for those of some means. Cars become mobile stages for individuals and groups with reputations to amplify what Heidir described as "party" or leisure life, as opposed to "drama" rap.

Heidir hailed me, LBC, and Kromo over to his car, and we took off. I realized that our cruising around curves and practically going nowhere logistically were parts of a game that included swerving, yelling out to everyone, and pumping a mix of Kova M–studio Kriolu rap and the latest tunes by Lil Wayne and 50 Cent. Heidir turned on the car's twelve-inch LCD screen and cued up a series of Jay-Z, 50 Cent, and Black Eyed Peas videos. Over the next hour or so, we made the rounds, stopping at this and that corner, asking to talk with so-and-so, and inquiring about the whereabouts of so-and-so's sister. While Heidir exchanged extended greetings with Kova M residents, LBC joked but with serious undertones that we were outlining the youth boundaries of the neighborhood, the *limiti di genti*, in our excursion. From an informational standpoint, very little was exchanged in these conversations, and inside the car, the sheer volume of sound precluded much chitchat. When we arrived back in the area close to Dona Anastácia's café and the funaná music, Heidir turned around and asked, "So, D, did you feel Kova M?"

The joyride was meaningful on several levels. As is per the norm in ethnographic research, it would only be later that I began to interpret Heidir's question as a provocation to consider the spatiality of the Kriolu keyword of *xinti*, "to feel," the base of "sentiment." *Feeling* affords an understanding of youth leisure and everyday drama. In effect, the videos doubled as inside entertainment for the passengers as well as a complement to the interior and exterior lighting of the car. We glided by bumping and illuminating trails in the neighborhood—a party pod in the name of Kova M.

## Kriolu Emplacement as a Form of Citizenship

Local rappers' use of Kriolu in Lisbon exemplifies what Nicholas de Genova (2010) has described as the conflict between an "autonomy of migration" and state sovereignty. Cape Verde was born out of an early Creole formation involving Portuguese sailors, West African traders, and displaced Muslims and Jews migrating out of Iberia. Movement as part of an overall spatial recognition is an essential part of Cape Verdean practices of language and identity. Most recently, the Portuguese state and third-party real estate developers have provided another scenario in the long series of (dis)emplacement dramas for Cape Verdeans as Lisbon administrations have pushed to demolish improvised housing and regroup people into social neighborhoods.

# CHAPTER 4

While in the United States, public opinion continues to reckon the housing "project" as a slum, a negative residue of modern architecture, and an obsolete form of urbanization, in Lisbon, as is the case in many other parts of the world, the project, or social, neighborhood is a primary response to postcoloniality made manifest in migration demographics and the reorganization of labor. The case of Lisbon housing fits within the spectrum of reactions and policies based on a set of expectations by European states regarding migrants, labor, and city space after World War II (Huttman, Saltman, and Blauw 1991; Karakayali and Rigo 2010). A convergence of increased labor demand in former European metropoles, increased political instability in African colonies, and, in the case of Portugal, persistent ethnocentric racism, cloaked in a national ideology of hierarchical multiculturalism (i.e., Lusotropicalism), occurred and helped create the political and market opportunity of social housing.

It is not the case that social housing is necessarily bad, and improvised housing is pure positivity but, rather, that the gradual shift of the working poor to the social neighborhoods in the Lisbon metro area has provoked many local youth to make more explicit their claims to place, not only because they try to combat stigma related to displacement but also because they strive to transform standardized urban planning into cultural identity. Moreover, the move to social housing has fortified the spirit of a cadre of activists to maintain improvised neighborhoods, such as Kova M, as distinct spaces. Cape Verdean Kriolu has emerged as one idiom with which youth work to reclaim control over their identification with space. From this perspective, the Kriolu case supports the current scholarship regarding diaspora and place, which argues that migrants are significantly invested in being active "subjects" rather than simply "objects" (Anderson and Lee 2005:15).

The relationship between urbanization policies and urban experiences is a problem of agency, that life path of connecting self to recognized social structures. The Kriolu distinction within the milieu of immigration and housing in the New Europe is embedded in the chronotopes of a relatively inclusive Portuguese colonialism with regard to Cape Verdeans and the differentiated linguistic practices of Cape Verdean Creole. Kriolu rap in Boba is an outburst of conflict, a rage against the machine. In Kova M, rappers also adopt this tone with respect to issues of employment, education, and immigration. However, they speak from more solid ground, and the sociospatial achievements of Cova da Moura facilitate a link between Kriolu and the pleasures of tourism, café life, day care, and parades. In the words of Heidir, there are simply many more "scenes" in Kova M.

The ethnographic cases of Kova M and Boba demonstrate that language and space are essential elements in identity formation because they mediate social history and citizenship politics, in this case, around the processes of migration, labor, gender, and race. Furthermore, the fact of territorial possession or leasing is not equal to the occupation of space. It is through occupation or emplacement that people invest value into space and are more or less recognized by the state as contributing to city or national culture. Kriolu scenes still do not resonate with the Portuguese state in any sustained systematic way and, thus, reveal part of the discontent between migrants and the state in postcolonial Portugal. Such case studies as this one provide insight into a global phenomenon—the interdependent and constitutive relationship between space and discourse in the milieu of postcolonial identity formation.

# CHAPTER 5

# Kriolu and European Interculturality

Dear Derek,
 No stress my friend
 *Poucos, mesmo muito poucos foram para CV, só alguns dos mais velhos (por acaso os meus pais foram).*
 *A maioria reimigrou para: Espanha, França, Suíça, Inglaterra, Luxemburgo, Alemanha, Angola, EUA, pois apesar da crise ser global, Portugal é muito pequeno e tem a* TROIKA.
 *Sim o Talude está na mesma situação que o 6 de Maio, fazem todos parte do mesmo circuito da 1ª grande vaga de imigração para Portugal.*
 *E pan flau, ami n'bem aprendi skrevi na krioulo dipos di 26 anus na portugal e n kumesa papea ku 14 ano na* TALUDE
 KEL ABRASU
 *DI BADIU PÉ RATXADU CRIADU NA DIASPORA*
 *Com os melhores cumprimentos, R*

[Dear Derek,
 No stress, my friend
 Very few CV immigrants have migrated back to CV, just some elderly (coincidentally, my parents went back).
 The majority have emigrated to Spain, France, Switzerland, England, Luxembourg, Germany, Angola, and the U.S., because despite the fact that the crisis is global, Portugal is more acutely affected due to its small size and the 'troika' austerity measures.[1]
 Yes, Talude is in the same situation as the neighborhood 6 de Maio; they are both products of the first big wave of CV migration to Portugal.
 (In Kriolu) I have to tell you, I have learned how to write in Kriolu only after 26 years living in Portugal. I started

speaking Kriolu more directly at around 14 years old here in
TALUDE NEIGHBORHOOD.
WARM REGARDS
FROM A PROUD BADIU BROUGHT UP IN THE DIASPORA,
R(olando)]

Given all of the heterogeneity within the identity category of Cape Verdean, the one aspect that all agree upon is that Cape Verdeans are essentially migrants. I never met a Cape Verdean who had not migrated at least once or whose immediate relative had not migrated to one of the many substantial communities throughout the Atlantic region, including the Americas, Western Europe, and West Africa. For the purposes of the overarching argument that there is something we can call "creole citizenship" and that it influences what it is to be "Portuguese," I am interested less in the motivations behind migration and more interested in the migration as a shaping force in the "host" country.[2]

The influence of Kriolu on ideologies, history, identities, and territories related to Portugal, specifically the Lisbon area, emerged and has been maintained through the encounter relationship. I have theorized such a relationship as a mode of being in the world and knowing the self and other. The last two chapters drew upon more material evidence and argued in more practical terms of neighborhood and housing politics. Recalling those discussions along with the historical evidence of race and labor relations in chapter 1, we are prepared to engage policy debates and test Kriolu as a model for citizenship. Moreover, I consider the Kriolu case within the more general milieu of the so-called New Europe. This leads to two questions: What does Kriolu tell us about the state of multiculturalism and interculturality as examples of European community ideals? Using the terminology of Phil Wood, Charles Landry, and Jude Bloomfield (2006), some of the original authors of the concept of interculturality, might Kriolu provide a special insight into "intercultural competence"?

I take the position that discussions of citizenship and migration necessitate a dialogue between experiences and policies. Migrants of all backgrounds think in this way as a matter of course in their identification paths coupling agency and structure. Using the email above, Talude, the place, signifies a braided set of conditions. Rolando, author of this email, told me when we met personally in 2013 that his family moved in 1984 from Santiago island to Talude, a neighborhood in Loures, a municipality to the north of Lisbon, on the suggestion of other settled Cape Verdean migrants and based on Talude's favorable ratio of rent to domicile size. In his account, Rolando jumped to 1993 as another landmark, the year when

FIGURE 15. The main entrance into the Talude community center. Photo by author, 2013.

his brother and he started the Talude Neighborhood Association for Improvements and Recreation (AMRT) (figure 15).

"We joined a dozen other families in Talude," Rolando explained. "There were connections from the islands, family relations . . . connections built on just knowing a place in Tarrafal or Orgãos or a neighborhood in the capital city of Praia [all on Santiago island]. This helped. And, then there are traditions in Cape Verde of collective work, giving a hand [*djunta mon*] that we just do." Rolando's stories of homesteading, a narrative of pioneering place, speak to the culturally specific diasporic practices of Cape Verdeans, things "we just do," the obligation of culture. In addition, this brief excerpt from Rolando's memories shows how migration experiences make places, such as Talude.

*Talude* is also a laden signifier that reflects state policy. In 2011 with hundreds of immigrant families living in increasingly precarious situations due to the ever-encroaching demolitions of PER (Special Program of Relocation) (as evident in figure 16) and the rising unemployment in Portugal (as well as Spain and much of southern Europe) since 2010, the Loures municipal officials decided to halt efforts to financially compensate residents in these illegal neighborhoods as incentive

FIGURE 16. Part of the Talude neighborhood seen from the neighborhood center. Photo by author, 2013.

for relocation. In sum, Rolando's email to me in 2012 demonstrates, beyond the linguistic code-switching between Portuguese, Kriolu, and English, a selective braiding of family and neighborhood experiences (homesteading, community activism, return, and serial migration), state and European Union (EU) policies (troika), and Kriolu as a coping mechanism and a way forward.

## Cultural Citizenship in Europe

Rolando's email, our conversations, and my subsequent interpretation are based on the assumption that culture shapes citizenship. What sort of influence do cultural expressions and practices have on ideologies of belonging and ultimately politics of citizenship? As discussed in the introduction, I posit that a Creole perspective on citizenship necessarily defines culture and identity as emergent from the self-other encounter rather than as products of collective insularity and consolidation. Such a perspective is particularly interesting in Europe because until the end of World War II, citizenship, on the whole, was strongly associated with nationalism and antithetical to immigration.

## CHAPTER 5

The work of Renato Rosaldo (1994) helps frame my discussion. He describes the concept as a peculiar attempt to include difference (culture) into a normative and universalist category (citizenship). As Nick Stevenson (2001), Christian Joppke (2010), and others have warned, this sort of combination could appear and, indeed, has manifested itself as a kind of violent racism. Hannah Arendt ([1951] 1973) wrote long ago that the innovation of totalitarianism was the implementation of governance as absolute public culture over private rights. Postwar Europe has been notably cautious about the conflation of culture, Arendt's "public," and citizenship, Arendt's espousal of a guarantee to the individual member of a polity.

Yet, a convergence has occurred. Over the past generation, everyday people and public policy analysts from various political stripes have increasingly understood culture as relatively fluid and reflective of practices instead of a concept based on traditionally located groups. In a parallel fashion, we recognize citizenship as not only a set of obligations, regulations, and laws but also an activity, indeed, an exercise that potentially affords power. This convergence, aided by the intensity of exchange as part of globalization, has made the idea of "cultural citizenship" a robust site for hegemony and grassroots empowerment.

How does migrancy, the mode of being and thinking where movement takes a central role, affect this formulation? The influence of immigration in the dynamics of citizenship policies is not only reflected in markets and employment (Weiler 1999; Collett 2014) but also in the development of the concepts of culture and identity as conditions for political rights and social status. The problem of contemporary citizenship designs in Europe, whether they are framed in terms of republicanism or *laïcité* (secularism) in France, the citizenship tests of Britain, Germany, and Denmark, or the Luso discourses embedded in intercultural programs in Portugal, is how to be simultaneously inclusive and distinctive. Elizabeth Collett in her study on the role of immigrants in the current fever of city branding describes a similar phenomenon. She analyzes the policies and discourses of municipal governments as a balance between the desire to attract high-skilled-labor populations and the maintaining of a "diversity-proof" identity (2014). The operating logic is that significant immigration disintegrates local identity and correlates with a shared feeling of loss and alienation.

In the case of Lisbon, *music* is both a key word in city branding and an alarm for development. According to ACIDI, the main state agency in Portugal responsible for the implementation of intercultural policies and general aid to immigrant communities, "music's creative mediation of cultural identity [in conjunction with] the migrant and intercultural experience in Portugal and abroad reveals that mobility offers a challenge to the notions of citizenship and national tradition, which is significant for those whose profession is in social science, politics and social work" (2010:11). Put a slightly different way, the question of municipal administrations and civil societies is: how can contemporary citizenship address both the liberalism of individuality and the communality of the nation (Brubaker 1989)? Following Joppke (2010:111–44), since all forms of citizenship are located inside polities, this relationship is unavoidable.

Contemporary Europe is a fascinating location to test cultural citizenship theories, especially ones related to migration, exchange, and expressive culture. One obvious reason for this is demographic. In 2005, 85 percent of population growth in Europe can be attributed to non-European immigration (predominantly from Africa and Asia with a minority from the Americas). State agencies and cadres of entrepreneurs have translated this reality of migration into market opportunities. For example, *Lusofonia*, a term discussed in chapter 1 as a "colonial legacy" (see also Jerónimo 2006:29), has become an effective brand in the areas of economic trade agreements, educational pedagogy, and the music industry for contemporary Portugal, especially Lisbon, to cash in on Portugal's "tradition" of racial and ethnic mixture during colonialism in the current milieu of globalization and marketing of multiculturalism and interculturality. This migrancy branding is discussed in more detail below in relation to the series of events connected to European Year of Intercultural Dialogue (EYID) in 2008.

The importance of migrancy and culture to the conceptualization and regulation of citizenship is also epistemological. According to Eurostat (2011:144), "while 77% of Europeans attribute importance to culture, 91% of them agree that culture and cultural exchanges contribute to greater understanding and tolerance and 92% consider that culture and cultural exchanges should have an important place in the EU." In other words, Europeans, at least those polled, believe that one of the primary values of culture is the understanding of difference, broadly construed. Even in countries such as Germany, whose governance and popular ideologies since the 1960s have rarely, if ever, espoused Germany as an immigrant country, integration occurs not only at the level of political participation but also cultural practices (Loch 2014). Nevertheless, we must begin with the *recognition* of difference as one element of citizenship and, thus, one factor in the creation of a condition of rights, status, belonging, and participation.

In the case of Portugal, Lusotropicalism has been a discourse that administrators, intellectuals, and common folk cite to explain social integration of difference and the national distinction of history. Lusotropicalism played a role in the composition and implementation of colonial categories, such as "indigenous" and "assimilated," in order to simultaneously feign inclusion and extract labor in Africa. Portuguese labor practices and their articulations with race demonstrate what Carlos Vélez-Ibáñez terms a "commodity-identity" in his work on Mexican migrants in the United States. Nicholas de Genova describes a situation with which many Cape Verdeans and Luso-Africans could identify, "the stigmatization of undocumented Mexicans—as a people reducible to the disposability of their labor for a price—has become central to the racialization of all Mexicans/Chicanos and other Latinos (regardless of immigration status or even U.S. citizenship)" (2010:48).

Moreover, in chapter 2, I showed that Cape Verdean elite were particularly interested in Luso discourses as a medium of pitching their high art as local Kriolu distinction and connecting it to cultural "success" stories, such as Brazil. In the end, though, throughout the twentieth century, there was a significant gap between Lusotropicalism as inclusive discourse and lived reality, even among Cape Verdeans, the Africans supposedly closest to the Portuguese, and even in the daily experiences of elite Cape Verdeans residing in Lisbon. Put bluntly, Lusotropicalism turned out to be lacking or, perhaps better, inexistent as a set of citizenship policies. Rather, it along with other Luso discourses is a set of dynamic ideologies.

While European countries, such as Belgium, Sweden, the Netherlands, and France, experimented with multiculturalist public policies in regional councils, voting, and race relations, as well as multicultural discourses of integration starting in the 1960s (Vertovec 1998), Portugal clung to Lusotropicalism, a paradigm of unrealized promises increasingly revealed as empty by disenchanted public servants at "home" in Portugal and militarized forces in the overseas African and Asian territories. Both Luso and multiculturalism would run their courses and, ultimately, fail to ameliorate difference with integration.

The problem of contemporary citizenship is a problem of recognition. The current approach in Europe is one that highlights the term *interculturality*, meaning social interaction among different cultural groups with the goal of not only recognition but also socioeconomic and political equality. This is different from multiculturalism in that interculturality asserts equality through interaction, and multiculturalism assumes equality as a natural outcome emergent from separate allocation (properties, state funding, etc.). Multiculturalism is essentially a disengaged recognition, while interculturality discourages enclaves and asserts the opposite, that recognition and citizenship in contemporary nation-states with significant immigrant populations are the results of engaged social interaction.

## Citizenship in Postcolonial Portugal

If interculturality is an answer to the problem of citizenship in Europe, then, perhaps, the experiences of postcolonial Portugal can serve as a lesson, after all. Perhaps, Cape Verdean Creole can serve as a model that brings together the Portuguese history of sustained encounters with an appreciation of cultural difference, where *appreciation* is understood to include productive tension and even *cultural* black opposition. The 1970s and the transition from dictatorship to democracy focused on socioeconomic class rather than race and migration. Changing demographics and a reassertion of Africanity in Lisbon over the ensuing decades have influenced what citizenship in Portugal has come to mean. The question continues to be: what is the relationship between experience and policy, lives and law?

In 1973, a year before the collapse of the Portuguese fascist regime and the beginning of independent governance in Portuguese Africa, the elite students lodged in the "houses" of Cape Verde, Angola, and so on, which by the mid-1940s had consolidated into the Home for the Students of the Empire (*Casa dos Estudantes do Império*), grappled with the implications of the current events on their residence and student status inside Lisbon. After all, these casas were where the likes of Amilcar Cabral; Pedro Pires, former president, Cape Verde–Guinea-Bissau; Graça Machel, politician and widow of former South Africa president Nelson Mandela and Mozambican president Samora Machel; Eduardo Mondlane, founding president of FRELIMO, the Mozambican Liberation Front; and Agostinho Neto, revolutionary leader and first president of Angola, had stayed during their studies in the 1950s and 1960s. Such student housing, located in the contemporary middle-class neighborhood referred to as the *Avenidas*, a region that was part of the approved social housing projects of mid-twentieth-century Lisbon, was targeted by the International and State Defense Police (PIDE), the Portuguese secret police, who did surveillance. The housing projects were also the sites of African assimilation as part of the long durée of Luso civilization (Faria 1997). As João Carlos (2012) explains, the casas frequently functioned as an intermediary point in the trajectory from the *Mocidade Portuguesa* (Portuguese youth), a Portuguese version of the Nazi youth groups of the 1930s and 1940s, to official posts back in their respective African countries.

Operating in a Portuguese version of double consciousness, Cape Verdean leaders of the era, such as Maria Mascarenhas, navigated between middle-class aspirations of professionalism inside Portugal and the identity work of being Cape Verdean and Kriolu at a moment when thousands of their proletariat compatriots began to immigrate to Lisbon as manual laborers and improvise neighborhoods near the new suburban construction sites and industrial plants.

Mascarenhas used her space at the Cape Verde student house to publish brief editorials about a range of Cape Verdean concerns. In particular, she tried to respond to the alarming news reports about Cape Verdean violence in these new, precarious neighborhoods. The centrality of the knife in the stereotypical depiction of Cape Verdean young men from chapter 2 is an example. In addition, Mascarenhas's bulletins represent an early document of immigration information before the Portuguese state created SEF and well before ACIME, later renamed ACIDI. Based on a survey of approximately four hundred Cape Verdean laborers in Lisbon, Mascarenhas identified some basic dimensions of the postcolonial diaspora of Cape Verdeans in Lisbon. For example, only 2 percent paid for their travel to the metropole from their own pockets or from family coffers. The great majority relied on loans from Portuguese institutions of labor or established Cape Verdean organizations, such as Apoio aos Trabalhadores Cabo-Verdianos, a Cape Verde workers support group. Only 5 percent of those interviewed said that they would not return to the islands even if their life conditions greatly improved (Mascarenhas 1973:5). In sum, these surveys show that, on the one hand, Cape Verdeans during this period maintained a strong connection to the archipelago. By contrast, they also demonstrate that the Portuguese state and industry as well as the Cape Verde diaspora had invested in Cape Verdean immigration. Kriolu as island pride and labor integration would transform into a more emplaced model of citizenship, one that strives to be in Portugal but change what Portuguese means.

After the collapse of the Salazar-Caetano regime in 1974, Portugal spent a decade in political reorganization with a series of ad hoc administrations ranging from Cuban-style communism to military juntas. In the mid-1980s, the consolidation of power under the Social Democratic Party (PSD), a centrist party of social democrats, dovetailed with Portugal's entry into the EU in 1986. EU membership stabilized the economy and also significantly affected immigration flows. As a result, new state agencies dedicated time and resources to this "problem."

## Institutions and Experiences

The EU overall began to recognize interethnic, racial, religious, and cultural conflict during the 1990s. Consequently, in 1995 the European Council espoused the importance for "intercultural education" to be implemented as part of mainstream pedagogy with special attention to "tolerance" and "racism." In Portugal, this political tone led to a legal experimentation in 1992 and 1993 with Law 13/92 and DL 212/92 as "the first process to regulate foreigners" under current circumstances (Malheiros 1996). Subsequently, the Portuguese state formed ACIME (later ACIDI). Its mission is to "collaborate in the creation, implementation and evaluation of sector, crosscutting and public policies concerned with the integration of immigrants and ethnic minorities, as well as to promote the dialogue between the various cultures, ethnic groups and religions." ACIDI promotes equality, open dialogue, hospitality, and other core values (ACIDI 2014:11).

The aim of ACIDI is to keep the public informed of immigrant and intercultural news and dialogues by providing links to intercultural groups and communities (such as the Roma communities) in Portugal as well as an emergency hotline for immigrants. The agency also produces a magazine, *BI, Boletins Informativos* (informational bulletins), that has more information about intercultural events and news in Portugal (current distribution is six thousand copies); advertises and works with the Centro Nacional de Apoio ao Imigrante (National Center of Immigrant Support) (CNAI) around Portugal; and does immigrant outreach and aims to simplify the process of formal citizenship and social integration. ACIDI also has television and radio programs, as well as seminars for communications professionals dealing with immigrant portrayal in the media (ACIDI 2013).[3]

With regard to interculturality's role in the exercise of citizenship, ACIME, in a 2005 report, summarizes its seven essential principles of operation. The commission underscores the idea of the immigrant as a "*cidadão de pleno direito*" (citizen from a universal right). Moreover, the ACIME authors assert: "more than a simple acceptance of the 'other,' the intercultural model proposes the inclusion of the 'other' and the transformation of both parties from this encounter" (2005:16). It is this final part about mutual change vis-à-vis the encounter that is the real question in Portugal and other parts of Europe invested in interculturality as a model of citizenship.

We find inconsistencies right away, even in the very language adopted by ACIME/ACIDI in its reports. In a summary report from the same 2005 document, ACIME announces the founding of a joint effort by Portugal and Cape Verde to address the "integration of these immigrants, one of the oldest and most representative communities." The objectives listed have nothing to do with interculturality and everything to do with assimilation with special emphasis given to creating "mechanisms to control the migration flow and combat clandestine immigration" (2005:267, 268).

In 2011 I attended an event celebrating ten years of Programa Escolhas (PE), an ACIDI flagship project oriented toward immigrant youth. Scholars and policy makers throughout Europe converged on the modernist, oval, white, cement building in Parque das Nações, an area completely renovated, reurbanized, and cleared of immigrant and working-class clutter for Expo 1998, to share comparative data from youth projects in education and community action aided by ACIDI partnerships.[4] The event was intended as a resounding vote of confidence for Portugal's role in the European movement toward interculturality. Films were made, and narratives were collected. In a brief interview, Rosário Farmhouse, a trained anthropologist and the then national coordinator of ACIDI, explained to me, "Cape Verdeans are wonderful participants in our projects, but Kriolu as a language of interculturality is somewhat controversial. At least, in the districts.... In general, they are not interested in bilingual projects in their schools. Make sure Pedro [the director of Programas Escolhas] gives you their recent publication. In it you'll find some insightful stories of Cape Verdeans and some real exciting practices of citizenship in today's Portugal" (personal communication, 2011).

I did, indeed, pick up the parting gift, a collection of 365 "life stories" selected from over a hundred thousand youth who participated in the Programas Escolhas projects over the past decade. The stories are short and purposefully underscore the positive impact of PE projects on the youths' lives as a way of creating a more inclusive atmosphere. The publication states: "Portugal welcomes you. This is a great place to live. Be an active participant and a good citizen" (ACIDI 2011:72). In the words of one young Cape Verdean, Vânia Martins, the presence of PE in the social neighborhood of Vale da Amoreira (in the so-called South Margin of Lisbon on the other side of the Tagus River from Lisbon proper) was good because the program always had "their doors open to receive us and talk to us about our problems" (ACIDI 2011:72). Another Cape Verdean youth relates that PE helped to show that "not all the social neighborhoods are bad.... I learned that rage isn't always a way out in life, it is better to invest in ourselves" (ACIDI 2011:70).

Yet, as I perused the stories from Cape Verdeans and other PALOP youth, I noted that many of the Cape Verdeans, unlike other immigrant youth, tended to mention something about Cape Verde, the place, or Cape Verdean-ness, in general, as a positive result from the PE project. For example, Solange participated in the project called *Geração Cool* (The cool generation), which comprised learning how to make and market clothes to residents of a nearby improvised neighborhood (*zona*). She was proud when she stated, "I hung out with all these people and learned many new things.... I worked with PE for seven years and I was able finally to fulfill my dream of going to Cape Verde, the birthplace of my parents, and check it out. It was unforgettable!" (ACIDI 2011:11).

However, the stories I heard from Kriolu rappers from Kova M and the social neighborhood of Arrentela were overtly critical of PE. Not published were the partnership accounts from rappers, who were excited to promote, for example, a new recording studio in Kova M but were offended by the way PE representatives imposed certain norms of lyrics, performance, and other event staging. In the end, many Kriolu rappers felt used by this state agency, and, again, interculturality was diluted into Luso.

The SEF monitors Portugal's borders and patterns of migrants. It emerged as a result of the Carnation Revolution of 1974, in which the Salazar-Caetano regime ceded to a process of political democratization. With the dissolution of PIDE and the fragmentation of the armed forces, SEF (SE until 1986) became the agency of authority with regard to security issues in Portugal.[5]

SEF not only controls the movement of people at the country's borders but also monitors the activities of foreigners during their time in Portugal. SEFSTAT is its statistics portal that holds statistical information on migrants moving in and out of Portugal. The agency has collected statistics since 1980 (its website dates back to 2000) in what it calls the "evolution" of Portuguese immigration. Each official report is a compilation of immigration statistics and trends for the year. These statistics include mode of transport into the country, breakdown of migrants by country of origin, and refusal-of-entry counts. There is also a detailed account of the different border-control measures being taken each year.

The general trends measured by SEF parallel the histories of labor and race discussed in chapter 1 in that Cape Verdeans, relative to other Luso-Africans, continue to have greater formal access to citizenship. Their petitions for Portuguese identification cards are more frequently granted. On the ground, however, in daily experience, Cape Verdeans also continue to be the immigrant community of a former Portuguese colony who most hold on to home-country identity. This would seem to support the notion that Portuguese citizenship for Cape Verdeans signifies a pragmatic status, a set of conditions for employment, educational, and housing opportunities and not a cultural-identity category.

"I go in between the worlds of Kriolu and tuga hip-hop," MC Tigre explains. She likes to present herself in this way and describe her place in the Lisbon scene. She is pleasantly gregarious and mingles just as well with the hardcore rappers of Kova M as with state employees of ACIDI. She had already struck up a giddy conversation with Vera, one of the coordinators of Interculturalcidade, a fusing of *intercultural* and *cidade* (city). Interculturalcidade is an NGO dedicated to promoting interethnic diversity as part of a particularly Lisboeta form of cultural citizenship. The organization has received funding from European agencies as well as the Portuguese state to hold artistic workshops, conduct sociological research on the São Bento neighborhood (part of what used to be the Mocambo region as chapter 1 describes),[6] and provide different immigrant communities, especially PALOP, a place to gather and share experiences. Vera and Janice seemed like old friends as they reminisced and discovered that they were both from Mindelo, the main city on São Vicente island, and moved early in life to Praia city and then on to various neighborhoods in Lisbon. MC Tigre/Janice comments on her new friend.

> It's funny. We know many of the same places back *na terra* [a common reference among Cape Verdeans to the archipelago, a home land of sorts] but here, she [Vera] is quite comfortable and enjoys living and working in the São Bento neighborhood. I think that's great, but she doesn't have so much to say when

conversation turns to some of my places like Chelas and 6 de Maio. I'm glad you brought me here. It's a great space, but no one has heard of this Interculturalcidade where I live. There needs to be more work to bring us all together. As you know I like to say, I go in between Kriolu and tuga hip-hop.

MC Tigre's reflections on meeting Vera and introduction to the organization Interculturalcidade demonstrate the lack of penetration of interculturality into immigrant neighborhoods. Chelas is a massive social neighborhood in northern Lisbon; 6 de Maio is an improvised neighborhood, somewhat similar to Kova M, located in a neighboring municipality of Amadora. Although Vera shares certain life experiences and place references with Janice, they have different views of what constitutes Lisbon. Both women, in fact, hold Portuguese citizenship, but they differ in how they exercise cultural citizenship.

## Cities and Citizenship

The example of Interculturalcidade is a reminder of the importance of space when discussing citizenship. The recognition of difference does not take place in a void; social experiences and political policies must be understood in spatial terms. The city has become the primary site for migration and correspondingly for citizenship policies. Globally speaking, urban population, what was once a slight majority of 52 percent in 2011, will be 67 percent of the world's population by 2050. Such an increase represents 2.7 billion more people living in cities (United Nations 2013:105–6). Specific to Europe, the EU sponsored a number of programs directly related to interculturality in the city. For example, Intercultural Cities Program (ICP) started in 2008. Lisbon joined the pilot group of eleven cities in 2010, and by the next year, Portugal added Oporto and Coimbra to form an internal network of three cities. The significance of ICP lies in its attempt to measure and interpret what interculturality means and how it is interpreted and implemented at the city and neighborhood levels. The sentiment of the reports is that reliable and inclusive metrics of interculturality will provide evidence as to the effectiveness of intercultural programs on issues of tolerance, violence, and basic bonds of civil society. Based on a complex survey of sixty-six questions about education, neighborhood, public services, business and labor markets, cultural and civil life, public spaces, mediation and conflict resolution, language, media, international outlook, intelligence competence, welcoming, and governance practices, ICP researchers created an intercultural index to evaluate twenty-nine European cities.[7]

The role of Kriolu comes to the fore in the data collected on Lisbon, Amadora, and Rotterdam. Amadora is the home of several rappers featured in this book, including LBC, MC Tigre, Ghoya, Boss, Hezbollah, and Kromo. The Cape Verdean population is relatively strong and consolidated. As told in Simão's story in chapter 4, Rotterdam, an industrial port city in the Netherlands, also has a significant Cape Verdean community. At 2.5 percent, Cape Verdeans are the fifth-largest immigrant community in Rotterdam, a city in which 48 percent of the total population—and 70 percent of the youth population—has an "immigrant background" (Entzinger and Engbersen 2014:4).

Amadora and Lisbon rank near the bottom of the general index of intercultural cities. According to an Intercultural Cities report, an intercultural city "has people with different nationality, origin, language or religion/belief. Political leaders and most citizens regard diversity positively, as a resource. The city actively combats discrimination and adapts its governance, institutions, and services to the needs of a diverse population. The city has a strategy and tools to deal with diversity and cultural conflict. It encourages greater mixing and interaction between diverse groups in the public spaces" ("Lisbon" 2014:2). Rotterdam is in the upper half.[8] My interest in these policy reports is not so much about the rankings themselves but about the categories where Lisbon and Amadora revealed certain contradictions. As suggested throughout this chapter, such efforts to quantify interculturality are only meaningful if used in a complementary fashion with personal narratives, contextual political history, and socioeconomic studies.

The policy analyses show that Lisbon's and Amadora's greatest intercultural weaknesses were in the pragmatic aspects of bringing together different sociocultural groups. For example, Lisbon scored the lowest of all participating European cities on projects that give a "positive image to migrant or minority languages." In addition, Lisbon's performance in conflict resolution, education, and intercultural neighborhood interaction was subpar. In more discursive categories, such as media, governance, and welcoming practices, Lisbon did remarkably well. Amadora faired a bit better overall mainly due to the fact that municipal agencies invested less in welcoming practices and more in public spaces and conflict resolution. The statistics suggest that Cape Verdeans and other PALOP residents, who make up more of a percentage of Amadora than of Lisbon, have been more active and, thus, more effective in transforming Amadora into an intercultural city relative to the touted Lisbon, the capital of Lusotropicalism and Lusofonia. Perhaps, the rubs and grinds of difference central to the screeds of LBC, Ghoya, and others are finding some traction and reasserting Creole as a path toward interculturality and a more robust migrant citizenship. The next section offers several provisional suggestions for intercultural policy along these lines.

In another EU-sponsored program aimed at using intercultural principles to reorganize city security, called Urban Safety, we find similar gaps between rhetoric and implementation. Lisbon officials were proud about receiving funding in 2010 and 2011 to carry out police training in three neighborhoods. The proposed idea of improving the relationship between police and community through intercultural methods and guiding principles was assumed to be easier among Lisbon police. A version of the Luso story surfaced, and police officers discussed their role as part of a cultural context. Curiously, two of the three neighborhoods were predominantly tourist areas with very few immigrant residents. In essence, Lisbon officials had transformed the intercultural security initiative into an opportunity to fund more police presence in the lucrative city spaces of Baixa, Chiado, and Alfama.

The crown jewel of Europe's policy initiatives around interculturality occurred when the European Parliament and the Council of the European Union issued a decision to designate 2008 as the European Year of Intercultural Dialogue (EYID).[9] The report, *Sharing Diversity*, supported by the European Commission, focuses on globalization and proposes a set of ideological and pragmatic goals for agencies of EU members to consider as they embark on funding application.

The key words of the initiative are *pluralism, solidarity*, and *coherence*. The first relates to the sociocultural reality of contemporary Europe. The second term refers to the stated intention of intercultural dialogue, that is, to foster a pragmatic sense of solidarity among individual and social groups for the common good of Europe. The first two key words articulate what Ginette Verstraete describes as the "worldwide marketing of unity-in-diversity" within the European identity project (2010:10). Finally, *Sharing Diversity* cites the third word, *coherence*, along with "cohesion" as objectives, which the commission should provide in its allocation of funds and supervision of member states' projects (European Institute for Comparative Cultural Research 2008:33–34).

Despite the fact that most of the EYID projects occurred elsewhere other than Portugal and despite its marginal status with regard to the "project of Europe," Portugal continues to be a rhetorical point of reference in the management of diversity in arenas of citizenship and expressive culture. In 2006 Portuguese legislators revised the Law of National Citizenship (*Lei da Nacionalidade*), thereby expanding citizenship in quantitative and qualitative terms, often citing the long tradition of Portuguese Lusotropicalism as a precursor to *interculturalidade* (interculturality). In 2008 the Portuguese shifted the legal theoretical framework around citizenship from one of jus sanguinis, moving toward to one of jus solis,[10] which extended legal rights to many residents whose parents were born abroad but who themselves were born in Portugal.

In the area of expressive culture, a range of individuals, NGOs, and businesses has attempted to promote Lisbon as a center of multiculturalism, mixture, hybridity, and intercultural conversation. For example, in *Lisboa Mistura* (Lisbon mix), a celebratory book of textual and photographic essays, sponsored by the Lisbon municipal government and published by the nonprofit organization Sons da Lusofonia (Lusophone sounds), a wide range of authors, scholars, and artists urges the reader to participate in diversity, with the hopes that Lisbon would realize its potential and see what it is—a creative, diverse metropolis and an exemplar of urban reflection, in particular, during 2008.

The EYID promoted interculturality on many different fronts. Beyond flashy catalogues, multicultural coffee-table books, and other forms of cultural tourism, the EYID facilitated investment in already established centers of expressive culture, entertainment, and community workshops in cities, such as Lisbon. During September and October 2009, I attended several performances as part of a series Dream of the World: Africa on Sundays at Bartô, a bar in the basement of Chapitô, an NGO dedicated to art education, social work on issues of equality, and expressive culture.

On one particular Sunday night, I waited for the group Belanafa to begin. According to the monthly program pamphlet, Belanafa consisted of virtuosic Guinean musicians on the guitar and kora and with voice (in the languages of Mandinga and the Guinean variant of Kriol) as well as Portuguese musicians holding down the rhythm section of the bass guitar and drum set. As I waited, stuck once again in a game of patience, hedging whether or not to order another drink, I decided to read for the third time the event program on the bar. My eyes had passed over the words without registering anything linguistic. On the third scanning, my eyes focused on a curious phrase toward the end of the band description—"a welcome accomplishment for World Music, made in Portugal by Portuguese." Belanafa finally arrived on stage and began to play while images from a British documentary film about the social uses and technical apprenticeship of the kora in rural Guinea-Bissau appeared on a screen behind the band.

In this example of sponsored inculturality, the spatial connotation of Portugal and otherness is reversed. Through cultural production, one supposedly can conjure directly a Portugal, expressed by others and transformed into a Portuguese entity. The Guineans, who do not possess Portuguese citizenship, become Portuguese in a gesture of honorary citizenship, at least insofar as entertainment advertisement.

However, I wonder to what extent the collages of popular culture represent a paradigm shift of Portuguese citizenship. In events, such as Lisboa Mistura and Festa do Jazz Português, or places, such as Teatro São Jorge and Chapitô, or with pop phenomena, such as Buraka Som Sistema, are we witnessing, as implied in a 2008 *Lisboa Mistura* essay by ACIDI's Farmhouse, a conversation (one-way) or a dialogue (two-way) between PALOP and Portugal?

## CHAPTER 5

## Turning Interpretation into Policy

In his opening statement of approval of the 2007 Immigration Integration Plan of ACIDI, the Portuguese Prime Minister José Sócrates admits that Portugal had no "global plan" and has yet to afford "co-responsibility" to immigrant communities in the formation of public policies of contemporary society (Sócrates 2007:3–4). In the sections "education" and "language and culture," the council resolution explicitly calls for a more systematic insertion of a pedagogy of Portuguese as a foreign language (*Portuguesa como a Língua Não-Materna*) into the national curriculum; however, there is no mention of bilingual or multicultural education per se (ACIDI 2007:16, 22). This omission has occurred despite state-sponsored scholarship and conferences held by academics, NGOs, and state employees.[11] Such observations demonstrate the operative contradictions between intercultural discourse and effective implementation in Lisbon and Amadora.

Corrective policy could include the formal recognition of Kriolu as an official language. It would not be unprecedented. In 1998 the Portuguese parliament officially recognized Mirandês, a language spoken by approximately fifteen thousand people in the northern regions of Bragança, Miranda do Douro, and Vimiosa. In addition, after various legislative sessions in Praia in late 2008 and early 2009, the parliament voted to implement ALUPEK as an official alphabet.

As demonstrated throughout this book in several different scenes and in various forms, Kriolu as a language is not only essential to Cape Verdean identity, even in consideration of the significant class, gender, and island hierarchies, but also formative of *ser português*, the mode of being Portuguese. Moreover, Kriolu language has contributed to the shaping of Lisbon spaces. There are historical material traces and active emplacement practices resulting from speaking Kriolu and Cape Verdean–Portuguese contact. For these reasons, the state, at least in the municipalities of Lisbon, Amadora, Seixal, Setúbal, Loures, and other Lisbon metro areas, should implement Kriolu language classes as part of the curriculum. Such policy is also not unprecedented. Public school teachers in Vale da Amoreira in the municipality of Seixal have periodically succeeded in implementing Kriolu language classes as part of the general curriculum.[12]

I return to the concept of chronotope, one of the key words of analysis in this book, as a guide in the following policy recommendations. Many who identify as Cape Verdean, Kauberdianu, or Kriolu are aware of the time-place convergences that make up Portuguese identity. They are institutionalized in monuments of Camões and towers of Belém. Kriolu rappers, in particular, strive to infuse their lyrics with alternative chronotopes to challenge these conventional configurations with chronotopes of African presence in Lisbon as well as time-place scenes of African and hip-hop diasporic dimensions. A policy of real interculturality should address this gap by redefining Portuguese cultural patrimony through concrete landmarks and new, Kriolu historiographies.

In a 2013 report EENC (European Expert Network on Culture) issued, Portugal boasts several sites of "cultural patrimony." They are national points of spatial distinction, the material complement to the discourse of *ser português*. The list includes what one might expect: selected vineyard regions, premodern city walls, and monasteries.[13] In fact, the Portuguese state invests more in "cultural heritage" proportionate to its gross domestic product (GDP) than any other European country (Dümcke and Gnedovsky 2013:11). There is no entry related to African presence or contribution. Such visibility is relegated to temporary exhibits in museums and shelved documents in archives. Is it not possible to conceptualize cultural patrimony in terms of migration? A site such as Kova M, for example, stands as a testament to migrancy, an increasingly significant factor in what Lisbon means. Moreover, Kova M represents spatially what census reports tell us about the shifts in citizenship data in Portugal and the overall trends in Western Europe. Kova M is, in part, Portugal. Is cultural patrimony just about relics, or can it not also include other types of representative territories made by residents?

Educational curricula and official landmarks are two obvious and conventional policy initiatives open for a government committed to interculturality. Another option is to embrace the globalized popular genre of hip-hop and invest in Kriolu and tuga rap, graffiti, DJs, and street dance as part of city branding. Such policy also has precedent in other cities, such as Diadema, a working-class, industrial suburb of São Paulo, Brazil. In 1999 the mayor, as advised by the secretary of culture, decided to invest in hip-hop by transforming a local cultural center into the first Hip-Hop Cultural House (*A Casa de Cultura Hip-Hop*) in Brazil. Diadema became known as the "hip-hop city." The "house" stands today and continues to be a local, national, and international reference of hip-hop. Based on informal interviews conducted since 1999, I can affirm that the Casa not only attracted artists, journalists, politicians, and researchers to Diadema, it also, and perhaps more important than the people the Casa attracted, inspired youth to care about their city (Pardue 2011). Such cultural investment gave a path for identification and a topos to exercise citizenship. Given hip-hop's broad networks of information exchange and its emphasis on wholesale borrowing and local scene building, Kriolu rap could become a vehicle for the thousands of PALOP residents on the outskirts of Lisbon to participate in a new paradigm of Portuguese citizenship and, thus, establish a more evenly distributed sense of interculturalidade.

CHAPTER 5

## Persistent Frustrations on the Ground

The difference between architects and urbanists and policy makers and social workers is one of structure and agency. Public policy can only work if there are healthy dialogue and participation with local constituents. Again, can we apply the lessons of Creole encounters into the process of writing and implementing policy?

Returning to Kova M, we can compare intercultural policies to migrant experiences and the everyday life of those who bear the weight of the stigma of being an immigrant independent of their actual place of birth. For rapper LBC, the new citizenship laws, for example, are "obscure." He has yet to obtain Portuguese citizenship, and during our conversation in the living room of his mother's apartment, LBC protested that as part of the precarious working class, he continues to feel marginal to the Portuguese state. According to the yearly statistic reports (INE 2013), the Portuguese government has received over twenty-five thousand requests from Cape Verdeans alone for legal status in Portugal since 2008, with an increasing number rejected resulting from actions taken to combat the economic recession and the accompanying high levels of unemployment. LBC states his reasoning.

> The new laws [2006 citizenship laws] are obscure. I mean, they are good in the sense that they did open up space for more applications and quicker results. But I feel that these laws, in fact, are a way of extending the law to control groups of people that will never quite be Portuguese. The bureaucracy is still tough, and it costs a lot of money. To me, anyway, I work. I have a job, and it is not an easy process. I am still waiting. Because, for me, I realize that some doors will open with Portuguese citizenship documentation. But, even as I say this, I hesitate, because this thing we discussed earlier, interculturalidade, with this, there is no dialogue, as they want to say, there is an imposition. It's like a different facet of Lusotropicalism.

One might attribute the frustration represented in the stories of LBC, Karlos, Chullage, Janice, and others as lamentable tales of impatient youth. However, the issue of invisibility remains a structural fact in Portuguese politics. During my fieldwork in 2009, Portuguese citizens prepared themselves for three general elections, most important, that of the seat of prime minister and of the leader of the parliament assembly. In following the debates on television and in the newspapers, I was struck by the lack of cultural diversity among participants on stage and in the crowds. In my informal chats with residents of Cape Verdean descent, PALOP, and white, or tuga, Portuguese social workers, it is certainly plausible that the invisibility of immigrants in the electoral process shows their marginality both equally in terms of local participation and political-party exclusion. There have been very few parliament members with PALOP heritage: Helder Amaral, born in Angola, of the center-right populist party and formerly of the conservative People's Party (PP); and Celeste Correira, a Cape Verdean woman from an elite family in Mindelo (the capital city of São Vicente) and a member of the PS (Socialist Party), which in Portugal refers to a center-left position. Currently, there are no members (out of twenty-two) of the European Parliament for Portugal who have any ethnic connection to PALOP.

LBC is what Antonio Gramsci would call an "organic intellectual," someone who dedicates his learning to his applied sociocultural position (2011:137–60). Not unlike an aspiring athlete, LBC proudly detailed his daily regimen of reading around issues of race and class. At meals and before sleeping are the two main periods that he explores texts and moves toward his goal to accumulate knowledge. He sat up tall in his mother's vinyl chair and glowed at the chance to demonstrate his command of the literature from Cabral to Machel to Frantz Fanon to Black Panther leader Fred Hampton. This litany of "fallen soldiers" acted as LBC's preface to describe his profession as class monitor in various intercultural schools throughout Lisbon. After recounting numerous incidents of self-correction, visible low self-esteem, and misrecognition by teachers, LBC underscored the importance of Kriolu rap and the Kriolu language, in general, as a fundamental part of any intercultural process. He summarized his feelings: "Kriolu belongs to me, to us Cape Verdeans, it is thus central to our self-esteem. Interculturalidade, whatever [it will look like], has to include this. Too many kids, so many of us, are not willing to give that up. Kriolu rap reminds us of this right."

The right of/to Kriolu is a contributive element to cultural citizenship in Lisbon, albeit absent from formal recognition. This chapter represents my attempt in academic discourse to do what rappers often do in their lyrics. From Racionais MCs in their paradigmatic song "Capítulo 4, Versículo 3" (chapter 4, verse 3), which infuses a reading of statistics highlighting the racialization of violence in late 1990s São Paulo, Brazil, to The Coup's many rap songs that index political policies of the day (e.g., the "no cruisin'" ordinances in Oakland and the 1 percent during the 2011 rallies of the Occupy Oakland movement), to Mentis Afro's and Ghoya's raps about specific policies of incarceration in contemporary Lisbon, cultural citizenship is best understood as a set of practices through which interest groups, such as young immigrant rappers, experiment in combining their knowledge of political policies and their aesthetic narratives of experience and sentiment.

In Lisbon, rapping in Kriolu, speaking in Kriolu, or general Kriolu identification is increasingly a medium to criticize or offer an alternative to the intercultural programs by the Portuguese state. The Kriolu alternative is not represented in the ethnic enclave or in simplistic Afrocentrism. Rather, Kriolu rappers are interculturally competent and, as we can glean from the personal stories above, committed to the interactional labor required to build bridges and create new forms of identity and belonging.

Lisbon officials in groups, such as ACIDI and Lisboa Mistura, as well as NGOs, such as Interculturalcidades, have tried to implement the concept of interculturality as a way of showing, if not celebrating, Lisbon as a city that naturally is able to address immigrant issues. It is not the case that ACIDI, for example, denies socioeconomic and educational problems of immigrant communities. Rather, ACIDI officials insist that Portugal's long history of multicultural encounters facilitates a smoother transition into democratic representation and a more complete exercise of citizenship. This is supposedly distinctive from other parts of Europe where this process has been violent and caused more separation than integration. In other words, what for the rest of the EU is a dawning of a postnational moment of citizenship, where the conditions of rights are more about current participation and networks rather than anthropological ties to the public sphere, the contemporary moment for Portugal is a reiteration of Portuguese national identity. Portuguese citizenship, for the gatekeepers, has always been light and malleable.

# Suggestive Conclusions

> There was an absence now of all forms of solace, a barrenness under the heading of consolation, and no way to return to what was. A sense of otherness had overtaken him—"otherness," a word in his own language to describe a state of being all but foreign to him.... My God, he thought, the man I once was! The life that surrounded me! The force that was mine! No "otherness" to be felt anywhere! Once upon a time I was a full human being.
>
> —Philip Roth

The acclaimed novelist Philip Roth speaks through his protagonist, an aging man once on top of the advertising world, a successful Mad Man with all the pleasures and trappings of the freewheeling post–World War II America. As the character comes to realize his life mistakes and begins to suffer the distress of an aging physique, he loses confidence in what we might call in today's world the "neoliberal self." In this passage Roth's dying everyman describes his general slide into decadence as a result of difference. In short, "otherness" disarms the ego and destabilizes identity. The sense that "otherness" shapes, rather than simply results from or is defined by, the encounters of daily life worries and, ultimately, fragments the protagonist beyond repair. He is no longer a "full human being." This concern has historically been a stigma against the Creole, a not fully enfranchised identity. Yet, the prevalence of the encounter with difference has become the ubiquitous dynamic of the postcolonial, globalized urban world. As demonstrated in this book, creolization is the "full human being" and deserves greater attention in the art and science of policy making, governance, and identity theory.

## Suggestive Conclusions

Portugal has thus entered an era of a new kind of expansionism, one in which the nation's perception of its historical ability to interact with other cultures, its intercultural sensitivity, and its ability to cooperate with other societies in the pursuit of technological advancement relates not only to how the Portuguese want to see themselves, but also the way they want the world—particularly the European Community and Africa—to see them. (Errante 1998:306)

This text began with a convergence, the musings of difference under colonial regimes of expansion and control, and the postcolonial policies of citizenship. The colonial school of Portuguese exploration (Sagres and Cabo da Roca) meets the information technology of diasporic exchanges (Uncle C's bank transfers). The open sea doubles as a symbol of Portuguese civilization and Cape Verdean culture. The sea morphs into the scattered ruins of BSF, of Talude, of Quinta da Serra, and of the dozens of other demolished or semi-demolished neighborhoods strewn about Lisbon's periphery. Another sea of nostalgia.

Writing at a moment in the late twentieth century, the year of the European Expo, an anxious time for Portugal to display more than the tired *caravela* ships, lateen sails, and melodramatic fado music, historian Antoinette Errante describes the everlasting trope of expansion among the Portuguese. Through a new European discourse of interculturality, expansion seems to be old hat to the Portuguese. The presences of all that old otherness are now fresh and, indeed, necessary to represent Portugal and Portuguese citizenship.

The nexus of migration, citizenship, and identity is like most social phenomena entangled in the tensions between agency and structure. To what extent are migration patterns and practices manifestations of intended choices or positioned reactions? Political scientists and policy analysts interested in migration foreground "actors," such as interest groups and institutions, to try and explain why certain policies around, for example, residence, labor, or family reunification, are more or less effective. In much of this literature, the state continues to be the privileged mediating force (Boswell 2007), at times, considered a unitary actor, invested in "patterns" of policy, which translates into a kind of durable power in terms of inclusion and exclusion.

Such durability can be explained by histories and stories that circulate and become ideology. In a recent volume the Smithsonian Institution produced about the sixteenth- and seventeenth-century Portuguese cultural encounters, Portuguese president Aníbal Cavaco Silva describes in the foreword that "the Portuguese simultaneously encompassed and embraced [the outside world], inviting reciprocal understanding and exchanges between its farthest points" (2007:8). In 1890 Portuguese chronicler Abreu Vasconcelos remarked that Portugal within Europe is only "tangentially linked to the great current of civilization ... [but] in Africa the situation is different. We are right along with England, France, Belgium and Germany. We must dedicate ourselves to the thickening of the civilization stew lest we lose ourselves within it" (1890:518). One can discern the beginnings of a Lusotropicalism discourse as national ideology in Vasconcelos's writings.

Moreover, in Pepetela's novel *Mayombe*, the reader can glean other encounters with the durability of state discourses. In Pepetela's story, we meet a number of Angolan fighters with programmatic noms de guerre, including Fearless, Struggle, and Theory. Their backgrounds of class, age, ethnicity, and education vary significantly. Theory opens the book with a provocative biographical statement.

> I was born in Gabela, in coffee country. From the land I received the dark color of coffee, from my mother's side, mixed with the off-white from my father, a Portuguese trader. I carry in me the irreconcilable and that is my driving force. In a Universe of yes or no, white or black, I represent maybe. Maybe says no for someone who wants to hear yes and means yes for someone who wants to hear no. Is it my fault if men insist on purity and reject compounds? Or must men accept the maybe? In the face of this essential problem, people are divided in my view into two categories: Manicheans and the rest. It is worth explaining that the rest are rare; the World generally is Manichean. (Pepetela 1996:2)

Kriolu rappers and Cape Verdeans, in general, have struggled with Manichean ways of viewing the world and categorizing its people. We have seen the repeated tension between Kriolu and tuga, between diasporic migrants and cultural nationalists. Nostalgia and the sea bring them together as labor and race pull them apart. Kriolu identification suggests that there are alternative paradigms of belonging to the nation-state and to a diaspora or to Afrocentrism.

The distinction of migrancy must figure into the current debates on citizenship. In this tussle over the state's role in regulating migration, *scale* is often lost in the shuffle. Due to the structural legitimacy and authority of various EU agencies (Europol, Eurostat, EC, European Central Bank), scholars and analysts are sensitive to the supranational dimension of policy and its impact on migrant experiences (Luedtke 2009). Why does mobility offer a challenge to citizenship? Scholars, such as Robyn Magalit Rodriguez (2013), have argued that the framework and operative experiences of globalization have fostered a "migrant labor transnationalism" that is essentially at odds with nation-based political subjectivity. Certainly, labor relations and labor geographies have shaped Kriolu, but can Kriolu be considered a form of postnational citizenship? Christian Joppke concludes in his 2010 book on migration and citizenship that due to the recognition of these contemporary conditions of migrancy, human rights, and identity politics, contemporary national citizenship has become more inclusive and more accessible and, thus, by logic has become less binding and valuable. This is "citizenship 'light' of rights without obligations, in itself socially inconsequential, and devoid of a particular cultural content" (Joppke 2010:33).

But does the balancing act of citizenship need to be conceptualized as a relationship between the private and the public or cultural specificities and universal human rights? A Creole perspective approaches citizenship as the relationship between the intersectionality of the encounter, for example, state/resident and individual distinction. This is the logic behind local rappers' insistence that Kriolu is neither tuga nor conventional Cape Verdean nostalgia. Kriolu is a Creole citizenship inside Portugal, and this is not the same presently as what passes for "Portuguese" or Portuguese iterations of interculturality.

The force of Kriolu rap as a postcolonial discourse and performance of identity cuts in multiple ways not only because many practitioners come from a range of PALOP, Cape Verdean diasporic, and local Lisbon experiences but also due to the historically grounded social fact that Kriolu is essentially a code of othering and difference. For multiculturalism to work as "intercultural dialogue," structural changes would need to take place in institutional forums of recognition, such as education (language and history), citizenship (law and everyday life), and cultural heritage (landmarks), as described in the previous chapter. Presently, the Portuguese state continues to imagine itself as a faint but progressive voice in the European citizenship debates. The current ideas of "Portuguese citizenship," despite their increasing leniency, still assume some sort of Luso lineage in the name of mixture. By contrast, Kriolu rappers and advocates of Kriolu identity politics, more generally, argue for "citizenship in Portugal."

Local rapper Biggie once reminded me, "You see, maybe Portugal is in the EU, but the PALOP aren't. We're just in Portugal . . . not quite Portuguese, not quite European . . . forever African and always black." From a Kriolu perspective, Luso dissolves, and Creole encounters become the paradigmatic condition from which policy makers can draft legislation and work toward new formulation of an "overlapping consensus." What I describe in this book as Creole citizenship exemplifies what political scientist Isabel Estrada Carvalhais theorizes as "postnational citizenship being accomplished *within* the state . . . with the state as a responsible actor in the whole process" (2007:4, italics in original). In this calculus, Portugal emerges as the vibrant place of Creole citizenship, of intertwining trajectories of language, labor, and exchange. A Kriolu perspective as local rappers articulate forces us to consider residents as Creole subjects in Portugal rather than stratified persons relative to a way of being Portuguese.

# Notes

## Introduction

1. The terms *social* and *improvised* in reference to housing and neighborhoods contain particular ideological connotations under debate in the context of contemporary Lisbon. I follow locals and urbanism scholars in using *improvised* to refer to informal methods of housing construction. Social housing is, generally, low-income housing funded by public-private partnerships with a mixture of government agencies, NGOs, and corporate entities. In Lisbon, social housing often takes the shape of a central plaza with apartment buildings around it and basic services nearby. There is a personal and often ad hoc aesthetic to these constructions.

2. Of course, Atlantic creolization occurred well before the cultural-linguistic term *Caribbean* was invented.

3. This is a phrase from the leading story in the first edition of the Cape Verdean newspaper *O Eco de Cabo Verde* in 1933. The headline reads, "1460–1933 Salve Portugal!" (1460–1933 Praise Portugal!"), 1460 being the year Portugal discovered and later named the archipelago Cape Verde.

4. See, for example, Joppke 2010, Zolberg and Litt Woon 1999, and Bowen 2007.

5. For more on Agualusa and his complex relationship with Lusofonia, see McNee 2012. Unlike most Kriolu rappers, Agualusa believes that Lusofonia has value because it allows for a critical hybridity. As McNee argues, Agualusa purposefully crafts his characters to occupy multiple ethnic, racial, and class positions in his novels and that this movement dramatized through various types of social encounter recuperates Lusofonia from a simplistic notion of Luso as assimilation.

6. The protagonist and the novel overall are references to Eça de Queirós, one of the most famous Portuguese novelists of the nineteenth century, and his text *Correspondência de Fradique Mendes*.

7. See David Leavitt, *The Two Hotel Francforts* (Bloomsbury 2013); Tomm Gabbay, *The Lisbon Crossing* (Harper 2007); Pascal Mercier, *A Night Train to Lisbon* (Grove 2008); and Robert C. Wilson, *A Small Death in Lisbon* (Berkley 2002).

8. For a similar scenario, see Burdick's discussion (2013, chapter 2) of the porous nature of evangelical rap production in São Paulo, Brazil.

## Chapter 1. Creole's Historical Presences

1. Al-Judami, appointed as governor of Lisbon in the eleventh century, was described as "*negro*" on his arrival to Badajoz, currently a Portugal-Spain border town (see A. Alves 1991).

2. Decades later, photographer Clifford Ashley would invoke the term *'Gee* to refer to the members of the "black crew" he discovered on *The Sunbeam*, one of the last whaling ships to leave the New Bedford, Massachusetts, docks. Ashley stated, "As for butter, the damned ''Gee' eats lard on his bread and thinks that the white man oughter" (1926:19).

3. For example, some scholars cite stories of precolonial occupations of Cape Verde as a refuge by the Jalofo tribe (Baptista 2002; Carreira 1972).

4. Until 1521, slaves were required to pass through Spain or Portugal to be "taxed and seasoned" before being transported to the Americas (Sweet 2003:15). By the 1830s, however, the Portuguese census takers eliminated racial categories from the census, thus making it difficult to track demographics in such terms. In part, this was due to the official abolition of slave trading in the ports of Lisbon and, most probably, also due to the effervescent ideologies of nation-building, including narratives of tradition, homogeneity, and superiority (Patterson and Kelley 2000).

5. Peter Mark in his work on Luso-African architecture cites the observations of the Dutch trader Pieter de Marees in 1602 regarding the ubiquity of Creole spoken throughout the Gambian region and Petite Côte just south of Dakar, Senegal (2002:15–16).

6. As mentioned earlier, there are several variants of Kriolu from Cape Verde. This variability is signaled in the very spelling of the language—*Crioulo* and *Kriolu*. I have opted for the latter throughout this text with the only exception being a citation of a published document. I spoke more with descendants of the island of Santiago, where the *K* spelling is preferred; this is also the rule per ALUPEK (Unified Alphabet for the writing of Cape Verdean). There is also a matter of politics and aesthetic taste connected to the *K*, as chapter 2 describes.

7. Skinheads em toda claque, será que,
   este pais só aceita um emigrante se for um craque.
   . . . . . . . . . . . . . .
   Será que, irmaos nao se apercebem que há que,
   Deixar que falar e sair para a rua em protesto
   Porque é lá que, vamos acabar com o racismo, capitalismo
   E todas as outras formas de saque.
   . . . . . . . . . . . . . .
   Será que.

8. From postindependence Africa until the present day, the relationship between migration and labor has accumulated other connotations. While Cape Verdeans continue to be

labor migrants, a significant percentage of other Luso-Africans and non-PALOP Africans are categorized as "refugee" migrants. According to state statistics, 65 percent of all requests in 2011 for refugee asylum in Portugal were from African citizens (SEF 2012:46–47).

9. Moreover, according to World Bank statistics published in 2011, Cape Verdean remittances constitute roughly 10 percent of the archipelago's gross domestic product (GDP). Despite the global recession since 2008, Cape Verdeans continue to send US$150 million back "home." As a percentage, this represents a significant decrease since the mid-1990s. The cited reason for this decline is an emergent tourism industry rather than a downturn in diasporic money transfers per se.

10. Author's translation of: "Que significa Portugal? Uma pátria da Europa, mas que, além da Europa, se completou e personalizou no encontro com os povos dos outros continentes. Convergência de etnias, expressa em relações humanas multiseculares que superaram as distâncias e as oposições raciais. Daí advém que o Ultramar português seja parte integrante e vital da Nação, nada tendo a ver com o colonialismo em que pretendem incluí-lo alguns observadores apaixonados, por falácia de generalização ilícita. Por que não admitir que os mares sejam tanto ou mais unitivos do que a continuidade terrestre?"

11. The Salazar apologists demonstrate what Maeve McCusker and Anthony Soares, in their edited volume on "Island" identification, describe as the connective qualities of the seas: "The very seas that would appear to act as guarantors of separateness have always been conduits, facilitating movement and exchange between peoples and cultures" (2011:xii–xiii).

12. The deployment of *vizinhança* is similar to what Jorge Cañizares-Esguerra describes in seventeenth-century México as a citizenship based on *vecinidad* and *naturaleza*, an inclusion based on "merit," that is, religion, property, marriage, residence, and space, manifested in neighborhood, municipal, and, ultimately, to the "natural" cohesion of what would become "nation" (2007:41).

13. Some of the retornados were Cape Verdean with Portuguese citizenship. Law Number 37, decreed on October 3, 1981, because it defined citizenship as based in blood, not soil, stripped most of these Cape Verdeans of their rights as the law also did to the more conventional "immigrant" Cape Verdeans. A minority of retornados escaped this cut based on their formal education and was able to emigrate and resettle not only in Portugal but in greater numbers in other Cape Verdean diasporas in Europe and the United States, where they saw more employment opportunities. See Gois 2008 for more details.

14. For more information, see "Prova de Língua Portuguesa para Aquisição de Nacionalidade."

## Chapter 2. Kriolu Interruptions of Luso

1. I thank Samuel Weeks for his personal comments to me regarding the complex role of the encounter in creolization. His suggestion that Creole cannot be entirely explained as the result of colonial encounters is important in any account of Kriolu agency.

2. The term *Lusotropicology* occasionally appears in the literature as a translation of Freyre's idea (Hammond 1967). Freyre himself prided himself on poetics and did write different versions of "Lusotropic" in his essays published during the 1950s.

3. Scholars such as Antoinette Errante have argued that Portuguese attempts at internationalism often smack of Lusotropicalism. For example, in the 1976 Constitution following the end of the fascist regime of Salazar-Caetano, Portuguese colonialism in Africa is referred to as "cooperation among nations" (Errante 1998:304). See also Thomaz 2000.

4. While virtually all Cape Verdeans continue to speak Kriolu in Portugal, the spirit of Kriolu as resistant difference introduced above certainly does not capture the totality of Cape Verdean identity formation and sociopolitical agency. Many Cape Verdeans, particularly those from affluent backgrounds connected to certain islands in the archipelago, embrace Lusofonia just as many elite Cape Verdeans identified with Lusotropicalism in the mid-twentieth century. However, even among those who are invested in accommodation, Kriolu has gained greater recognition as a valuable distinction. In the world of pop music, for example, Cape Verdean performers, such as Sara Tavares, Mayra Andrade, and Lura, now enjoy global success due in great part to their reapproximation with the Kriolu language and Cape Verdean musical repertoires (Arenas 2011).

5. Richard Price cites a letter written in 1928 by Jonkeer L. C. van Panhuys to Melville Herskovits as the first documented use of the term *creolisation* to describe cultural change, in this case referring to Suriname Maroons (2010:57).

6. Scholars, such as Palmié 2002 and Gilroy 1993, argue that *Creole* and *Black Atlantic*, respectively, were central in the formation of modernity, once considered a purely European conceptualization.

7. For historical and ethnographic details on the Cape Verdean diaspora in the United States, see Halter 1993; Britto 2002; Sieber 2005. For more on Cape Verdean diaspora in Europe, particularly France, Italy, and Holland; Africa, particularly Senegal and São Tomé e Príncipe; and the Americas, particularly Argentina, Brazil, and Uruguay, see Lobban and Halter 1988:49–50 and Carling 2004.

8. As Errante argues, the utility of the Lusotropicalism discourse was not only in service of an imagined antiracism but also by the late 1950s and early 1960s an attempt to essentially link Portugal to its remaining African colonies (1998:296). For example, *Presença*, a propaganda magazine of the 1960s and 1970s, printed in color, often features a pair of children, one a black native of Angola or Mozambique and the other a white native of Portugal. Ensuing interviews and reports frame the white youth as identifying with Angola, and the text equates this sentiment with a Portuguese identity as well.

9. This absence is, indeed, curious given that in Ferreira's collection of nonfiction essays, *A Aventura Crioula*, he agrees with scholar Teixeira da Mota of the "crioulo dialect" in Guinea-Bissau that *crioulo* is "essentially an idiom of contact" (1967:120).

10. For example, with regard to his notion of "Africa" in his poems as solely North Africa, Cardoso's evocations of Egypt and culture represent a myopic view.

11. For example of Bordalo's work, see the cartoon "Herança Histórica" (History's inheritance), a Bordalo political cartoon from 1900 and depicts the foolhardy, myopic exploitation of the African colonies by Portuguese administration, through the analogy of an "anthropophagic banquet." Portuguese officials in blackface gorge themselves on Zambezia and Nyassa, provinces in contemporary Mozambique, while politician and businessman

Cecil Rhodes and, by extension, British entrepreneurial interests patiently and calculatingly observe. In 1895, as part of the fallout from the British Ultimatum in 1890, an embarrassing admission on the part of the Portuguese state of British hegemony in southern Africa, Rhodes was able to transfer much of Zambezia into a new state of Rhodesia.

12. Veiga's analysis of Kriolu is a response to the book by Baltasar Lopes, a member of the Claridosos, who had published a linguistics text written in Portuguese in 1957. Veiga's discourse of *badiu* as matrix has been central to his argument since the 1980s, including in his remarks during the release of a dictionary he published in 2011. See his comments in Veiga 2011.

13. The original text in Portuguese: "Ora, a expressão mais perversa da Lusofonia é a amnésia sobre o passado pré-colonial dos países africanos ou de Timore, de algum modo, a repetição dessa expressão do colonialismo que foi 'a descoberta' destes povos—que só passaram a ter história no momento em que os 'descobridores' os encontraram. A Lusofonia é, pois, a última marca de um império que já não existe."

## Chapter 3. Lisbon Rappers and the Labor of Location

1. See Guilbault 1993 for an ethnomusicological discussion of the use of Creole in pop music among various French Antilles Islands nations as part of a postcolonial identity project.

2. According to A. P. B. Horta (2008:184–85), the actual history of Cova starts in 1940 with rural, white migrants in search of arable land.

3. Tuga is not a style of rap per se but, rather, a general term of place-designation. My intention is not to reify tuga as a historically stable category within popular culture or national history. However, when hip-hoppers discuss perennial topics, such as the development of hip-hop, they employ *tuga* to mean simply *national* (i.e., relating to the Portuguese nation-state).

4. Similar to other hip-hop locales in which I have conducted research, Brazil, the United States, and Cape Verde, the national hip-hop movement in Portugal is anchored by a foundational and controversial recording, *República*, a compilation album in 1994. For scholarly discussions on the controversy around "Rapper's Delight" (1979) in the United States, see Forman 2002; on "Hip Hop Cultura de Rua" (1987) in Brazil, see Pardue 2011. In the case of Cape Verde, sociologist Redy Lima has been the primary voice in rap scholarship (2010, 2012). From these texts and personal conversations, one can glean the controversies about foundational recording and artists in Cape Verde. For example, it is well known among rappers on the islands of Santiago and São Vicente that there were many rap recordings throughout the 1990s; however, many cite Black Side as foundational because the group managed to record in Holland and, thus, create a product of higher technological value. For more on *República*, see Fradique 2003 and Calado 2007. Judging from the consistent citation by hip-hoppers during my fieldwork in Lisbon, the value of *República* within national hip-hop continues to be formidable, despite a number of personal conflicts that emerged due to the level of visibility the recording generated.

5. *Batuko* involves only women and consists of a series of call-and-response forms over a steady polyrhythm of hand percussion. *Coladera* is also a national genre; the tempo is

## Notes to Chapters 3 and 4

usually faster than in morna, and the lyrics often relate to current social issues. *Funaná* is an upbeat dance music consisting of accordion, bass, percussion, occasional brass, and the distinct scraping sound of the *ferrinho*, an iron slab. Funaná is native to the island of Santiago, but since independence in 1975 and, particularly, in the past decade, the genre has become popular throughout the archipelago and the diaspora. *Morna*, a song genre with a long history throughout Cape Verde, is a lyrical lament that takes the form of romantic, nostalgic ballads. The voice takes front stage and is usually accompanied by nylon-stringed guitar, clarinet and other winds, occasional keyboard, and light percussion. *Tabanka*, a genre that is related to the carnivalesque tradition of ridicule, features the sounds of the conch shell. An exception to the absence of traditional musical influences in Cape Verdean rap is the music of São Vicente rapper Expavi, which includes participation by Cesária Évora and Princezito. For more, see David 2011.

6. According to Baganha 2005, approximately five hundred thousand retornados settled in Portugal during the late 1970s and early 1980s, with 59 percent born in Portugal and 41 percent born in Africa of various ethnicities.

7. Political scientists, such as Keith Banting and Will Kymlicka 2013, have argued more recently that European states are much more variable in their treatment of multiculturalism and interculturality in the (post)recession era.

## Chapter 4. Spatial Politics of Kriolu Presence in Lisbon

1. I use *space* and *place* somewhat interchangeably. In English and Portuguese, the connotations of *place* are rooted in a boundedness and a specificity and are seemingly closer to identity formation; the meaning of *space* is generally more abstract, universal, and less articulated. However, as cultural geographers, such as Doreen Massey 1994 and Edward Soja 1996, following Henri Lefebvre 1991, point out, this dichotomy is a false one. *Place* necessarily includes more than the local just as *space* is always located "somewhere" vis-à-vis human practices. For either term to be salient in analysis, one must account for practices, such as language and labor, in a dynamic temporality.

2. The official spelling is *Fontaínhas*, but on multiple occasions residents referred to it as *Fontainha*. The difference is maintained as per the speaker's choice.

3. In any discussion of Fontaínhas, it is important to cite the cinematic work of Pedro Costa and Kiluanje Liberdade. In his trilogy of films depicting daily life in the Lisbon periphery during late 1990s and early 2000s, Costa chose the case of Fontaínhas to represent migration, youth, class, and displacement as a struggle for recognition burdened by the stigmas of racism and machismo. The viewer takes on a gaze that penetrates the neighborhood of Fontaínhas through discourses of personal frustrations and machines ripping gradually at the precarious residential infrastructure. Through long scenes of intimacy, the viewer occupies the perspectives of local perpetrators of sexual violence and masochistic intravenous-drug abusers. Costa's representation of the increasingly visible scenes of marginality in the Lisbon metropolitan area unfolds as a depressing and addictive banality through the intense images of sustained stares and the jarring sounds of buses and stray dogs. Despite his an-

thropological approach to casting and set production, Costa does not explain "otherness" or urban renewal in his triptych, which includes *Ossos* (Bones) (1998), *O Quarto da Vanda* (Vanda's room) (2002), and *Juventude em Marcha* (Colossal youth) (2006). Rather, as an aesthete, Costa imposes a sentiment of marginality. The role of Cape Verdeans and Kriolu is fleeting, a few sexual and moral encounters for the main actors to negotiate. In *Juventude em Marcha*, Costa does focus more on movement than squalor and the struggle of internal, intra-urban migrants to make place. For the most part, Costa privileges class over race and, thus, holds Kriolu at a distance (Arenas 2011). *Outros Bairros*, directed by Liberdade, Vasco Pimentel, and Inês Gonçalves, is a film about the management of "otherness" in urbanization projects. Exploring the dynamics of Fontaínhas, the filmmakers mix visual art and ethnographic storytelling in an account of demolition and urban renewal. The film employs the power of Cape Verdean Creole rap as a sound track and in the process transforms the viewer from a voyeur into a witness. *Outros Bairros* is a robust document of reality and a sensitive piece of aesthetics.

4. See also Märzhäuser 2009 and 2011 regarding the adoption of some Kriolu vocabulary from Kriolu rap by non-Kriolu speakers in Lisbon.

5. For more information about the support of Programa Escolhas and the music studio, see Super User (2009).

## Chapter 5. Kriolu and European Interculturality

1. *Troika* is the tripartite division of institutional financial reform directed toward the most severely affected European countries in the present economic crisis. The three institutions are the European Commission, European Central Bank, and International Monetary Fund.

2. See, for example, theories of migration as a set of "push and pull factors" (Ravenstein 1885), migration and its relations with labor (Bartoli 1966), and a typology of migration, including "primitive migration"—ecological impulse, "forced migration," "self-propelled migration," and "mass migration" (Petersen 1958)—which consider migration as less of an individual choice and more of a collective social pattern.

3. Cape Verdean and Portuguese community activists often referred me to the ACIDI website.

4. For more on the Expo, see Sieber 1999, 2007.

5. Originally, the transition government passed a law, "Decreto-Lei, number 215/74," on May 22, 1974, authorizing that this new organ, SE, would control foreigners within the national territory, issue foreign passports, and manage the bureaucratic process of foreigners who petitioned to enter the country. A separate entity, Guarda Fiscal, was responsible for actual border patrol. In 1986 these two spheres of operation were consolidated, and SE and Guarda Fiscal became SEF.

6. See, for example, Alves, Raposo, and Pereira 2004.

7. For the entire report, see "The Outcomes and Impact of the Intercultural Cities Programme 2008–2013."

8. For individual city reports, see "Intercultural Cities Index."

## Notes to Chapter 5

9. For more information on the decision, No. 1983/2006/EC, see European Institute for Comparative Cultural Research 2008.

10. I write "moving toward" because the law's requirements are still based on length of official residence of the applicant's parents, the applicant's formal school level, and, in the case of a person born in Portugal but with foreign parents, Portuguese proficiency. For more information on the debate on language, see Healy 2011:99–103.

11. ACIDI lists three documents under "bilinguismo" on its website and fifty events related to Crioulo including language courses.

12. See, for example, S. R. Oliveira 2010. In addition, the work of Nezi Brito, Marlyse Baptista, and others in the public schools of the Dorchester neighborhood in Boston, Massachusetts, deserves mention (Baptista 2010).

13. For more information on the 2011 report, see Dümcke and Gnedovsky 2013. The list includes the following sites and entry dates of cultural heritage sites: PT Central Zone town of Angra do Heroismo, Azores, 1983; Convent of Christ, Tomar, 1983; Monastery of Batalha, 1983; Monastery of the Hieronymites and Tower of Belém, Lisbon, 1983; historic center, Évora, 1986; Monastery of Alcobaça, 1989; cultural landscape of Sintra, 1995; Historic Center of Oporto, 1996; prehistoric rock-art sites, Côa Valley and Siega Verde, 1998; Alto Douro Wine Region, 2001; Historic Center, Guimarães, 2001; and landscape, Pico Island Vineyard Culture, 2004.

# References

ACIDI. 2007. *Plano para a Integração dos Imigrantes.* Resolução do conselho de Ministros, no. 63-A/2007. Lisbon: ACIDI.
———. 2010. "Música e Migração." Special issue. *Revista Migrações* 7 (October). Coordenação científica de Maria de São José Côrte-Real. Accessed June 2013. http://www.oi.acidi.gov.pt/modules.php?name=Content&pa=showpage&pid=119.
———. 2011. *10 Anos Programa Escolhas.* Lisbon: ACIDI.
———. 2013. Home page. Accessed June 2013. http://www.acidi.gov.pt/.
———. 2014. *More Diversity, Better Humanity.* Lisbon: ACIDI.
ACIME. 2005. *Relatório de Actividades.* Lisbon: ACIME.
———. 2006. *Media, Imigração e Minorias Étnicas II.* Lisbon: ACIME.
"Actividade da S.G.L." 1938. *Boletim da SGL,* ser. 56 (1): 135–45.
Agualusa, José Eduardo. 2002. *Creole.* London: Arcadia.
Åkesson, Lisa. 2004. "Making a Life: Meanings of Migration in Cape Verde." PhD diss., Department of Social Anthropology, Gotëburg University.
Alim, Samy H. 2003. "'We Are the Streets': African American Language and the Strategic Construction of a Street-Conscious Identity." In *Black Linguistics: Language, Society, and Politics in Africa and the Americas,* edited by Sinfree Makoni, Geneva Smitherman, Arnetha F. Ball, and Arthur K. Spears, 40–59. New York: Routledge.
———. 2004. *You Know My Steez: An Ethnographic and Sociolinguistic Study of Styleshifting in a Black American Speech Community.* Publication of the American Dialect Society, 89. Durham: Duke University Press.
———. 2009. "Straight Outta Compton, Straight aus München: Global Linguistic Flows,

## References

Identities, and the Politics of Language in a Global Hip Hop Nation." In *Global Linguistic Flows: Hip Hop Cultures, Youth Identities, and the Politics of Language*, edited by H. Samy Alim, Awad Ibrahim, and Alastair Pennycook, 1–22. New York: Routledge.

Almada, Andre Alvares d'. (1594) 1984. *Brief Treatise on the Rivers of Guinea*. Annotated by P. E. H. Hair. Liverpool, UK: University of Liverpool.

Almada, Maria Dulce de Oliveira. 1961. *Cabo Verde: Contribuição para o Estudo do Dialecto Falado no seu Arquipélago*. Lisbon: JIU.

Almeida, Miguel Vale de. 2007. "From Miscegenation to Creole Identity: Portuguese Colonialism, Brazil, Cape Verde." In C. Stewart 2007, 108–32.

Alves, Adalberto. 1991. *O Meu Coracão é Arabe: A Poesia Luso-Arabe*. Lisbon: Assírio e Alvim.

Alves, Jorge Fernandes. 1999. "Emigração portuguesa: O exemplo do Porto nos meados do século XIX." *Revista de História* 9:267–89.

Alves, Marta, Otavio Raposo, and Patricia Pereira. 2004. *Rotas Cruzadas: Imigrantes no Coracão de Lisboa*. CISSEI (Centro de Investigação em Serviço Social e Estudos Interdisciplinares). Programa de Iniciativa Comunitária. Lisbon: Projeto InterculturalCidade.

Anderson, Wanni W., and Robert G. Lee. 2005. "Asian American Displacements." In *Displacements and Diasporas: Asians in the Americas*, edited by Wanni W. Anderson and Robert G. Lee, 3–22. New Brunswick: Rutgers University Press.

Andrade, Mário Pinto de. 1951. "Aspectos da Literatura Negro-Africana: Ensaio." *Casa Comum*. Accessed March 3, 2015. http://hdl.handle.net/11002/fms_dc_83522.

Antunes, Antonio Lobo. 2008. *Os Cus de Judas*. 3rd ed. Alfragide, Portugal: Leya.

Arenas, Fernando. 2011. *Lusophone Africa: Beyond Independence*. Minneapolis: University of Minnesota Press.

Arendt, Hannah. (1951) 1973. *On Totalitarianism*. Orlando: Harcourt.

Ashley, Clifford. 1926. *The Yankee Whaler*. New York: Dover.

Baganha, Maria I. 1999. "Migracões internacionais de e para Portugal: O que sabemos e para onde vamos." *Revista Crítica de Ciências Sociais* 52–53: 229–80.

———. 2005. "Política de imigração: A regulação dos fluxos." *Revista Crítica de Ciências Sociais* 73: 9–44.

Bakhtin, M. M. 1981. "Forms of Time and of the Chronotope in the Novel: Notes towards a Historical Poetics." In *The Dialogic Imagination*, edited by Michael Holquist, 84–258. Translated by Caryl Emerson and Michael Holquist. Austin: University of Texas Press.

Bammer, Angelika, ed. 1994. *Displacements: Cultural Identities in Question*. Bloomington: Indiana University Press.

Banting, Keith, and Will Kymlicka. 2013. "Is There Really a Retreat from Multiculturalism Policies? New Evidence from the Multiculturalism Policy Index." *Comparative European Politics* 11: 577–98.

Baptista, Marlyse. 2002. *The Syntax of Cape Verdean Creole: The Sotavento Varieties*. Amsterdam: John Benjamins.

———. 2010. "Cape Verdean Creole in Education: A Linguistic and Human Right." Co-authored with Inês Brito and Saídu Bangura. In *Creoles and Education*, edited by Bettina Migge, Isabelle Léglise, and Angela Bartens, 273–96. The Creole Language Library. Amsterdam: John Benjamins.

## References

Baraka, Amiri (LeRoi Jones). (1963) 2000. "The Changing Same (R and B and the New Black Music)." In *The LeRoi Jones/Amiri Baraka Reader*, edited by William J. Harris, 186–209. New York: Thunder's Mouth Press.

Barbosa, Carlos Elias, and Max Ruben Ramos. 2009. "Vozes movimentos de afirmação: os filhos de cabo-verdianos em Portugal." In *Comunidade(s) Cabo-Verdiana(s): As Múltiplas Faces da Imigração Cabo-Verdiana*, compiled by Pedro Góis, 173–91. Lisbon: ACIDI.

Barros, Victor. 2008. "As Sombras da Claridade: Entre o discurso de Integração Regional e a Retórica Nacionalista." In *Comunidades Imaginadas: Nação e Nacionalismos em África*, compiled by Luís Reis Torgal, Fernando Tavares Pimenta, and Julião Soares Sousa, 193–217. Coimbra, Portugal: Imprensa da Universidade de Coimbra.

———. 2009. "Sob o signo da celebração do império: o discurso colonial e o mito da especificidade Caboverdiana." In *Sociedades Desiguais: Género, Cidadania, Identidades*, compiled by Muleka Mwewa, Gleiciani Fernandes, and Patrícia Gomes,151–85. São Leopoldo, Brazil: Editora Nova Harmonia.

Bartoli, H. 1966. "Les migrations de la main d'oeuvre." *Cahiers de ISEA* (Institute of Applied Economic Science) 177: 135–86.

Batalha, Luís. 2004a. *The Cape Verdean Diaspora in Portugal: Colonial Subjects in a Postcolonial World*. New York: Lexington Books.

———. 2004b. "A elite portuguesa-caboverdiana: ascensão e queda de um grupo colonial intermediário." In *A Persistência da História: Passado e contemporaneidade em África*, edited by Clara Carvalho and João Pina Cabral, 191–225. Lisbon: Imprensa de Ciências Sociais.

Batalha Luís, and Jørgen Carling, eds. 2008. *Transnational Archipelago: Perspectives on Cape Verdean Migration and Diaspora*. Amsterdam: Amsterdam University Press.

Bellamy, Richard. 2004. "Introduction: The Making of Modern Citizenship." In *Lineages of European Citizenship: Rights, Belonging, and Participation in Eleven Nation-States*, edited by Richard Bellamy, Dario Castioglione, and Emilio Santoro, 1–20. New York: Palgrave.

Bennett, Andy. 2000. *Popular Music and Youth Culture: Music, Identity, and Place*. London: Macmillan.

Bhabha, Homi. 1983. "The Other Question." *Screen* 24 (6): 18–36.

———. 1990. "The Third Space: Interview with Homi Bhabha." In *Identity, Community, Culture, Difference*, edited by Jonathan Rutherford, 207–21. London: Lawrence and Wishart.

Blommaert, Jan. 2003. *Sociolinguistics of Globalization*. Cambridge: Cambridge University Press.

Bocage. (Elmano Sadino). (1799) 2007. "Os cães domésticos e o cão montanhês." In *Obra completa de Bocage*, edited by Daniel Pires, 23–24. Vol. 3. Oporto, Portugal: Caixotim.

Bolland, O. Nigel. 1992. "Creolisation and Creole Societies: A Cultural Nationalist View of Caribbean Social History." In *Intellectuals in the Twentieth-Century Caribbean, vol. 1: Spectre of the New Class: The Commonwealth Caribbean*, edited by Alistair Hennessy, 50–70. London: Macmillan.

Bordalo Pinheiro, Raphael. 1900. "Herança Histórica." *Faculdade de Letras da Universidade de Lisboa*, 2007. http://bibliotecadigital.fl.ul.pt/ULFLOM466988_26/ULFLOM 466988_26_master/ULFLOM466988-10/ULFLOM466988-10_item1/P67.html.

Bosniak, Linda. 2006. *The Citizen and the Alien*. Princeton: Princeton University Press.

# References

Boswell, Christina. 2007. "Theorizing Migration Policy: Is There a Third Way?" *International Migration Review* 41 (1): 75–100.

Bourgois, Philippe. 2003. *In Search of Respect: Selling Crack in El Barrio*. 2nd ed. New York: Cambridge University Press.

Bousetta, Hassan. 1997. "Citizenship and Political Participation in France and the Netherlands: Reflections on Two Local Cases." *New Community* 23 (2): 215–31.

Bowen, John. 2007. *Why the French Don't Like Headscarves*. Princeton: Princeton University Press.

Bretell, Caroline B., and Deborah Reed-Danahay. 2010. *Civic Engagements: The Citizenship Practices of Indian and Vietnamese Immigrants*. Stanford: Stanford University Press.

Brito-Semedo, Manuel. 1995. *Caboverdiamente ensaiando*. Praia, Cape Verde: Ilhéu.

Britto, Lena. 2002. *YankeeMericana: My Cape Verdean Odyssey*. Middleborough, MA: Rock Village.

Brochmann, Grete, and Idunn Seland. 2010. "Citizenship Policies and Ideas of Nationhood in Scandinavia." *Citizenship Studies* 14 (4): 429–43.

Brubaker, William James. 1989. Introduction. In *Immigration and the Politics of Citizenship in Europe and North America*, edited by R. Brubaker. Lanham, MD: University Press of America.

Bull, Benjamin Pinto. 1989. *O Crioulo da Guiné-Bissau: Filosofia e Sabedoria*. Lisbon: Instituto de Cultura e Língua Portuguesa.

Burdick, John. 2013. *The Color of Sound: Race, Religion, and Music in Brazil*. New York: New York University Press.

Butler, Judith. 1990. *Gender Trouble: Feminism and the Subversion of Identity*. London: Routledge.

Cabral, Amílcar. 1974. *Textos Políticos*. Lisbon: Edições Afrontamento.

———. 1978. *Obras Escolhidas*. Porto: Seara Nova.

Cahen, Michel. 2012. "Indigenato before Race? Some Proposals on Portuguese Forced Labor Laws in Mozambique and the African Empire (1926–62)." In *Racism and Ethnic Relations in the Portuguese-Speaking World*, edited by Francisco Bethencourt and Adrian J. Pearce, 149–71. Proceedings of the British Academy. Oxford: Oxford University Press.

Calado, Pedro. 2007. "Não Percebes o Hip Hop: geografia, (sub)culturas e territorialidade." Master's thesis, Department of Geography, Universidade de Nova Lisboa.

Callixto, Vasco. 1974. *Viagem a Cabo Verde*. Lisbon: privately published.

Cañizares-Esguerra, Jorge. 2007. "Creole Colonial Spanish America." In C. Stewart 2007, 26–45.

Cardoso, Ana, and Heloísa Perista. 1994. "A Cidade Esquecida: Pobreza em Bairros Degragados de Lisboa." *Sociologia: Problemas e Práticas* 15: 99–111.

Cardoso, Pedro. 1913. "A Manduco . . ." *A Voz de Cabo Verde* 75, January.

Carling, Jørgen. 2002. "Migration in the Age of Involuntary Immobility: Theoretical Reflections and Cape Verdean Experiences." *Journal of Ethnic and Migration Studies* 28 (1): 5–42.

———. 2004. Emigration, Return, and Development in Cape Verde: The Impact of Closing Borders. *Population, Space, and Place* 10 (2): 113–32.

## References

Carling, Jørgen, and Lisa Åkesson. 2009. "Mobility at the Heart of a Nation: Patterns and Meanings of Cape Verdean Migration." *International Migration* 47 (3): 123–55.

Carlos, João. 2012. "Casa dos Estudantes do Império: berço de líderes africanos em Lisboa." *Deutsche Welle*. Accessed January 2014. http://www.dw.de/casa-dos-estudantes-do-imp%C3%A9rio-ber%C3%A7o-de-l%C3%ADderes-africanos-em-lisboa/a-16233230.

Carneiro, Costa. 1970. "Que significa Portugal?" *Permanência* 1 (1).

Carreira, Antonio. 1972. *Cabo Verde: formação e extinção de uma sociedade escravocrata (1460–1878)*. Lisbon: Centro de estudos da Guiné Portuguesa.

Carter, Katherine, and Judy Aulette. 2009. "Creole in Cape Verde: Identity, Language and Power." *Ethnography* 10 (2): 213–36.

Carter, Paul. 1992. *Living in a New Country: History, Traveling and Language*. London: Faber and Faber.

Carvalhais, Isabel Estrada. 2007. *Postnational Citizenship and the State: Political Integration of Non-national Residents in Portugal*. Oporto, Portugal: Celta.

Casimiro, Augusto. 1935. *Ilhas Crioulas*. Lisbon: Edições Cosmos.

———. 1940. *Portugal Crioulo*. Lisbon: Edições Cosmos.

Castelo, Cláudia. 1998. *O Modo Português de Estar no Mundo: O luso-tropicalismo e a ideologia colonial portuguesa (1933–1961)*. Oporto, Portugal: Afrontamento.

César, Amândio. 1970. "A Propósito de Eugénio Tavares." *Permanência* 1 (5): 26–27.

Chabal, Patrick, with Moema Parente Augel, David Brookshaw, Ana Mafalda Leite, and Caroline Shaw. 1996. *The Post-Colonial Literature of Lusophone Africa*. Evanston: Northwestern University Press.

Challinor, Elizabeth Pilar. 2008. "Home and Overseas: The Janus Face of Cape Verdean Identity." *Diaspora* 17 (1): 84–104.

Chambers, Iain. 1994. *Migrancy, Culture, Identity*. New York: Routledge.

Chaplin, Joyce E. 2007. "Creoles in British America: From Denial to Acceptance." In C. Stewart 2007, 46–65.

Chilcote, Ronald. 1966. "Developmental Nationalism and Lusotropicology Concepts for Comparative Study of Portuguese Africa?" Paper given at Ninth Annual Meeting of the African Studies Association, October 29. Bloomington, IN.

———. 1968. "The Political Thought of Amilcar Cabral." *Journal of Modern African Studies* 6 (3): 373–88.

Cidra, Rui. 2010. "Música e migração." "Brasil." "Cabo Verde." In *Enciclopédia da Música em Portugal no Século XX* [Encyclopedia of music in Portugal in the twentieth century], coord. Salwa Castelo-Branco, 773–89, 174–79, and 195–98. Lisbon: Círculo de Leitores.

Clements, J. Clancy. 2009. *The Linguistic Legacy of Spanish and Portuguese: Colonial Expansion and Language Change*. Cambridge: Cambridge University Press.

Clifford, James. 1988. *The Predicament of Culture*. Cambridge, MA: Harvard University Press.

Coelho, F. Adolfo. 1882. "Os Dialectos Românicos ou Neo-Latinos na África, Ásia, e América." *Boletim da SGL* 3 (8): 451–512.

Cohen, Robin, ed. 1995. *Cambridge Survey of World Migration*. Cambridge: Cambridge University Press.

## References

———. 2010. "Social Identities, Diaspora, and Creolization." In *Diasporas: Concepts, Identities, Intersections*, edited by Kim Knott and Seán McLoughlin, 69–73. London: Zed Books.

Cohen, Robin, and Olivia Sheringham. 2008a. "Introduction: Islands and Identities." *Diaspora* 17 (1): 1–5.

———. 2008b. "The Salience of Islands in the Articulation of Creolization and Diaspora." *Diaspora* 17 (1): 6–17.

Collett, Elizabeth. 2014. "The City Brand: Champion of Immigrant Integration or Empty Marketing Tool?" *Migration Policy Institute*, 2001–15. Accessed September 1, 2014. http://www.migrationpolicy.org/research/city-brand-champion-immigrant-integration-or-empty-marketing-tool.

Condry, Ian. 2006. *Hip-Hop Japan: Rap and the Paths of Cultural Globalization*. Durham: Duke University Press.

Connell, John, and Chris Gibson. 2003. *Sound Tracks: Popular Music, Identity, and Place*. London: Routledge.

Contador, António. 2007. "Lisboa quer ser negra outra vez?" *Ípsilon* June 29, 11–15.

Cornelius, Wayne A. 1994. "Spain: The Uneasy Transition from Labor Exporter to Labor Importer." In *Controlling Immigration: A Global Perspective*, edited by Wayne A. Cornelius, Philip L. Martin, and James F. Hollifield, 331–70. Stanford: Stanford University Press.

Correia, Mendes. 1945. "Palestra de Abertura." *Boletim da SGL* ser. 63: 3–7.

Crooks, Peter, and Timothy Parsons, eds. 2014. *Empires and Bureaucracy from Late Antiquity to the Modern World*. Cambridge: Cambridge University Press.

Dash, Michael. 1996. "Psychology, Creolisation, and Hybridisation." In *New National and Post-Colonial Literatures: An Introduction*, edited by Bruce King, 45–58. Oxford: Clarendon Press.

David, Carina. 2011. "O novo álbum de Expavi: 'História k' nunca esh contop.'" *A Semana*. Accessed June 2013. http://www.asemana.publ.cv/spip.php?article62495.

Davidson, Basil. 1989. *The Fortunate Isles: A Study in African Transformation*. Trenton, NJ: Africa World Press.

Dent, Alexander Sebastian. 2009. *River of Tears: Country Music, Memory, and Modernity in Brazil*. Durham: Duke University Press.

Duarte, Dulce Almada. 2003. *Bilinguismo ou Diglossia? As relações de força entre o crioulo e o português na sociedade cabo-verdiana*. Praia, Cape Verde: Spleen Edições.

Duffy, James. 1961a. "Portugal in Africa." *Council on Foreign Affairs*, 2002–15. April 1. Accessed January 3, 2014. http://www.foreignaffairs.com/articles/71625/james-duffy/portugal-in-africa.

———. 1961b. "Portuguese Africa (Angola and Mozambique): Some Crucial Problems and the Role of Education in Their Resolution." *Journal of Negro Education* 30 (3): 296–301.

Dümcke, Cornelia, and Mikhail Gnedovsky. 2013. "The Social and Economic Value of Cultural Heritage: Literature Review." EENC. Accessed March 25, 2015. eenc.org.

Durão, Susana. 2011. "Opportunities, Politics, and Subjectivity in Rio de Janeiro and Lisbon's Non-governmental Organizations." In *Europe in Black and White: Immigration, Race, and*

## References

*Identity in the "Old Continent*," edited by Manuela Ribeiro Sanches, Fernando Clara, João Ferreira Duarte, and Leonor Pires Martins, 101–20. Chicago: Intellect Press.

Eagleton, Terry. 2000. *The Idea of Culture*. Oxford: Blackwell.

Eaton, Martin. 1993. "Foreign Residents and Illegal Aliens: Os negros em Portugal." *Ethnic and Racial Studies* 16 (3): 536–62.

Ennes, Antonio. (1893) 1971. *Mozambique—Report Presented to the Government*. 4th ed. Lisbon: Agência Geral do Ultramar.

Entzinger, Han, and Gottfried Engbersen. 2014. *Rotterdam: A Long-Time Port of Call and Home to Immigrants*. Washington, DC: Migration Policy Institute.

Epifânio, Renato. 2013. "'Para acabar de vez com a lusofonia'?! Resposta a António Pinto Ribeiro." *GeoPol*, January 23. Accessed June 2013. http://www.geopol.com.pt/?p=530.

Errante, Antoinette. 1998. "Education and National Personae in Portugal's Colonial and Postcolonial Transition." *Comparative Education Review* 42 (3): 267–308.

European Institute for Comparative Cultural Research. 2008. *Sharing Diversity: National Approaches to Intercultural Dialogues in Europe: Study for the European Commission*. Bonn: European Institute for Comparative Cultural Research. http://www.interculturaldialogue.eu/web/files/14/en/Sharing_Diversity_Final_Report.pdf.

Eurostat. 2011. *Cultural Statistics*. Eurostat Pocketbooks. Luxembourg: European Union.

Évora, Iolanda. 2011. "Djunta-mon em três tempos: pós-independência, imigração e transnacionalismo. Aspetos da experiência associativa Cabo Verdiana." Paper presented at X Congresso Luso-Afro-Brasileiro de Ciências Sociais. Moinho, Portugal, Febraury. Accessed February 2012. http://pascal.iseg.utl.pt/~cesa/files/publicacoes/OP11.pdf.

Ezequiel, E. 1944. "Os Tactores da Riqueza das Nossas Ilhas Atlânticas." *Boletim da SGL* 62 (5): 306–67.

Faria, Antonio. 1997. *A Linha Estreita da Liberdade: A Casa dos Estudantes do Império*. Lisbon: Edições Colibri.

Farmhouse, Rosário. 2008. "Lisboa—cidade intercultural." In *Lisboa Mistura*, 30. Lisbon: Sons da Lusofonia.

Feldman-Bianco, Bela. 1993. "Multiple Layers of Time and Space: The Construction of Class, Ethnicity, and Nationalism among Portuguese Immigrants." In *Towards a Transnational Perspective on Migration*, edited by Nina Glick, 145–74. New York: Academy of Sciences.

Ferreira, Manuel. (1962) 1972. *Hora di Bai*. Lisboa: Plátano.

———. 1967. *A Aventura Crioula*. Lisbon: Editora Ulisseia.

Fikes, Kesha. 2009. *Managing African Portugal: The Citizen-Migrant Distinction*. Durham: Duke University Press.

Filho, João Lopes. 1995. "O Estigma da Faca: Cabo-Verdianos em Portugal." *Etnologia* 3–4: 71–79.

Filho, Wilson Trajano. 2009. "The Conservative Aspects of a Centripetal Diaspora: The Case of the Cape Verdean Tabancas." *Africa* 79 (4): 520–42.

Forman, Murray. 2002. *The 'Hood Comes First: Race, Space, and Place in Rap and Hip-Hop*. Middletown: Wesleyan University Press.

## References

Forrest, Joshua. 2003. *Lineages of State Fragility: Rural Civil Society in Guinea-Bissau.* Athens: Ohio University Press.

Foucault, Michel. 1984. "Of Other Spaces." *Architecture, Mouvement, Continuité* 5: 46–49.

Fox, Aaron A. 2004. *Real Country: Music and Language in Working-Class Culture.* Durham: Duke University Press.

Fradique, Teresa. 2003. *Fixar o Movimento. Representações da música rap em Portugal.* Lisboa: Publicações Dom Quixote.

French, Jan Hoffman. 2009. *Legalizing Identities: Becoming Black or Indian in Brazil's Northeast.* Chapel Hill: University of North Carolina Press.

Freyre, Gilberto. 1953a. *Aventura e Rotina: sugestões de uma viagem à procura das constantes portuguesas de carácter e accão.* Rio de Janeiro: José Olympio.

———. 1953b. *Um Brasileiro em Terras Portuguêsas.* Rio de Janeiro: José Olympio.

Gallagher, Mary. 2007. "The *Creolité* Movement: Paradoxes in a French Caribbean Orthodoxy. In C. Stewart 2007, 220–36.

Gaspar, Vitor. 2013. "RE: Swedes Shaken by Second Night of Riots in Stockholm Suburb Triggered by Police Shooting." blog, May 24. *Total War Center.* http://www.twcenter.net/forums/showthread.php?601703-Swedes-shaken-by-second-night-of-riots-in-Stockholm-suburb-triggered-by-police-shooting/page5.

Genova, Nicholas de. 2010. "The Deportation Regime: Sovereignty, Space, and the Freedom of Movement." In *The Deportation Regime,* edited by Nicholas de Genova and Nathalie Peutz, 33–65. Durham: Duke University Press.

Gibau, Gina Sánchez. 2005. "Contested Identities: Race and Ethnicity in the Cape Verdean Diaspora." *Identities* 12: 405–38.

Gidé, André. 1949. *The Immoralist.* New York: Alfred Knopf.

Gilroy, Paul. 1993. *Black Modernity: Modernity and Double-Consciousness.* Cambridge, MA: Harvard University Press.

Glissant, Édouard. 1989. *Caribbean Discourse: Selected Essays.* Charlottesville: University of Virginia Press.

———. 1997. *Poetics of Relation.* Translated by Betsy Wing. Ann Arbor: University of Michigan Press.

Gois, Pedro. 2008. "Entre Janus e Hydra de Lerna: As Múltiplas Faces dos Cabo-Verdianos em Portugal." In *Comunidade(s) cabo-verdiana(s): as múltiplas faces da imigração cabo-verdiana,* org. Pedro Góis, 9–24. Lisbon: ACIDI.

Gomes, Pinharanda. 1970. "José Osório de Oliveira e a cultura portuguesa do Ultramar." *Permanência* 1 (4): 28–29.

Goodwin, Charles. 2007. "Participation, Stance, and Affect in the Organization of Activities." *Discourse and Society* 18 (1): 53–73.

Graham, Richard. 1990. *The Idea of Race in Latin America.* Austin: University of Texas Press.

Gramsci, Antonio. 2011. *The Prison Notebooks.* Edited by Joseph A. Buttigieg. New York: Columbia University Press.

Grassi, Marzia. 2009. "Identidades Plurais na Europa Contemporânea: Auto-Percepções e Representações nos Jovens de Origem Africana em Portugal." In *Comunidade(s) Cabo-*

# References

*Verdiana(s): As Múltiplas Faces da Imigração Cabo-Verdiana*, org. Pedro Góis, 155–72. Lisbon: ACIDI.

Greenberg, Michael. 2014. "The Daggers of Jorge Luis Borges." *New York Book Review of Books* January 9. http://www.nybooks.com/articles/archives/2014/jan/09/daggers-jorge-luis-borges/.

Guilbault, Jocelyn. 1993. *Zouk: World Music in the West Indies*. Chicago: University of Chicago Press.

Guimarães, Ângela. 1984. *Uma Corrente do Colonialismo Português. A Sociedade de Geografia de Lisboa, 1875–1895*. Lisbon: Livros Horizonte.

Hall, Stuart. 1995. Negotiating Caribbean Identities." *New Left Review* 1 (209): 3–14.

Halter, Marilyn. 1993. *Between Race and Identity: Cape Verdean American Immigrants, 1860–1965*, Urbana: University of Illinois Press.

Hamilton, Russell G. 1991. "Lusofonia, Africa, and Matters of Languages and Letters." *Hispania* 74 (3): 610–17.

Hammond, Richard J. 1967. "Race Attitudes and Policies in Portuguese Africa in the Nineteenth and Twentieth Centuries." *Race and Class* 9: 205–16.

Hannerz, Ulf. 1987. "The World in Creolisation." *Africa* 57: 546–59.

———. 1996. "Stockholm: Doubly Creolizing." In *Transnational Connections*, edited by Ulf Hannerz, 150–59. New York: Taylor and Francis.

Harris, Wilson. 1999. "Creoleness: The Crossroads of a Civilization?" In *Selected Essays of Wilson Harris: The Unfinished Genesis of the Imagination*, edited by A. J. M. Bundy, 237–47. New York: Routledge.

Havik, Philip J. 2007. "Kriol without Creoles: Rethinking Guinea's Afro-Atlantic Connections (Sixteenth to Twentieth Centuries)." In *Cultures of the Lusophone Black Atlantic*, edited by Nancy Priscilla Naro, Roger Sansi-Roca, and David H. Treece, 41–73. New York: Palgrave.

Healy, Claire 2011. *A Cidadania Portuguesa: A Nova Lei de Nacionalidade de 2006*. Lisbon: ACIDI.

Hebdige, Dick. 1987. *Cut n' Mix: Culture, Identity and Caribbean Music*. London: Methuen Press.

Henriques, Isabel Castro. 2009. *A Herança Africana em Portugal—séculos XV–XX*. Lisbon: Correios de Portugal.

———. 2011. *Os Africanos em Portugal: Memória e Cultura, Séculos XV–XIX*. Lisbon: Projeto UNESCO.

———. 2012. "Africans in Portuguese Society: Classification Ambiguities and Colonial Realities." In *Imperial Migrations: Colonial Communities and Diaspora in the Portuguese World*, edited by Eric Morier-Genoud and Michel Cahen, 72–103. New York: Palgrave.

Heywood, Linda, and John Thornton. 2007. *Central Africans, Atlantic Creoles, and the Foundation of the Americas, 1585–1660*. New York: Cambridge Press.

Holm, John, Jürgen Lang, Jean-Louis Rougé, and Maria João Soares, eds. 2006. Cabo Verde: origens da sua sociedade e do seu crioulo. Tübingen, Germany: Gunter Narr.

Horta, Anna Paula Beja. 2001. "Transnational Networks and the Local Politics of Migrant Grassroots Organizing in Postcolonial Portugal." ESRC Research Programme, University of Oxford, WPTC-02-03.

## References

———. 2008. *A Construção da Alteridade: Nacionalidade, Políticas de Imigração e Acção Coletiva Migrante na Sociedade Portuguesa Pós-Colonial*. Lisbon: Fundação Calouste Gulbenkian.

Horta, Jose da Silva. 2000. "Evidence for a Luso-African Identity in 'Portuguese' Accounts on 'Guinea of Cape Verde' (Sixteenth–Seventeenth Centuries)." *History in Africa* 27: 99–130.

Huttman, Elizabeth, Juliet Saltman, and Wim Blauw. 1991. *Urban Housing Segregation of Minorities in Western Europe and the United States*. Durham: Duke University Press.

Ifekwunigwe, Jayne O. 2010. "'Black Folk Here and There': Repositioning Other(ed) African Diaspora(s) in/and 'Europe.'" In *The African Diaspora and the Disciplines*, edited by Tejumola Olaniyan and James H. Sweet, 313–38. Bloomington: Indiana University Press.

INE [National Statistical Institute]. 1981. *Statistical Yearbook of Portugal, 1981*. Lisbon: INE.

INE [National Statistical Institute]. 2007. *Statistical Yearbook of Portugal, 2007*. Lisbon: INE.

INE [National Statistical Institute]. 2013. *Statistical Yearbook of Portugal, 2013*. Lisbon: INE.

"Intercultural Cities Index." Council of Europe. Accessed June 2013. http://www.coe.int/t/dg4/cultureheritage/culture/Cities/Index/default_en.asp.

Intercultural Cities Report 2012. "The City of Rotterdam: Intercultural Profile." *Council of Europe*. https://www.coe.int/t/dg4/cultureheritage/culture/Cities/RotterdamProfile_en.pdf.

Irvine, Judith T., and Susan Gal. 2000. "Language Ideology and Linguistic Differentiation." In *Regimes of Language: Ideologies, Polities, and Identities*, edited by Paul V. Kroskrity, 35–83. Santa Fe: School of American Research Press.

Ishemo, Shubi L. 1995. "Forced Labour and Migration in Portugal's African Colonies." In *Cambridge Survey of World Migration*, edited by Robin Cohen, 162–65. Cambridge: Cambridge University Press.

Jackson, Shona N. 2012. *Creole Indigeneity: Between Myth and Nation in the Caribbean*. Minneapolis: University of Minnesota Press.

Jerónimo, Miguel Bandeira. 2006. "Os Missionários do Alfabeto nas Colónias Portuguesas (1880–1930)." In *Estudos de Sociologia da Leitura em Portugal no Século XX*, edited by Diogo Ramada Curto, 29–65. Lisbon: Fundação Gulbenkian.

———. 2012. "The 'Civilization Guild': Race and Labor in the Third Portuguese Empire, c.1870–1930." In *Racism and Ethnic Relations in the Portuguese-Speaking World*, edited by Francisco Bethencourt and Adrian J. Pearce, 173–99. Proceedings of the British Academy. Oxford: Oxford University Press.

João, Maria Isabel. 1998. "Organização da Memória." In *História da Expansão Portuguesa*, edited by Francisco Bethencourt and Kirti Chaudhuri, 6:376–402. Lisbon: Circulo de Leitores.

Jones, LeRoi. *See* Amiri Baraka.

Joppke, Christian. 2010. *Citizenship and Immigration*. Malden, MA: Polity Press.

Kaczorowski, Jacqueline. 2014. "Os limites da Lusofonia." *Revista Língua*, Accessed January 2014. http://revistalingua.uol.com.br/textos/99/os-limites-da-Lusofonia-304206-1.asp.

Karakayali, Serhat, and Enrica Rigo. 2010. "Mapping the European Space of Circulation." In *The Deportation Regime*, edited by Nicholas de Genova and Nathalie Peutz, 123–44. Durham: Duke University Press.

## References

Keane, Webb. 2011. "Indexing Voice: A Morality Tale." *Journal of Linguistic Anthropology* 21 (2): 166–78.

Keese, Alexander. 2012. "Imperial Actors? Cape Verdean Mentality in the Portuguese Empire under the *Estado Novo*, 1926–1974." In *Imperial Migrations: Colonial Communities and Diaspora in the Portuguese World*, edited by Eric Morier-Genoud and Michel Cahen, 129–48. New York: Palgrave.

Kelley, Robin. 1997. *Yo' Mama's Disfunktional! Fighting the Culture Wars in Urban America*. Boston: Beacon Press.

Kenny, Mary Lorena. 2013. "The Contours of Quilombola Identity in the Sertão." *Luso-Brazilian Review* 50 (1): 140–64.

Khan, Aisha. 2001. "Journey to the Center of the Earth: The Caribbean as Master Symbol." *Cultural Anthropology* 16 (3): 271–302.

———. 2004. *Callaloo Nation: Metaphors of Race and Religious Identity among South Asians in Trinidad*. Durham: University of Duke University Press.

———. 2007. "Creolization Moments." In C. Stewart 2007, 237–53.

Kiesling, Scott. 2001. "Stances of Whiteness and Hegemony in Fraternity Men's Discourse." *Journal of Linguistic Anthropology* 11 (1): 101–15.

Koopman, Ruud. 2010. "Trade-Offs between Equality and Difference: Immigrant Integration, Multiculturalism, and the Welfare State in Cross-National Perspective." *Journal of Ethnic and Migration Studies* 36 (1): 1–26.

Krims, Adam. 2007. *Music and Urban Geography*. New York: Routledge.

Kroskrity, Paul V. 2000. "Regimenting Languages: Language Ideological Perspectives." In *Regimes of Language: Ideologies, Polities, and Identities*, edited by Paul V. Kroskrity, 1–34. Santa Fe: School of American Research.

Kymlicka, Will. 1995. *Multicultural Citizenship*. Oxford: Oxford Press.

Laguerre, Michel S. 1998. *Diasporic Citizenship: Haitian Americans in Transnational America*. New York: St. Martin's.

Lang, George. 1996. "Literary *Crioulo* since Independence in São Tomé, Guinea-Bissau and Cape Verde." *Luso-Brazilian Review* 33 (2): 53–63.

———. 2005. "Basilects in Creole Literatures: Examples from Sranan, Cape Verdean Crioulo, and Antillean Kr'eyol." *Journal of Pidgin and Creole Languages* 20 (1): 85–99.

Lefebvre, Henri. 1991. *Critique of Everyday Life*. Vol. 1. London: Verso.

"Legislação." *Procuradoria-Geral Distrital de Lisboa, 2011–15*. Accessed June 2013. http://www.pgdlisboa.pt/pgdl/leis/lei_mostra_articulado.php?nid=614&tabela=leis.

Leite, Mario. 1937. "Apontamentos para a história das ilhas de Cabo Verde: O actual povo caboverdiano." *Boletim da SGL* series 55 (5): 196–203.

Levenson, Jay A., ed. 2007. *Encompassing the Globe: Portugal and the World in the 16th and 17th Centuries*. Washington, DC: Smithsonian Institution.

Lima, Mesquitela. 1959. "Coexistência." *Boletim da SGL* 35 (403): 3–4.

Lima, R. W. 2010. "Thugs: vítimas e/ou agentes da violência?" *Revista Direito e Cidadania*, special issue. *Política Social e Cidadania* 30: 191–220.

# References

———. 2012. "Rappers cabo-verdianos e participação política juvenil." *Revista Tomo (Dossiê: Juventudes, expressividades e poder em perspectivas cruzadas)* 21: 263–94.

Lipski, John M. 1994. "Afro-Portuguese Pidgin: Separating Innovation from Imitation." Paper presented at annual meeting, the American Association of Teachers of Spanish and Portuguese, Philadelphia, August. Accessed April 2010. http://www.researchgate.net/publication/237631981_Afro-Portuguese_pidgin_separating_innovation_from_imitation.

"Lisbon: Results of the Intercultural Cities Index 2014." 2014. *Council of Europe*. Accessed June 2014. http://www.coe.int/t/dg4/cultureheritage/culture/Cities/Index/Lisbon_en.pdf.

Lobban, Richard. 1995. *Cape Verde: Crioulo Colony to Independent Nation*. Boulder, CO: Westview Press.

Lobban, Richard, and Marilyn Halter. 1988. *Historical Dictionary of the Republic of Cape Verde*. 1st ed. Plymouth, UK: Scarecrow.

Loch, Dietmar. 2014. "Immigration, Segregation, and Social Cohesion: Is the 'German Model' Fraying at the Edges?" *Identities* 21 (6): 675–92.

Lochery, Neill. 2011. *Lisbon: War I the Shadows of the City of Light, 1939–1945*. New York: Public Affairs.

Lopes, Baltasar. 1956. *Cabo Verde Visto por Gilberto Freyre: Apontamentos lidos ao microfone do Rádio Barlavento*. Praia, Cape Verde: Imprensa Nacional.

———. 1957. *O dialecto crioulo de Cabo Verdo*. Lisbon: Imprensa Nacional de Lisboa.

Lopes, Edmundo Correia. 1941. "Dialectos crioulos e etnografia crioula." *Sociedade de Geografia de Lisboa* 59 (9–10): 415–35.

Luedtke, Adam. 2009. "Uncovering European Union Immigration Legislation: Policy Dynamics and Outcomes." *International Migration* 2: 1–27.

Macedo, Donaldo Pereira. 1979. *Descarado*. Amsterdam: Atlantis.

Machado, Fernando Luis. 1994. "Luso-Africanos em Portugal: nas margens da etnicidade." *Sociologia: Problemas e Práticas* 16: 111–34.

Machado, Igor José de Renó. 2004. "Imigrantes brasileiros no Porto: Aproximação à perinidade de ordens racias e coloniais portuguesas." *Lusotopie* 1: 121–40.

Malheiros, Jorge Macaísta. 1996. *Imigrantes na região de Lisboa: Os Anos da Mudança: Imigração e Processo de Integração de Origem Indiana*. Lisbon: Edições Colibri.

———. 1998. "Immigration, Clandestine Work and Labour Market Strategies: The Construction Sector in the Metropolitan Region of Lisbon." *Southern European Society and Politics* 3 (3): 169–85.

———. 2002. "Ethni-cities: Residential Patterns in the Northern European and Mediterranean Metropolises: Implications for Policy Design." *International Journal Population Geography* 8: 107–134.

———. 2010. "De-Segregation, Peripheralisation and the Social Exclusion of Immigrants: Southern European Cities in the 1990s." With the assistance of Sónia Arbaci. *Journal of Ethnic and Migration Studies* 36 (2): 227–56.

———. 2011. "Portugal 2010: The Return of the Country of Emigration?" *Observare* 2 (1): 127–36.

## References

Mark, Peter. 2002. *"Portuguese" Style and Luso-African Identity: Precolonial Senegambia, Sixteenth–Nineteenth Centuries*. Bloomington: University of Indiana Press.

Märzhaüser, Christina. 2009. "Portugiesisch und Kabuverdianu im Kontakt: Muster des Code-switching und lexikalische Innovationen. Eine empirische Untersuchung von Raptexten aus Lissabon." Dissertation, Department of Language and Literary Criticism, Ludwig-Maximilians-Universität.

———. 2011. "Cape Verdean Creole in Lisbon: The Young Generation's Perspective." In *Postcolonial Linguistic Voices: Identity Choices and Representations*, edited by Eric A. Anchimbe and Stephen A. Mforteh, 299–322. Berlin: de Gruyter.

Mascarenhas, Maria. 1973. "Situação dos trabalhadores Cabo-verdianos na Metrópole." *Presença Crioula* 1 (3): 5.

Massey, Doreen. 1994. *Space, Place, and Gender*. Minneapolis: University of Minnesota Press.

Maxwell, Ian. 2003. *Phat Beats, Dope Rhymes: Hip Hop Down under Comin' Upper*. Middletown: Wesleyan University Press.

McCusker, Maeve, and Anthony Soares, eds. 2011. *Islanded Identities: Constructions of Postcolonial Cultural Insularity*. Leiden, The Netherlands: Brill Press.

McNee, Malcolm K. 2012. "José Eduardo Agualusa, and Other Possible Lusofonias." *Luso-Brazilian Review* 49 (1): 1–26.

Meintel, Deidre. 1984. *Race, Culture, and Portuguese Colonialism in Cabo Verde*. Syracuse: Syracuse University Press.

———. 2002. "Cape Verdean Transnationalism, Old and New." *Anthroplogica* 44: 25–42.

Melville, Herman. (1851) 2001. *Moby-Dick*. New York: Penguin. Citations are to the Penguin edition.

———. (1856) 2013. "The 'Gees." *Harper's New Monthly Magazine*. Biblioklept, January 27. Accessed June 2013. http://biblioklept.org/2013/01/27/the-gees-herman-melville/. Citations are to the website.

Mintz, Sidney. 1971. "The Socio-historical Background to Pidginization and Creolization." In *Pidginization and Creolization of Languages*, edited by Dell Hymes, 437–43. Cambridge: Cambridge University Press.

Miranda, Nuno de. 1971. "Mar: Imagem e Palavra." *Permanencia* 1 (10): 31.

Moehn, Frederick. 2012. *Contemporary Carioca: Technologies of Mixing in a Brazilian Music Scene*. Durham: Duke University Press.

Morgan, Marcyliena. 2009. *The Real Hip Hop: Battling for Knowledge, Power and Respect in the L.A. Underground*. Durham: Duke University Press.

Morier-Genoud, Eric, and Michel Cahen. 2012. "Introduction: Portugal, Empire and Migrations: Was There Ever an Autonomous Social Imperial Space?" In *Imperial Migrations: Colonial Communities and Diaspora in the Portuguese World*, edited by Eric Morier-Genoud and Michel Cahen, 1–30. New York: Palgrave.

Moura-Ramos, Rui Manuel Gens de. 1984. *Do Direito Português da Nacionalidade*. Coimbra, Portugal: Coimbra Editora.

Narayan, Kirin. 2010. "Placing Lives through Stories: Second-Generation South Asian Americans." In *Everyday Life in South Asia*, edited by Diane P. Mines and Sarah Lamb, 472–86. Bloomington: Indiana University Press.

Newitt, Marilyn. 2004. *A History of Portuguese Expansion Overseas, 1400–1668*. New York: Routledge.

Nogueira, Rodrigo de Sá. 1957. Prologue. In *O Dialecto Crioulo de Cabo Verde*, 7–25. Lisbon: Imprensa Nacional de Lisboa.

Núcleo. 2008. Interview with rapper Núcleo. Translated by author. *Hip Hop Tuga*. Accessed May 2010. http://www.h2tuga.net/artigos-h2t/entrevistas/2418-supa-nucleo-gab-e-dj-ride.html (post discontinued).

Oliveira, Mário António Fernandes de. 1970. "A política portuguesa de integração lingüística." *Permanência* 20–21.

Oliveira, Osorio de. 1936. "Palavras sobre Cabo Verde para serem lidas no Brasil." *Claridade* 2, August.

Oliveira, Marques de. 1955. *Cabo Verde: Boletim de Propaganda e Informação* 4 (43): 24.

Oliveira, Sara R. 2010. "Alunos imigrantes: Integração facilitada." *ACIDI*. Accessed August 28, 2014. http://www.acidi.gov.pt/pesquisa/crioul.

Osário, Oswaldo. 1980. *Cantigas de trabalho: Tradições de Cabo Verde*. Lisboa: Plâtano Editora.

"The Outcomes and Impact of the Intercultural Cities Programme 2008–2013." 2014. *Council of Europe*. www.coe.int/interculturalcities.

Palmié, Stephan. 2002. *Wizards and Scientists: Explorations in Afro-Cuban Modernity and Tradition*. Durham: Duke University Press.

———. 2006. "Creolization and Its Discontents." *Annual Review of Anthropology* 35: 433–56.

Pardue, Derek. 2010. "Making Territorial Claims: Brazilian Hip Hop and the Socio-geographical Dynamics of *Periferia*." *City and Society* 22 (1): 48–71.

———. 2011. *Brazilian Hip Hoppers Speak from the Margins: We's on Tape*. New York: Palgrave.

Parekh, Bhiku. 2000. *Rethinking Multiculturalism: Cultural Diversity and Political Theory*. Cambridge, MA: Harvard University Press.

Parsons, Elsie Clews. 1921. "Folk-lore of the Cape Verde Islanders." *Journal of American Folklore* 34 (131): 89–109.

Patterson, Tiffany Ruby, and Robin D. G. Kelley. 2000. "Unfinished Migrations: Reflections on the African Diaspora and the Making of the Modern World." *African Studies Review* 43 (1): 11–45.

Pedaliu, Effie. 2013. "The Making of Southern Europe: An Historical Overview." *A Strategy for Southern Europe*, SR17, 8–14. London: London School of Economics and Political Science.

Pennycook, Alastair. 2010. *Language as a Local Practice*. New York: Routledge.

Pepetela [Artur Carlos Maurício Pestana]. 1996. *Mayombe*. Oxford: Heinemann.

Pépin, Ernest, and Raphael Confiänt. 1998. "The Stakes of Créolité." In *Caribbean Creolization: Reflections on the Cultural Dynamics of Language, Literature and Identity*, edited by Kathleen M. Balutansky and Marie-Agnès Sourieau, 96–100. Gainesville: University of Florida Press and University of the West Indies Press.

Pereira, Nuno Teutônio. 1994. "Pátios e vilas de Lisboa, 1870–1930: A promoção privada de alojamento operário." *Análise Social* 29 (127): 509–24.

## References

Pereira, Sonia. 2013. Replacement Migration and Changing Preferences: Immigrant Workers in Cleaning and Domestic Service in Portugal." *Journal of Ethnic and Migrations Studies* 39 (7): 1141–58.

Perl, Matthias. 1982. "Acerca de alguns aspectos históricos do Português Crioulo em África." *Biblios* 58: 1–12.

Perry, Imani. 2005. *Prophets of the Hood: Politics and Poetics in Hiphop*. 2nd ed. Durham: Duke University Press.

Pestana, Artur Carlos Maurício. *See* Pepetela.

Peterson, Charles F. 2007. *Dubois, Fanon, Cabral: The Margins of Elite Anti-Colonial Leadership*. New York: Lexington Books.

Petersen, William. 1970. "A General Typology of Migration." *American Sociological Review* 23: 256–66.

Pires, R. 1999. "A Imigração." In *História da Expansão Portuguesa*, edited by Francisco Bethencourt and Kirti Chaudhuri, 5:197–213. Lisbon: Círculo dos Leitores.

Pombal, Marquis de. 1761. Livro 9 de Leis [The ninth book of laws], fl. 160v., and Maço [papers] 6 de Leis, no. 402. Instituto dos Arquivos Nacionais [National Archives Institute], Torre do Tombo, Portugal.

"Portugal Youth Unemployment Rate: 1983–2015." 2015. *Trading Economics*. http://www.tradingeconomics.com/portugal/youth-unemployment-rate.

Pratt, Mary Louise. 1992. *Imperial Eyes: Travel Writing and Transculturation*. London: Routledge.

Price, Richard. 2010. "African Diaspora and Anthropology." In *The African Diaspora and the Disciplines*, edited by Tejumola Olaniyan and James H. Sweet, 53–74. Bloomington: Indiana University Press.

"Prova de Língua Portuguesa para Aquisição de Nacionalidade." 2015. *Portaria* 176. *Governo de Portugal*. Accessed March 24, 2015. http://www.dgidc.min-edu.pt/projetosinterministeriais/index.php?s=directorio&pid=7.

Raimundo, Gabriel. 2008. *Sodade de Cabo Verde*. Lisbon: privately published.

Raimundo, Jacques. 1933. *O Elemento Afro-Negro na Língua Portuguesa*. Rio de Janeiro: Renascença Editora.

Ramos, Belmiro. 1985. "ACTAS do Congresso sobre a situação atual da Língua Portuguesa no Mundo." Lisbon, ICALPE, 1:229. In *A Língua Portuguesa no Mundo*, edited by Silvio Elia, 44. São Paulo: Editora Ática.

Ramos, Rui. 2004. "Portuguese, but Not Citizens: Restricted Citizenship in Contemporary Portugal." In *Lineages of European Citizenship: Rights, Belonging, and Participation in Eleven Nation-States*, edited by Richard Bellamy, Dario Castiglione, and Emilio Santoro, 92–112. New York: Palgrave Macmillan.

Raposo, Otávio. 2007. "Niggaz, Brothers, Blacks, soldados, ou gangsters: os jovens Red Eyes Gang." Paper presented at Center for Research and Studies in Sociology conference, Lisbon, Portugal, June 12.

———. 2010. "'Heart there and body here in Pretugal': Between Mestizagem and the Affirmation of Blackness." *Buala*, October 21, 2010. Accessed September 2014. www.buala.org/en/.

# References

Ravenstein, E. G. 1885. "The Laws of Migration." *Journal of Statistic Society of London* 48 (2): 167–235.

Reckless, Walter. (1933) 1969. *Vice in Chicago*. Montclair, NJ: Patterson Smith.

Rego, Márcia. 2008. "Cape Verdean Tongues: Speaking of 'Nation' at Home and Abroad." In *Transnational Archipelago: Perspectives on Cape Verdean Migration and Diaspora*, edited by Luís Batalha and Jørgen Carling, 145–59. Amsterdam: Amsterdam University Press.

Ribeiro, António Pinto. 2013. "Para acabar de vez com a Lusofonia." *Público*, January 18. *Buala*. Accessed June 2013. http://www.buala.org/pt/a-ler/para-acabar-de-vez-com-a-Lusofonia.

Rivera, Raquel Z. 2003. *New York Ricans from the Hip Hop Zone*. New York: Palgrave.

Rodrigues, Isabel Fêo P. B. 2011. "Literary Encounters with Intimacy in Cape Verde." In *The Power of Gender, The Gender of Power: Women's Labor, Rights, and Responsibilities in Africa*, edited by Toyin Falola and Bridget Teboh, 449–67. Trenton, NJ: Africa World Press.

Rodriguez, Robyn Magalit. 2013. "Beyond Citizenship: Emergent Forms of Political Subjectivity amongst Migrants." *Identities* 20 (6): 738–54.

Rogozen-Soltar, Mikaela. 2012. "Managing Muslim Visibility: Conversion, Immigration, and Spanish Imaginaries of Islam." *American Anthropologist* 114 (4): 611–23.

Rosaldo, Renato. 1994. "Cultural Citizenship and Educational Democracy." *Cultural Anthropology* 9 (3): 402–11.

Rosas, Fernando, and J. M. Brito, coords. 1996. *Dicionário de história do Estado Novo*. Lisbon: Bertrand Editora.

Rose, Tricia. 1994. *Black Noise: Rap Music and Black Culture in Contemporary America*. Hanover: University Press of New England.

Rothwell, Phillip. 2000. "A Tale of Two Tensions: Synthesis and Separation in Portuguese National Identity." *Forum for Modern Language Studies* 36 (3): 322–30.

Rumsey, Alan. 1990. "Wording, Meaning, and Linguistic Ideology." *American Anthropology* 92 (2): 346–61.

Saint-Maurice, Ana de. 1997. *Identidades Reconstruídas: Cabo-Verdianos em Portugal*. Lisbon: Celta Editora.

Salazar, Antonio de Oliveira. 1939. *Discursos e Notas Políticas*. Vol. 1. Coimbra, Portugal: Coimbra Editora.

Samuels, David. 2009. "Singing Indian Country." In *Music of the First Nations: Tradition and Innovation in Native North America*, edited by Tara Browner, 141–59. Urbana: University of Illinois Press.

Santos, Boaventura de Sousa. 2002. "Between Prospero and Caliban: Colonialism, Postcolonialism, and Inter-identity." *Luso-Brazilian Review* 39 (2): 9–43.

Sardinha, João. 2010. "Identity, Integration, and Associations: Cape Verdeans in the Metropolitan Area of Lisbon." In *Identity Processes and Dynamics in Multi-Ethnic Europe*, edited by Charles Westin, José Bastos, Janine Dahinden, and Pedro Góis, 233–56. Amsterdam: Amsterdam University Press.

Sassen, Saskia. 2001. *The Global City*. Princeton: Princeton University Press.

Serviço de Estrangeiros e Fronteiras (SEF). 2006. "Distribuição da População Estrangeira

## References

Total por distrito, nos anos de 2000, 2003 e 2006." Section 2:12–15. *Relatório de Atividades Imigração, Fronteiras e Asilo.* Lisbon: SEF.

———. 2012. *Annual Immigration Report on Borders and Asylum.* Lisbon: SEF.

Shakespeare, William. 2004. *The Tempest.* Edited by Barbara A. Mowat and Paul Werstine. New York: Simon and Schuster.

Shank, Barry. 1994. *Dissonant Identities: The Rock 'n' Roll Scene in Austin, Texas.* Middletown: Wesleyan University Press.

Sieber, Timothy. 1999. "Intervenção nas frentes de água das cidades americanas." In *A cidade da Expo '98, Uma reconversão na frente ribeirinha de Lisboa*, edited by V. M. Ferreira and F. Indovina, 63–77. Lisbon: Bizâncio.

———. 2005. "Popular Music and Cultural Identity in the Cape Verdean Post-Colonial Diaspora." *Etnográfica* 9 (1): 123–48.

———. 2007. "City Streets and Public Sociability: The View from Lisbon." In *The Street as a Place*, edited by Graca Indias Cordeiro and Frederic Vidal, 47–64. Lisbon: Livros Horizonte.

Silberling, Louise. 2003. "Displacement and *quilombos* in Alcântara, Brazil: Modernity, Identity, and Place." *International Social Science Journal* 55 (75): 145–56.

Silva, Aníbal Cavaco. 2007. Foreword to *Encompassing the Globe: Portugal and the World in the Sixteenth and Seventeenth Centuries*, edited by Jay A. Levenson. Washington, DC: Smithsonian Institution.

Silva, Tomé Varela da. 1988. *Natal y kontus.* Praia, Cape Verde: Institutu Kauberdianu di Libru.

Silverstein, Michael. 1979. "Language Structure and Linguistic Ideology." In *The Elements: A Parasession on Linguistic Units and Levels*, edited by R. Clyne, W. Hanks, and C. Hofbauer, 193–247. Chicago: Chicago Linguist Society.

Simmel, Georg. (1908) 1971. "Group Expansion and the Development of Individuality." In *Georg Simmel: On Individuality and Social Forms*, by Georg Simmel, edited by Donald Levine, 251–93. Chicago: University of Chicago Press.

Siu, Lok C. D. 2005. *Memories of a Future Home: Diasporic Citizenship of Chines in Panama.* Stanford: Stanford University Press.

Skidmore, Thomas E. 1992. *Black into White: Race and Nationality in Brazilian Thought.* Durham: Duke University Press.

Sócrates, José. 2007. "The Council of Ministers Resolution no. 63-A/2007, May 3rd." *Plan for Immigrant Integration*, 3–4. Lisbon: ACIDI.

Soja, Edward W. 1996. *Thirdspace: Journeys to Los Angeles and Other Real-and-Imagined Places.* Cambridge, MA: Blackwell.

Sousa, Albano Neves de. 1971. "Hora di Bai." *Permanência* 1 (10): 32.

Soysal, Yasemin Nohuglu. 1994. *Limits of Citizenship: Migrants and Postnational Membership in Europe.* Chicago: University of Chicago Press.

Stam, Robert, and Ella Shohat. 2011. "The Cultural Wars in Translation." In *Europe in Black and White: Immigration, Race, and Identity in the "Old Continent,"* edited by Manuela Ribeiro Sanches, Fernando Clara, João Ferreira Duarte, and Leonor Pires Martins, 19–35. Chicago: Intellect Press.

# References

Stasiuk, Andrzej. 2009. *Fado*. London: Dalkey Archive Press.
Stevenson, Nick, ed. 2001. *Culture and Citizenship*. Thousand Oaks, CA: Sage.
Stewart, Charles, ed. 2007. *Creolization: History, Ethnography, Theory*. Walnut Creek, CA: Left Coast Press.
Stewart, Kathleen. 1996. *A Space on the Other Side of the Road: Cultural Poetics in an "Other" America*. Princeton: Princeton University Press.
Stokes, Martin. 2007. "On Musical Cosmopolitanism." Paper 3. *Macalester International Roundtable*. Accessed March 7, 2013. http://digitalcommons.macalester.edu/cgi/viewcontent.cgi?article=1002&context=intlrdtable.
Straw, Will. 1991. "Systems of Articulation, Logics of Change: Scenes and Communities in Popular Music." *Cultural Studies* 5 (3): 368–88.
Suárez-Navaz, Liliana. 2004. *Rebordering the Mediterranean: Boundaries and Citizenship in Southern Europe*. New York: Berghahn Books.
"Subsidio para o estudo comparativo do ensino colonial no estrangeiro." 1910. *Boletim da SGL* 10: 312.
Super User. 2009. "Estúdio 'KM: o céu é o limite.'" *Moinho de Juventude*. Accessed June 2013. http://www.moinhodajuventude.pt/index.php/en/kola-san-jon/111-estudio-de-gravacao.
Sweet, James H. 2003. *Recreating Africa: Culture, Kinship, and Religion in the African-Portuguese World, 1441–1770*. Chapel Hill: University of North Carolina Press.
Teixeira, Cônego A. da Costa, ed. 1898. "Lusíadas." Canto 5.°, stanzas 8 and 9. Chegada Ás Ilhas de Cabo-Verde. *Revista Portuguesa Colonial e Marítima* 1 (2): 566.
Tenreiro, Francisco José. 1963. "Processo poesia." *Mensagem* 14 (1): 5–11.
Terkourafi, Marina. 2010. "Introduction: A Fresh Look at Some Old Questions." In *Languages of Global Hip Hop*, edited by Marina Terkourafi, 1–18. New York: Continuum Books.
Thomaz, Omar Ribeiro. 2000. "Uma retórica luso-tropical." Insert. *Folha de São Paulo, Revista Mais!* March 12. BibliotecaVirtual Gilberto Freyre.
Tinhorão, José Ramos. 1988. *Os Negros em Portugal*. Lisbon: Caminho.
Trouillot, Michel-Rolph. 1995. *Silencing the Past: Power and the Production of History*. Boston: Beacon Press.
"Unemployment Rate by Sex and Age Groups: Annual Average, %." 2015. *Eurostat*. http://appsso.eurostat.ec.europa.eu/nui/show.do?dataset=une_rt_a&lang=en.
United Nations Population Fund (UNPFA). 2013. "World Population Policies." New York: United Nations.
Vanspauwen, Bart Paul. 2012. "A importância de implementar uma noção de *Lusofonia* na educação cultural e cívica em Portugal, argumentado por alguns músicos oriundos de países 'lusófonos' em Lisboa." In *Anuário Internacional de Comunicação Lusófona 2011: Lusofonia e Cultura-Mundo*, edited by Moisés de Lemos Martins, Rosa Cabecinhas, and Lurdes Macedo, 67–83. Coimbra, Portugal: CECS.
Vasconcelos, Abreu G. de. 1890. "O Instituto oriental e ultramarino Português." *Boletim da SGL* 10: 517–22.

## References

Vaughan, Megan. 2005. *Creating the Creole Island: Slavery in Eighteenth-Century Mauritius.* Durham: Duke University Press.

Vaz, Claúdia. 2011. "Tatuagens, Graffitis e Letras de Rap: Formas de Expressão e/ou Rebeldia? Identidade de Jovens da Cova da Moura." Paper presented at the annual conference of Congresso Luso Afro Brasileiro de Ciências Sociais, Moinho, Portugal, August 9.

Veiga, Manuel. 1982. *Diskrison Strutural di Lingua Kabuverdianu: um ensaio.* Praia: ICL (Instituto da Cooperação da Língua).

———. 2011. "Manuel Veiga lança dicionário Caboverdiano-Português." *diárioliberdade.* Accessed August 20, 2014. http://www.diarioliberdade.org/africaasia/cultura-m%C3%BAsica/13969-manuel-veiga-lanca-dicionario-caboverdiano-portugues.html.

Vélez-Ibáñez, Carlos G. 1996. *Border Visions: Mexican Cultures of the Southwest United States.* Tucson: University of Arizona Press.

Vergès, François. 2007. "Indian-Oceanic Creolizations: Processes and Practices of Creolization on Réunion Island." In C. Stewart 2007, 133–52.

Verstraete, Ginette. 2010. *Tracking Europe: Mobility, Diaspora, and the Politics of Location.* Durham: Duke University Press.

Vertovec, Steven. 1998. "Multicultural Policies and Modes of Citizenship in European Cities." *UNESCO, International Social Science Journal* 50 (156): 187–99.

Weeks, Samuel. 2012. "'As you receive with one hand, so should you give with the other': The Mutual-Help Practices of Cape Verdeans on the Lisbon Periphery." MA thesis, Institute of Social Sciences, University of Lisbon.

Weiler, Joseph. 1999. *The Constitution of Europe.* Cambridge: Cambridge University Press.

Weiss, Brad. 2002. "Thug Realism: Inhabiting Fantasy in Urban Tanzania." *Cultural Anthropology* 17 (1): 93–124.

Wheeler, Douglas L., and Walter C. Opello Jr. 2010. *Historical Dictionary of Portugal.* Lanham, MD: Scarecrow Press.

Winford, Donald. 2003. "Ideologies of Language and Social Realistic Linguistics." In *Black Linguistics: Language, Society, and Politics in Africa and the Americas*, edited by Sinfree Makoni, Geneva Smitherman, Arnetha F. Ball, and Arthur K. Spears, 40–59. New York: Routledge.

Wood, Phil, Charles Landry, and Jude Bloomfield. 2006. "How Can We Unlock the Potential of Cultural Diversity in Cities?" *JRF.* Accessed June 15, 2013. http://www.jrf.org.uk/publications/how-can-we-unlock-potential-cultural-diversity-cities.

Woolard, Kathryn. 1994. "Language Ideology." *Annual Review Anthropology* 23: 55–82.

World Bank. 2011. *Migration and Remittances Factbook 2011.* Washington, DC: World Bank.

Zolberg, Ari, and Long Litt Woon. 1999. "Why Islam Is like Spanish." *Politics and Society* 27 (1): 5–38.

## Discography

Araphat. 2009. "Ka Ta Mesti Apresentason." Independent.
Boss AC. 2005. "Sabim." *Ritmo, Amor e Palavras.* No Stress Records.

Buraka Som Sistema. 2006. *From Buraka to the World*. Enchufada Records.
Chullage. 2001. *Represálias*. Lisafonia Records.
———. 2004. *Rapensar*, Lisafonia Records.
———. 2012. *Rapressão*. Lisafonia Records.
The Coup. 1993. "I ain't the nigga." *Kill My Landlord*. Wild Pitch Records.
Ghoya. 2008. "The Other Side of the Law." Sonoterapia Records.
———. 2009. "Vida é assi." Independent.
Hezbollah. 2009. *Entri lagrimaz y rimas*. Mixtape, Independent.
Karlos. 2009. "Kotidianu." Independent.
LBC/Soldjah. 2009. *Lagrimaz di Sangui*. Mixtape, Independent.
———. 2010. "Liberta Palestina." Independently produced.
Mentis Afro. 2012. *Mundo Infernal*. Independent.
Rapública. 1994. Compilation album. Independent.
Soares, Armando Zeferino. 1950s. "Sodade." Morna.
Tribe Called Quest. 1991. "Buggin' Out." *Low End Theory*. Jive Records.
TWA (Third World Answer). 2002. "Miraflor." *Miraflor*. Independent.
Veloso, Caetano, and Gilberto Gil. 1993. *Tropicália 2*. Polygram.

# Index

ACIDI: and Cape Verdean experiences in Lisbon, 82; definition of, xi; grants to Zulu Nation, 111–13; immigrants and policies toward, 139–43, 147–48; and interculturality, 152; on music and cultural identity, 136; referrals to, 163n3; relationships between Africans and Portuguese, 24, 26
African Party for the Independence of Guinea-Bissau and Cape Verde (PAIGCV), xi, 44, 108
africanity, 24, 28, 29, 32–33, 48, 72, 139
agency: Creole as vocabulary of, 60; creolization and Kriolu citizenship, 74–78; social, 7–8, 29, 52, 116; state, 26, 82, 111–12; and structure, 130, 133, 150, 154
Agualusa, José Eduardo, 11, 12–13, 43, 57, 157
Alim, Samy, 79, 85, 92, 93, 95, 102
Al-Judami, 28, 158n1
Almeida, Miguel Vale De, 10, 62, 74
Alto da Cova da Moura (Kova M.), 121–30; and blackness, 57; Cape Verdean population, 46–47; as emplacement site, 112; Kriolu language growth and change, 104, 109; and Kriolu rappers, 142–43; Kromo's description of, 16, 87–88; and language politics, 91–93; and LBC, 97–98, 115–16; and migrancy, 149–50
ALUPEK, ix, xi, 89, 148
Alves, Jorge Fernandes, 3
Alyson, 128
Amadora (municipality): Alto da Cova da Moura (Kova M.), 87, 125–29; Buraca, 97; Kriolu language programs, 148; and Kriolu rappers, 120–22, 144–45; structure and population of, 41, 111, 117
Anastácia, Dona, 128, 129
Andrade, Mário Coelho Pinto de, 44
Andrade, Mayra, 95, 160n4
Antunes, Antonio Lobo, 74
Apoio aos Trabalhadores Cabo-Verdianos (CV Workers Support group), 140
Araphat, 93
Arco do Cego (neighborhood), 117–18
Arenas, Fernando, 160n4, 163n3
Arendt, Hannah, 136
Arrentela (neighborhood), 80–82, 96, 101, 119, 123, 142
Asilo 28 de Maio, 80, 101
Associação Sons da Lusofonia, 78, 147
Aubyn, Antonio Saint, 9–10

# Index

autoconstructed communities, 2, 29, 31, 46, 112, 118

B. Leza (Francisco Xavier da Cruz), 76, 78
*badiu* (vagabond): definition of, 28; and diaspora, 132–33; as identity marker, 57; as a Kriolu matrix, 161n12; Kriolu rappers and sociocultural identity, 65–66, 67, 75–77; and Kriolu variations, 40; in LBC song, 114–16; use in Kriolu rap, 48
Bairro de Santa Filomena ("BSF," neighborhood), vii, 1, 119, 120, 154
Bakhtin, Mikhail, 86
Bana, 76
Baptista, Marlyse, 82, 89, 158n3, 164n12
Barbosa, Elias, 82
Barbosa, Jorge, 70–72
*barlavento* (windward islands), 9, 67
*batuko*, 95, 161n5
Belém (neighborhood), 29, 32, 148, 164n13
belonging: and citizenship, 7–8, 11, 17, 18, 25, 135, 137; and identity, 14–15, 57, 100, 152, 155; and place, 69, 79, 92–93, 101, 106
Bhabha, Homi, 31, 81
"Black Atlantic," 25, 41, 160n6
Black Panthers, 22
black/blackness (as identity): badiu and culutural stigmatization, 67, 76; Black Atlantic scholars, 25; "Black Boston," 15; and ghetto, 49; as identity of Cape Verde, 73; and Kriolu consciousness, 57; and Kriolu language, 42–43; and Kriolu rappers, 17–18, 61–62, 93, 128; and Lusotropicalism, 8; and slave trade in Portugal, 12–13; and urban culture expression, 31–33
Boba, 120–24, 125, 130
Bocage, 38
Bordalo Pinheiro, Rafael, 73, 160n11
Borges, Jorge Luis, 59, 64
Bulimundo, 76–77
Buraka Som Sistema, 97, 147
Butler, Judith, 92

Cabo da Roca (Roca Cape), vii, 1–2, 154
Cabral, Amílcar, 38–39, 44, 66, 78, 108, 139, 151
Cahen, Michel, 27, 31, 50–53
Caliban, 23–24, 38–40, 64

Callixto, Vasco, 40–41
*calunga*, 13
*Cambridge Survey of World Migration*, 10
Camões, Luís Vaz de, 1, 39, 65, 67, 71, 148
Cape Verde: population demographics, 6–7; and slave routes, 12–13
Cape Verdeans: as migrants worldwide, 15
Cardoso, Pedro, 37, 69, 70, 88, 160n10
Carling, Jørgen, 76, 89, 108, 160n7
Carreira, Manuel, 42, 158n3
Carter, Paul, 18–19
Carvalhais, Isabel Estrada, 53, 156
Casa dos Estudantes do Império (Home for the Students of the Empire), 44, 139
Casal da Boba (neighborhood), vii, 120–25, 130
Casimiro, Augusto, 27, 88
CDS-PP (Social Democratic–People's Party), 114
Challinor, Elizabeth, 50
Chambers, Iain, 19–20, 22, 31, 38, 63, 84, 89
Chapitô bar/restaurant, 147
Chelas (neighborhood), 52–53, 111, 144
Chilcote, Ronald, 45, 62, 68
chronotope: and Cape Verdean identity, 148–49; Creole, as variable, 75–76; of ghetto, 49; Kriolu as, 95, 101–4; linguistic practice of Cape Verdean Creolo, 130; meaning of citizenship, 8; rap and identity formation, 86, 91–92
Chullage (Nuno Santos): control of linguistic inheritance, 39–40; and cultural diversity, 150; Kriolu and meaning, 18; *kritikam* and *djam bai*, 124; and links among migration, race, and labor, 47, 50; "N.I.G.G.A.S.," 90–91; "Nu bai," identity, and belonging, 14–16, 96, 100–104; transformation of housing to cultural center, 119; use of contentious words, 80–82
citizenship: and civil rights, 62; cultural, 25, 81, 112, 135–38, 143–48, 151–56; European, 103, 113, 156; and immigration, 4–11; and laws, 10, 17–18, 24, 50–55, 118, 150, 159n13, 164n10; and nationality, 53–57, 144; postcolonial, 138–41; in postcolonial Portugal, 139–46; and race, 29–34, 46–50, 74, 113–16, 133, 137–39; recognition, 35, 71, 87, 92–93, 106, 111, 119–24;

# Index

rights, 11–14, 24–25, 50–58, 62, 136–38, 146, 152, 155–56, 159n13; as universal right, 58. *See also under* migration
Claridosos, 44, 70, 76, 161n5
Cohen, Robin, 10
Collett, Elizabeth, 136
colonialism: and African culture in Portugual, 28–35; Cape Verdeans and, 17; Creole as by-product, 13; Creole rappers, 130; in globalization and branding, 137; Kriolu and, 44, 49–54, 70–77; and Lusofonia, 79, 161n13; and Lusotropicalism, 160n3; Portuguese, 2–8, 54, 159n10
Community of Portuguese Language Countries (CPLP), 3–6
Confiänt, Raphael, 11
Contador, Antonio, 33
Correia, Mendes, 71
Corsino ("Uncle C"), vii, 1–3, 65, 66, 107–8, 154
Costa, Pedro, 162–63n3
The Coup (US rap group), 45, 151
Cova da Moura. *See* Alto da Cova da Moura (Kova M.)
CPLP (Community of Portuguese Language Countries), 3–6
Creole: in the Carribean, 11, 13, 61, 65, 85, 157n2; definition of, ix, 2, 6; linguistics, 75, 161n2; in West Africa, 15, 41, 42, 103, 109, 129
*Creole* (Agualusa), 12–13
creolization: Atlantic, 157n2; and citizenship, 83, 153; definition, 8; and identity formation, 8–13; and policy, 50; as population/characteristic identity, 60–65; relationship to Kriolu and Kriolu identity, 35, 41, 57; as transformative force, 77, 159n1
crime fiction, 13
*criollo*, 59, 64
Cruz, Francisco Xavier da. *See* B. Leza (Francisco Xavier da Cruz)
cultural patrimony, 71, 149
Curaçao, 4

Dakar, Senegal, 6, 15, 35, 89, 158n5
D'Almada, André Álvares, 36–37, 40
Damaia (neighborhood), vii, 31, 111, 118–19
Dani, 109–11

Davidson, Basil, 35, 125, 127
de Marees, Pieter, 158n5
decolonization: contradictions of Lusotropocalism, 74; language as inheritance, 38–39; and laws of citizenship, 54–55; and Organic Law 1953, 62; and PAIGCV, 108; use of Kriolu by Cape Verde youth, 109; and use of "rural" label, 51; wars of 1960s and 1970s, 17, 20, 91
Def, 64
Dent, Alexander Sebastian, 86
diaspora: and Afrocentrism, 155; Cape Verde immigration, 140; Cape Verdean presence in Lisbon and, 7, 22; and challenge of language, 115–16; creolization, 64, 159n1; economic and racialized dimensions of, 65–66; *Funaná*, 76, 161–62n5; and Kriolu, 9, 69, 98–99, 103, 109, 130; LBC on, 48, 60; PALOP and language as identity marker, 89; rappers' narrative of, 15, 18, 82–83, 86–87, 96; Rolando on, 132–33; in the United States, 160n7
displacement: as creator of Creole, 25; as creator of Kriolu, 35, 41–42; fighting the stigma, 130; and Kriolu rappers, 16–17, 29; in literature about Cape Verde, 69; migrant, 112; as part of occupation and settlement, 106; shift to new culture, 85; symbolized by Fontaínhas, 162–63n3
*djuguta* (daily struggle), 16, 94
*djunta mon* (joining hands), 49, 134
drama. *See under* Kriolu/Crioulo
Duffy, James, 21, 37, 45, 51
Durão, Susana, 23

education: African occupants of Lisbon, 31; and citizenship heirarchy, 54–58, 159n13; and experience, 140–52; identity recognition, 72; as integrating force, 15, 25; and language politics, 10, 35–37; "Marcus Garvey University," 22, 43–46; MIPEX tracking of, 4; rap and Kriolu identity, 91, 101
EENC (European Expert Network on Culture), 149
emplacement: Chullage's narrative of, 40; Kriolu, 87; and Kriolu citizenship, 128–31, 148; and Kriolu rappers, 16–17; and language, culture, and identity, 60; migration

and housing, 106–7; as response to displacement, 28–31; and scenes and topos, 109–17
encounter: centrality of, 19–20; and Creole citizenship, 135, 150–56, 159n1; Creole speakers and writers, 74–77; inter-identity, 4–12; rap and, 60–64; theory of identity and Kriolu, 25–28, 99, 133; "third space," 31–35; Tuga and Kriolu, 91
Ennes, Antonio, 28, 31
Errante, Antoinette, 154, 160n3, 160n8
European Commission, 9, 26, 146, 163n1
European Union (EU): and the *barro de lata*, 121; entrance of Portugal, 17, 58, 76, 113; and interculturality, 8–9, 26; Kriolu as a coping mechanism, 136; "New Europe" concept, 12; Portugal compared to rest of, 81
European Year of Intercultural Dialogue (EYID), 137, 146–47
Eurostat, 4, 137, 155
Évora, Cesária, 56, 76, 95, 161, 162n5
Expavi, 161, 162n5
experience: lived, 17, 86, 96, 106; migrant, 10, 63, 104, 150, 155;
Farmhouse, Rosário, 141, 147
Fema D, 111
Ferreira, Manuel, 43–44, 68–70, 160n9
Ferro Gaita, 76–77
Fikes, Kesha, 48
Firmino, Gregório, 78–79
Fontaínhas (neighborhood), 121–25, 162nn2–3
Forman, Murray, 114
Foucault, Michel, 105, 109
Fox, Aaron A., 86
Fradique, Teresa, 161n4
França, 111–12
Freyre, Gilberto, 50, 62, 67, 68, 71–74, 115, 159–60
*funaná*, 76–77, 95, 128–29, 161–62n5

Garvey, Marcus, 22, 46–50, 57, 98
Ghoya, 61, 113, 121–24, 145, 151
Gibau, Gina Sanchez, 89, 114
Gilroy, Paul, 87, 114, 160n6
Gilson, 52–53
Glissant, Edouard, 61, 77–78

globalization, 24, 78, 83, 99, 136–37, 146, 155
Guinea-Bissau, 4

Hair, P. E. H., 37
Hall, Stuart, 77–78
Halter, Marilyn, 97, 108, 160n7
Havik, Philip J., 42
Heidir, 127–30
Henriques, Isabel Castro, 29–32, 38, 51, 62
*A Herança Africana em Portugal*, 32
heterotopic space, 109–11
Hezbollah, 22, 61, 96–100, 104, 145
High Commission of Immigration and Ethnic Minorities (ACIME). *See* ACIDI
High Commission of Immigration and Intercultural Dialogue (ACIDI). *See* ACIDI
*Hora di Bai* (Ferreira), 69
Horta, Anna Paula Beja, 161n2
Horta, Jose da Silva, 35
housing, 14, 19, 31, 80, 86, 104–7, 143policy about, 113, 121, 134social, vii, 107, 116–22, 129–30, 139, 157n5. *See also under* migration
hybridity: ambiguities of, 61–63; and citizenship, 4, 50; and Creole, 65; and identity formation, 104; and Kriolu, 114; Lisbon as center of, 146–47; and Lusofonia, 157n5; meaning to Cape Verde, 8; and "third space," 31

identity. *See* black/blackness (as identity) cultural citizenship"inter-identity"Kriolu/CriouloLusofonia (Portugueseness)
ideology: language, 85, 91–93, 99; state/national, 2–12, 19, 25, 49, 58, 62, 68, 112, 130, 154–55
immigration. *See* migration
Immigration and Borders Service. *See* SEF (Immigration and Borders Service)
INE (National Census Bureau), 15, 57
Intercultural Cities Program (ICP), 144
Interculturalcidade, 143–44, 152
interculturality: in Cape Verde, 72; European treatment of, 162n7; Kova M, 14; and Kriolu, 26, 65–66, 132–56; and Lusofonia myth, 8–9, 11; as new idea, 113; and NGOs and immigration, 21; rejection of projects by policy makers, 104; and state policies of

citizenship, 58. *See also* ACIDI; European Union (EU)
"inter-identity," 6
International and State Defense Police. *See* PIDE (International and State Defense Police)
intersectionality, 10, 156

Jerónimo, Miguel Bandeira, 21
Joppke, Christian, 6, 8, 136–37, 155–56, 157n4
Jorginho, 82, 102, 107, 109

Karlon, 64
Karlos, 16–17, 65–67, 81, 93–96, 150
Khan, Aisha, 11, 65
Khapaz Association, 80–81, 119, 128
Kova M. *See* Alto da Cova da Moura (Kova M.)
Kriol, 17, 66, 81, 82, 147
Kriolu/Crioulo: and citizenship, 9; definition of, 2, 6; drama of, 11, 16, 23, 69–72, 86, 95–99, 104, 123–29; as identity, 57–59, 72, 98, 112, 156; inside Portugal, 14–16; as interruption, 59–63, 82–83; as presence, 31, 106–13, 121–31; and rap music, 16–17; as unofficial language, ix, 15–18, 42–45, 74, 88–89, 124, 148, 164n4
Kromo, 16, 87–88, 91–92, 96, 103, 129, 145
*kuduro* music/dance, 97
Kymlicka, Will, 24, 162n7

*ladinização*, 42
*lançados*, 41–42
LBC: Amadora as home, 145; *badiu*, 114–16; on citizenship laws, 150; and Kova M, 127–29; Kriolu as critique/back talk, 40, 103–4; *kritikam* and *djam bai*, 124; Lusotropicalism, 77; process of interruption, 66; rap as spatial politics, 60–62; rap as voice of Kriulo, 95–100; on social problems and human geography, 31; Tuga and rap as competitive interests, 91–92; use of *bitch*, 48; use of *nigga*, 80; whitening of hip-hop worldwide, 89. *See also* Alto da Cova da Moura (Kova M.)
*Leis Pombalinas* (Pombaline Reforms), 30
Liberdade, Kiluanje, 162–63n3

Lima, Aristides, 56
Lima, Eugênio, 115–16
Lima, Mesquitela, 44
Lima, Redy Wilson, 161n4
"Linha Sintra," 97
*Lisboa Mistura*, 15, 146–47
Lisbon, 13–14
*The Lisbon Crossing*, 13–14
Lobban, Richard, 160n7
locality, 48, 82–83, 103, 116, 122, 128
Lochery, Neill, 14
Lopes, Baltasar, 70–71, 88, 161n12
Lopes, Manuel, 70
Lopi, Sema, 77
Lord G, 16
Loures (municipality), 117, 133–34, 148
Lura, 95, 160n4
Luso: inclusive but distinctive identity problems, 136–39; Kriolu interruptions of, 59–62; lineage, 156; as myth, 8; rapper challenges to, 25–26, 78–81; worldview and Cape Verde, 73. *See also* Lusofonia (Portugueseness); lusotropicalism
Luso-Africa (Luso-Africans): compared to other Cape Verdeans, 142–43; Gregorio Firmino on, 78; history collection in Lisbon, 32; and housing politics, 106–7; Jose da Silva Horta on, 35; Miguel Bandeira Jerónimo on, 21; and Kriolu identity, 57; in Lisbon, 38, 98; Fernando Luis Machado on, 83; Peter Mark on, 52, 158n5; Portuguese collective memory and, 27–28; rappers and identity, 67; as "refugee migrants," 158–59n8; represented in fiction, 12–17; state discourse vs. racism and xenophobia, 50; as stigmatized people, 137–38
Luso-Creole, 28
Lusofonia (Portugueseness): Agualusa's relationship with, 157n5; and belonging, 78–79; and Cape Verdean identity, 160n4; as identity brand, 137; and interculturality, 145; and Kriolu rappers, 25; and linguistic identity, 3–6, 11–12, 62; as multiculturalism, 113; pervasiveness of, 161n13
lusotropicalism: and Cape Verdean identity, 112–13; as categorizing discourse, 137–38; and Creole, 66–78; ethnocentric racism disguised as, 130; Kriolu rap as interrup-

tion, 62; language of Cape Verde, 160n4; LBC on, 150; linking Portugal with colonies, 160n8; Lisbon as capital of, 145–46; as national ideology, 155; as organizing ideology, 24–29; and Portugal's attempt at internationalism, 160n3; rap as response to, 60. *See also* Luso-Africa (Luso-Africans)
lusotropicology, 159n2

Macedo, Donald, 84
Machado, Igor, 74
Machine, 100
Malheiros, Jorge Macaísta, 47
marginality, 109, 124, 150, 162–63n3
Marilene, 111, 118
Mark, Peter, 52, 158n5
*Mayombe* (Pepetela), 13
MC Tigre, 143–45
Meintel, Deirdre, 55
Melo, Sebastião José de Carvalho, 29
Melville, Herman, 33–35
*Merka* (America), 97
migrancy, 13, 19, 83, 96, 136–37, 149, 155
Migrant Integration Policy Index (MIPEX), 4
migration: and citizenship, 6–12, 16, 23–29, 56–57, 80, 113–14, 129–30, 136–44, 154–55; and demography, 76, 86, 143, 162n2; and housing, 104–8, 116, 120, 125, 132–35, 162n3
Minao Soldjah, 97–98, 115
MIPEX (Migrant Integration Policy Index), 4
Miraflores (neighborhood), 109
Mirandês, 148
Mocambo, 32, 143
Moinho da Juventude (cultural association), vii, 46, 125–27
Morier-Genoud, Eric, 27, 31
*morna*, 56, 69–72, 76, 95, 162n5
*mouros* (moors), 28

Narayan, Kirin, 112
National Citizenship Laws, 10
negritude, 18, 33, 44, 61, 114
neighborhoods. *See* autoconstructed communitiessocial/state-sponsored project housing*and entries for specific neighborhoods*
"New Europe," 8, 12, 124, 130, 133
"nigga": Chullage's *Rapressão*, 90; "false nigga," 124; and Kriolu relationship to race and class, 45–49, 80–84; M.I.N.A.O. 2009, 115; and rap's antiracial message, 16, 75; "vagrant" as euphemism for, 57
Nigga Poison, 61, 64, 84
*A Night Train to Lisbon*, 13–14
nostalgia, 6, 16, 20, 28, 65–66, 70, 120, 154–56. *See also* sea (mar/calunga)
"Nu bai" (Chullage), 14–16, 15, 96, 100–102, 107
Núcleo, 77

Olímpia, Ana, 13
Organic Law 1953, 62

PAIGCV (African Party for the Independence of Guinea-Bissau and Cape Verde), xi, 44, 108
PALOP. *See* Portuguese as the Official Language (PALOP) countries
Paris, Tito, 76
Parque das Nações (neighborhood), 52–53, 80, 120, 127, 141
PE (Programas Escolhas), 141–42
Pedreira dos Húngaros (neighborhood), 109
Pennycook, Alastair, 79, 85, 92
People's Party (PP), 151
Pepetela (Artur Carlos Maurício Pestana), 13, 155
Pépin, Ernest, 11
PER (Special Program of Relocation), 26, 121, 134
periphery neighborhoods: Lisbon, 15, 31, 51, 76, 102, 109, 115, 154, 162n3; Stockholm, 60
PIDE (International and State Defense Police), 139, 142
Plataforma Gueto, 46
pluralism, 23, 146
policy: citizenship, 10, 22, 57, 104, 133, 145–46; housing, 113, 121, 134; immigration, 4, 10, 16, 26, 134; public, 2, 4, 57, 136, 148–50, 153–56
Portugal: citizenship, 7–10; and Kriolu/Crioulo, 14–16; and Luso-Africa in fiction, 12–14; marginal position of, 23–24, 105, 146; migration flows, 2–6; slave trade routes, 12–13

Portuguese as the Official Language (PALOP) countries: areas included, 4; and Cape Verdean identity, 89; and Cape Verdean migration, 83; and Cape Verdeans and Africans, 57, 65; and Lusophone, 79; rappers and, 81, 92–93, 103–4, 142–50, 156; "refugee migrants," 158–59n8; residents in Lisbon political lobby, 22
Portuguese emigration, 3–4, 23, 25, 53
Portuguese empire, 12, 31, 60, 113
Portugueseness. *See* Lusofonia (Portugueseness)
PP (People's Party), 151
Praia city, 9, 67; Alyson's stories on, 128; author's fieldwork in, 21–22, 40, 56; and corrective policy, 148; Ferro Gaita, 76–77; Ghoya's stories on, 124; Gil's story and, 120; LBC on, 104, 115–16; Rolando on, 134; Vera and Janice on, 143
*Presença* (magazine), 160n8
*pretugal*, 39
*pretuguês*, 37–39
Price, Richard, 75, 160n5
Princezito, 162n5
Prior Velho (neighborhood), vii, 106–7
Programas Escholhas (PE), 141–42
PS (Socialist Party), 151
PSD (Social Democratic Party), 140

Q-Tip, 90
Queirós, Eça de, 43, 157n6
*quiandas*, 13
Quinta da Lage (neighborhood), vii, 110–12
Quinta da Serra (neighborhood), vii, 106–7, 154

racialization, 29, 42, 49, 138, 151
racism: and the combination of culture and citizenship, 136; and creolization, 62; in Cuba, as contrast to Lisbon, 49; and intercultural education, 140; Lusotropicalism, 160n8; in Portugal, 114, 130; rap as antiracial communication, 18, 40, 47, 158n7; scientific, 28–29, 34; "social," 52; works of Fontaínhas, 162n3
Raimundo, Jacques, 37–38
Ramos, Max Ruben, 82
rap music: history in Portugal, 14, 16, 22, 33, 72, 88, 117; and sociolinguistics, 86, 94, 102, 114
Raposo, Otávio, 80, 82, 123, 163n6
*Rapública* (album), 161n4
Rego, Márcia, 42
retornados ("returnees"), 55, 87, 102, 159n13, 162n6
Rogozen-Soltar, Mikaela, 113
Rolando, 19, 133–35
Rosaldo, Renato, 112, 136
Roth, Philip, 153
Rothwell, Phillip, 11

Saint-Maurice, Ana de, 15, 107, 113
Salazar, Antonio, 2; apologists, 159n11; collapse of regime, 140–42; housing and clandestine neighborhoods, 117–18; *indigenous* and *assimilated* as labels, 51; jus sanguinis introduced, 54; Lisbon's reputation under, 13–14; and Lusotropicalism, 21, 62; regime's effect on Portugal, 23–25; and "there is no wealth but life," 71
Santiago (island of Cape Verde): Almada as respresentative, 37; Alyson's narrative, 128; *badiu*, 28, 40, 57, 158n6; freedom of slaves, 125–26; Freyre's narrative, 72–73; *Funaná*, 161–62n; hip hop movement on, 161n4; LBC migration from Kova M, 115–16; as matrix of Creole, 75–77; rapper Gilson, 52–53; as the "real" Cape Verde, 67; Rolando's narrative, 133–34; *txada*, 107–8
Santos, Boaventura de Sousa, 6
São Paulo, Brazil, 15, 20, 109, 149, 151, 158n8
São Tomé and Príncipe, 4–5, 12, 15, 51, 55–56, 69, 81, 119, 160n7
Saramago, José, 35
scene (Kriolu rap): Kriolu and tuga in Lisbon rap scene, 89–92; MC Tigre in Lisbon scene, 143; and neighborhoods, 114–20; and Portuguese identity, 148–49; social consciousness and hip-hop, 101–4; story of, in Lisbon, 109–13
sea (mar/calunga): and commerce, 32, 33; and death, 12–13; as image of history and desires, 1, 20, 27; nostalgia of Cape Verdeans, 65, 79; as symbol of Portuguese and Cape Verdean culture, 154–55; as symbol of separateness, 159n11

# Index

SEF (Immigration and Borders Service), xi, 53, 57, 140, 142–43, 159n8, 163n5
6 de Maio (neighborhood), 132, 144
Seixal (municipality), 117, 148
SGL (Geographical Society of Lisbon), xi, 21, 43, 45
Shakur, Tupac, 48, 80, 95, 99, 104
Sieber, Timothy, 79, 160n7, 163n4
Silva, Aníbal Cavaco, 154
Silva, Tomé Varela da, 75–76
Simmel, Georg, 7
Siu, Lok C.D., 62, 79, 106, 108, 112
6 de Maio (neighborhood), 132, 144
slave trade routes, 12–13
*A Small Death in Lisbon*, 13–14
Social Democratic Party (PSD), 140
social imaginary, 116, 124
Socialist Party (PS), 151
social/state-sponsored project housing, 26, 107, 112, 116, 118, 119, 130, 139, 157n1
Sócrates, José, 148
*sodadi* (nostalgia), 16, 56, 57, 76
Sons da Lusofonia, 78, 147
*sotavento* (leeward islands), 9, 67
Special Program of Relocation (PER), 26, 121, 134
Suárez-Navaz, Liliana, 113–14, 122
Sweet, James, 41, 75, 158n4

*tabanka*, 95, 162n5
Talude (neighborhood), vii, 132–35, 154
Tavares, Eugênio, 69–71
Teatro São Jorge, 147
territories: African, 23, 138; d'Almada descriptives of, 36–37; decolonization wars, 55; Kriolu's influence on, 133; Luso-Creole, 28; management of overseas, 24, 71; Portugal's significance, 54
"third space," 31
Tinhorão, José Ramos, 35
Tribe Called Quest, 90
*troika*, 79, 132, 135defined, 163n1
tuga (white Portuguese): Def lyrics, 64; definition of, 61, 161n3; Gilson on, 52–53; and Kova M, 127–28; Kriolu as alternative to, 86–95; MC Tigre on, 143–44; rap, 116, 149; rappers' use of term, 100–103; tension between Kriolu and, 155–56
TWA (Third World Answer), 16, 109
*The Two Hotel Francforts*, 13–14

Uncle C (Corsino). *See* Corsino ("Uncle C")
Unified Alphabet for Cape Verdean Writing (ALUPEK), ix, xi, 89, 148
urbanization, 14–15, 19, 26, 29, 80, 87, 107, 122, 130, 163n3

Vale da Amoreira (neighborhood), 142, 148
Vanspauwen, Bart, 78–79
Vasconcelos, Abreu, 154–55
Veiga, Carlos, 115
Veiga, Manuel, 39–40, 75, 161n12
Vicente, Gil, 38
Vierira, Paulino, 95
*vizinhança* (neighborhood), 54, 159n1

Wallerstein, Emmanuel, 10
Weeks, Samuel, 151n1
worldview, 40, 73

DEREK PARDUE is an assistant professor in the Department of Culture and Society at Aarhus University and author of *Ideologies of Marginality in Brazilian Hip Hop*.

INTERPRETATIONS OF CULTURE
IN THE NEW MILLENNIUM

Peruvian Street Lives: Culture, Power, and Economy among Market Women of Cuzco
    *Linda J. Seligmann*
The Napo Runa of Amazonian Ecuador    *Michael Uzendoski*
Made-from-Bone: Trickster Myths, Music, and History from the Amazon
    *Jonathan D. Hill*
Ritual Encounters: Otavalan Modern and Mythic Community    *Michelle Wibbelsman*
Finding Cholita    *Billie Jean Isbell*
East African Hip Hop: Youth Culture and Globalization    *Mwenda Ntaragwi*
Sarajevo: A Bosnian Kaleidoscope    *Fran Markowitz*
Becoming Mapuche: Person and Ritual in Indigenous Chile    *Magnus Course*
Kings for Three Days: The Play of Race and Gender in an Afro-Ecuadorian Festival
    *Jean Muteba Rahier*
Maya Market Women: Power and Tradition in San Juan Chamelco, Guatemala
    *S. Ashley Kistler*
Victims and Warriors: Violence, History, and Memory in Amazonia    *Casey High*
Embodied Protests: Emotions and Women's Health in Bolivia    *Maria Tapias*
Street Life under a Roof: Youth Homelessness in South Africa    *Emily Margaretten*
Reinventing Chinese Tradition: The Cultural Politics of Late Socialism    *Ka-ming Wu*
Cape Verde, Let's Go: Creole Rappers and Citizenship in Portugal    *Derek Pardue*

The University of Illinois Press
is a founding member of the
Association of American University Presses.

---

University of Illinois Press
1325 South Oak Street
Champaign, IL 61820-6903
www.press.uillinois.edu